The Art of Mark Twain

FOLLOWING THE EQUATOR (HARTFORD: AMERICAN PUBLISHING COMPANY, 1897)

FACSIMILE PAGE FROM THE AUTHOR'S NOTEBOOK

After struggling unsuccessfully to write a maxim about the inventor of the cuckoo clock, Mark Twain makes a maxim about maxim-making.

THE ART OF
MARK TWAIN

William M. Gibson

New York
OXFORD UNIVERSITY PRESS
1976

for

Barbara, Julia, Jeffrey, Thomas, and Benjamin

Prefatory Note

In matters of literary taste readers are often so securely imprisoned in their own times that it takes a strong effort to break free. Do we now address ourselves to the best of Mark Twain's work, openly, as that best work deserves? I do not think so. If we read Mark Twain at all, we tend to see myopically, through a fog of whiskey advertisements and notions about "Americanism," cartoon images of a "funny man" and writer who is supposed by some to have wasted his talent.

Is there a better, or conceivably an ideal, condition for the ever-renewed encounter of readers with the figures and actions and voices created by Samuel L. Clemens, Mark Twain? I suspect there is. The new edition of his *Works*, from the University of Iowa, and that of the *Mark Twain Papers*, from the University of California at Berkeley (both to be issued by the University of California Press), will make it possible for the reader to choose and evaluate for himself. But while the two editions are still under construction, such a reader is invited to follow and to test one critic's choice of Mark Twain's "best."

Mark Twain's contemporaries by the thousands had the chance to hear that consummate actor-reader tell his stories on the lecture platform. Many thousands more encountered his anecdotes and sketches and even such sequences as "Old Times on the Mississippi" in their local newspapers—lifted from the newly published books or from the latest issue of the *Atlantic Monthly*. Some fortunate few came to know Clemens the man, as well as Mark Twain the public mask—and found the man as captivating and vital as were his books among the books of the day.

Subsequently, when copyright law tightened so that the stories could no longer be picked up free in the daily press, and after the death of their author in 1910, these opportunities disappeared. But even before his death there were collected editions of his writings, first from the American Publishing Company (his own firm) and then from Harper & Brothers. As late as the 1930s, by way of building circulation, newspapers made available gaudily bound sets of the "National Edition" very cheaply. What good fortune it was, for young readers especially, to draw the books several at a time from the local Carnegie Free Public Library or to find a set of Mark Twain on the shelves at home. Though some parents might object to his "irreverence," as young T. S. Eliot's parents in St. Louis apparently did, or to the vulgarity of Huckleberry Finn's adventures, the chance to pick and choose or to "read straight through" was a golden one—and of course literature "hooked on the sly" or read on one's own, as the boy Sam Clemens himself learned early, is always especially tasty.

Older, more critical readers in the 1920s and 1930s, moreover, were drawn more or less consciously into one side or the other in a sharp controversy over the success or failure of Mark Twain as writer. As Albert Bigelow Paine, his first literary editor, continued to publish volumes from the mass of the Mark Twain papers, such readers began to suspect that Paine was withholding controversial pieces from publication and that he was "editing" the Mark Twain *oeuvre* to suit daughter Clara Clemens Gabrilowitsch's views, or his own, or the publisher's. The battle opened with publication of Van Wyck Brooks's "cautionary" biography, *The Ordeal of Mark Twain* (1920), in which it was argued that the author had wasted his talent out of a mistaken regard for the prejudices of his wife, his editor, and his age. It was Brooks's rhetorical point that the young writers of the 1920s should recognize Mark Twain's errors and avoid them. The critical war was fully joined when Bernard DeVoto heatedly defended Mark Twain as an artist springing from an indigenous Western culture much richer than Brooks, the New Englander, could understand. The whole conflict now appears as part of the inevitable revolt of Second American Renaissance writers in the 1920s against their forebears—but the specific issues no longer seem vital. Questions enough remain in interpreting the paradoxes of Clemens's life. The quarrel between Brooks and DeVoto dwindles in the perspective of only half a century.

Contemporary readers of Mark Twain, who are more numerous than ever, both at home and abroad, will profit from the new Iowa and California editions as they appear; from inexpensive reprints made from these textually sound editions; and particularly, I believe, from the reappearance of inaccessible shorter pieces and the first publication of certain manuscript materials. But while the two editions—which will include notebooks, letters, and all the autobiographical dictation and scattered political writing—are being completed, I wish to deal as directly as I can with three questions.

First, what truly are Mark Twain's best pieces of writing? Putting the question this way implies that many pieces in the great mass of his writings are five-finger exercises, or exerted a momentary interest now past, or were disjointed and unstructured from the first, or are now for still other reasons dead and unresurrectible. The question implies, conversely, that critics of the past five decades whose taste has been equal to their knowledge have been constantly distinguishing the best from the less good, the worse, and the worst and treating this substantial body of "best" with the close regard and the solid respect that have characterized good modern criticism. I hope to consolidate their effort and to extend it.

Second, what are Mark Twain's best pieces in the various kinds of writing that he essayed? My question assumes that he was a writer talented in many modes and genres. Mark Twain became a writer, much as did Cooper and Melville and Conrad, while he was a young man leading a most vigorous active life under the pose of loafing. He learned the art of the "picaresque" romance rather late, but he mastered early the tall tale, the burlesque sketch, the fable, the travel record, and the humorous or serious story told by a sufficiently complex vernacular narrator, though he remained an amateur playwright, and though his biography of Joan of Arc is flawed by heroine-worship. He valued history and memoir as literary forms and combined the two with striking success in *Roughing It*. He attempted the rhetoric of praise only fitfully; but he practiced the polemical art with peculiar verve, and to this art he brought great power: whether at vituperation, or burlesque, or humor of the high order that simultaneously protests the absurd and the inhumane and despairs of change.

Howells called this Mark Twain's "prophetic function." Late in life he turned to maxims and epigrams—concentrated, flashing, poetic. First and last he wrote effective public letters and ebullient private correspondence. Mark Twain, in short, was more a man of letters in the traditional sense of the term than anyone has yet argued, and if one is to find his best, he must search for it through the many kinds of writing he put his hand to.

Finally, it is my assumption throughout this book that, for reasons I do not wholly understand, and hereby challenge the reader to discover, Mark Twain was at his brilliant best in his shorter works. It was chiefly in these shorter pieces that he became a "veteran trader in shadows," as he put it with mingled self-deprecation and pride. The notions of Mark Twain as clown or as a "jack-leg novelist" or as a Gilded Age entrepreneur are partial or grotesque or beside the point when we consider him at his substantial best. He then becomes master, in his own phrase, of a "high and delicate art."

Madison, Wisconsin   William M. Gibson
August, 1975

Acknowledgments

My study of Mark Twain owes a very large debt to the John Simon Guggenheim Memorial Foundation earlier, and the National Endowment for the Humanities more recently, for fellowships and free time—that inexpressibly valuable gift to engaged academics and slow writers. The Research Committee of the University of Wisconsin at Madison provided research assistance as I was completing the manuscript, and Mary Bradish performed this task with devotion and intelligence. Jane Renneberg deciphered my handwriting and typed the printer's copy of the manuscript. Luisa Melelli of the Magistero Library in Florence made me welcome when I was beginning the book. Mary Ellen Evans in editing the manuscript clarified and persuaded me to clarify my meaning. Thomas G. Chamberlain, President of the Mark Twain Company, has kindly granted me permission to quote a number of unpublished Pudd'nhead Wilson maxims from the Mark Twain Papers in Berkeley, California. I thank them all.

My special thanks go to Walter Blair, John C. Gerber, Henry Nash Smith, and Frederick Anderson for many of the insights into Mark Twain's ideas and forms and artistry assembled in this book.

W. M. G.

Contents

And so I am become a knight of the Kingdom of Dreams and Shadows! A most odd and strange position, truly, for one so matter-of-fact as I.
   —The Prince and the Pauper

The humorous story is strictly a work of art—high and delicate art—and only an artist can tell it.
   —"How to Tell a Story"

Every day the feeling of the day before is renewed to me—the feeling of having been in a half-trance all my life before—numb, sluggish-blooded, sluggish-minded—a feeling which is followed at once by a brisk sense of being out of that syncope and awake! awake and alive; alive to my finger-ends. I realize that I am a veteran trader in shadows who has struck the substance. I have found the human race.
   —"The Refuge of the Derelicts"

The Art of Mark Twain

Chapter 1

◆

MARK TWAIN'S STYLE

That "fatal music of his voice." — The "word with the bark on it." — "Obituary eloquence." — The language of printing. — "Compound stran-gulated sorosis of the valvular tissues." — A prose style "as natural as breathing." — Mark Twain's "strong hold," metaphor. — Donning the vernacular mask.

That Mark Twain (the pen name of Samuel Langhorne Clem-ens) was an authentic stylist is not a universally accepted opinion, nor is he always and automatically thought of as a lit-erary artist. Of course it is a nice question whether a writer must be a stylist to be considered a true literary artist—one can pile up evidence for either position; yet the conviction grows that the American Mark Twain fashioned one of the great styles of literature in English—even though it took an English novelist of German extraction, Ford Madox Ford (born Ford Madox Hueffer) to say so first. Like his own raftsman Dick Allbright in *Life on the Mississippi*, Mark Twain learned to "curl his tongue around the bulliest words in the language when he was a mind to, and lay them before you without a jint started anywheres."

A lion in the path of such acceptance—really a paper lion, I believe—is the easily confirmed view that Mark Twain took little interest in literary theory beyond the practicalities necessary to his own writing. He did not consistently think of himself as a novelist or even a man of letters—that is, a committed and consummate stylist. Henry James, for instance, seems to have considered him a raconteur, a humorist, a public figure. Even his trusted friend of forty years, William Dean Howells, who witnessed the birth and growth of almost all his major works, reveals something of the same attitude in two prime critical documents. In the first, the lecture "Novel-Writing and Novel-Reading," he never mentions Mark Twain, though he covers the entire range of fiction up to Henry James. In the second, *My Mark Twain*, Howells insists that his friend was different from all the literary men he had known, in three generations of American and European writers, and calls him "the Lincoln of our literature." [1]

It is a great tribute and just, but it implies a definition of literature rather looser than usual for Howells, however profoundly humane. Is it not striking that T. S. Eliot of St. Louis, Missouri, who read so much of the best of so many literatures, should have discovered *Adventures of Huckleberry Finn* only when he was nearing the age of sixty? [2] One is forced to conclude that Clemens did not in his own day appear to be a "man of letters" in the sense that James and Howells and Eliot were men of letters, and that he exercised his art less consciously than they did, and with less interest in theory. It follows as well that his art must be defined chiefly in his practice—and his best practice, at that. This is not to say that he wrote no literary criticism or that he was not keenly aware of certain mysteries of literary expression, but rather that his few written ventures into the area of theory and technique serve at best to confirm or enlarge what is discoverable, pragmatically, from his best writing in many modes.

"The difference between the *almost right* word and the *right* word," Mark Twain affirmed, "is really a large matter—'tis the difference between the lightning-bug and the lightning." [3] Throughout his writing life he respected the search for the exact word as whole-heartedly as Gustave Flaubert, and he took as much pleasure in finding it as that other word-connoisseur, the New England poet Emily Dickinson. In fact, he learned so many right words from his reading and his listening to the talk of thousands of men and women, of every sort and condition, and he mastered so thoroughly the art of "sentencing" them (the word is Robert Frost's), that he became the prime mover and shaker in a revolution in the language of fiction, a "renewal of language," as Frost was to put it. Just as Emerson had called for an American poet who spoke the language of the street, phrases strong as the oaths in a New England farmer's mouth, sentences that if cut "they bleed," and Whitman consciously answering the appeal created a new lingo for poetry, so Mark Twain responding to other appeals such as Southwestern humor created a new language for prose. Words in the mouth translated to the page with a skill that no one yet has properly measured—this is the base of his literary expression. His friend the Reverend Joseph Twichell, Howells, A. B. Paine (his official biographer), the thousands of Americans and Englishmen and Australians and Germans who flocked to hear Mark Twain in person, the continuing success of Hal Holbrook impersonating him and reciting his pieces with disarming simplicity—all attest to his astute use of a varied, rich, vital vocabulary. "The stately word" pleased his ear, but the colloquial word and phrase pleased it even more. He "caressed them all with his affectionate tongue," [4] as his farmer John Backus caressed his words when naming cattle breeds. All the contrasting words fell then into place, serving nearly every kind of literary effect, permeated with "that fatal music of his voice." [5]

The pungent variety of Mark Twain's language, the written and apparently the spoken, too, stems from a bewildering variety of sources. On the side of the written word, one suspects that he came to know and absorb the styles of more writers than anyone has yet observed, though Walter Blair's *Mark Twain and Huck Finn* and Howard Baetzhold's *Mark Twain and John Bull* reveal a great many. He had read the whole Bible at a tender age. For months, on the Mississippi, he read and talked about and quoted Shakespeare under the tutelage of the river pilot Horace Bixby. He developed a strong taste for the clarity and the balance between style and mind in Goldsmith's *Citizen of the World* and Swift's *Gulliver's Travels,* even as he reacted against the verbosity and slovenly diction of the sentimental fiction of his day, both juvenile and adult, and against "obituary eloquence" in the newspapers. Proof of this verbal sophistication lies in his own writing: he imitated or parodied or used in some serious fashion all these writers and works. How keen an ear and how tenacious a memory he had for poetry appears in the supremely funny bad poem composed by the prematurely deceased Emmeline Grangerford of *Huckleberry Finn* fame, her "Ode to Stephen Dowling Botts, Dec'd," or in the wildly mangled quotations from Emerson, Holmes, Whittier, and Lowell in the Whittier Birthday Speech delivered before these worthies in December of 1877.

In two slashing attacks on James Fenimore Cooper's novels, and especially on their stilted dialogue, Mark Twain revealed that he had read Cooper thoroughly, and probably with enthusiasm, as a boy. Well known is the report of the boundless pleasure he took in the rhythms of Sir Thomas Malory's *Morte D'Arthur,* and the role played by Malory's "stately" prose in his writing of *A Connecticut Yankee,* his mood torn between admiring imitation and playful burlesque. But by this time he was probably re-encountering Malory, for an earlier skit, "The 'Tournament' in A.D. 1870," makes fun of knighthood and Malory's language.[6] After reading Cable's *The Grandissimes* he went around for days talking Cable's soft Creole English with Howells.

The evidence is strong that Mark Twain was peculiarly sensitive to the sound appeal of words, whether musical or cacophonic. He loved the spoken word on the stage. He was a master hand at "yellocution," reading aloud from the page not only his own work but, especially during the mid–1880s, the poetry of Browning. He was, above all, as Franklin Rogers has shown,[7] expert in burlesquing the styles of other writers, from Shakespeare to his own contemporaries, and of profiting himself from this practice. One has only to think of Poe's "How to Write a Blackwood Article," (1838), Whitman's *Franklin Evans, or the Inebriate* (1842), Bret Harte's *Condensed Novels* (1867), or Bayard Taylor's *Diversions of the Echo Club* (1876) to realize that Mark Twain was working a popular vein. Nineteenth-century American readers loved burlesques. On the stage good burlesques were so popular with audiences that in any one town a current stage success on tour was almost certain to be followed up a week later by an equally successful burlesque.[8]

The written word, including more than a few of French, Italian, and especially German provenance, furnished Mark Twain with a rich word-hoard, particularly on the "stately" side. It was his extraordinary grasp of the American vernacular, however, that enabled him to use words "as if they had never been used by other writers," as Howells said: "the word with the bark on it" in Mark Twain's own metaphor.[9] He secured that grasp only by the "Arabian Nights" life he early led, jack-of-many-trades and master-of-several, throughout the United States and in many countries abroad. He had been, as he once claimed, "everything, from a newspaper editor to a cowcatcher on a locomotive." [10] In a letter to an unknown correspondent he sums up the experiences of these *Wanderjahren:*

> I was a *soldier* two weeks once at the beginning of the war, and was hunted like a rat the whole time. Familiar? My splendid Kipling himself hasn't a more burnt-in, hard-baked and unforgetable familiarity with that death-on-the-pale-horse-with-hell-following-after which is a raw soldier's first fortnight in the field—and which, without any doubt is the most tremendous fortnight and the vividest he is ever going to see.
>
> Yes and I have shoveled silver tailings in a quartz mill a couple of weeks, and acquired the last possibilities of culture in *that* direction. And I've done "pocket-mining" during three whole months in the one little patch of ground in the whole globe where Nature conceals gold in pockets—or *did,* before we robbed all of those pockets and exhausted, obliterated, annihilated the most curious freak Nature ever indulged in. . . .
>
> And I've been a prospector and know pay rock from poor when I find it—just with a touch of the tongue. And I've been a silver *miner* and know how to dig and shovel and drill, and put in a blast. And so I know the mines and miners *interiorly.* . . .
>
> And I was a newspaper reporter four years in cities, and so saw the inside of many things and was reporter in a legislature two sessions and the same in Congress one session—and thus learned to know personally three sample bodies of the smallest hearts and the selfishest souls and the cowardliest hearts that God makes.
>
> And I was some years a Mississippi pilot and familiarly knew all the different kinds of steamboatmen—a race apart and not like other folk.
>
> And I was for some years a traveling "jour" printer, and wandered from city to city—and so I *know* that sect familiarly.
>
> And I was a lecturer on the public platform a number of seasons and was a responder to toasts at all the different kinds of banquets—and so I know a great many secrets about audiences—secrets not to be gotten out of books but only acquirable by experience. . . .
>
> And I am a publisher and did pay to one author's widow the largest copyright checks this world has seen—aggregating more than $80,000 in the first year.
>
> And I have been an author for 20 years and an ass for 55. [11]

It is an extraordinary record of occupations, all of which except for the bit of guerrilla soldiering provided the developing artist with their own special lingo. Even so, the record fails to account in full for the luxuriance of his expression. The sketch called "Buck Fanshaw's Funeral," which is Chapter 47 of *Roughing It* (1872), unfolds a whole series of Western activities and amusements, each with its special vocabulary. The story is in fact a kind of "language experiment," as Whitman sometimes spoke of his *Leaves of Grass,* since it hinges on the comic possibilities for misunderstanding between a polysyllabic fledgling from an Eastern theological seminary who is new to Nevada, and the "stalwart rough," Scotty Briggs, who speaks only in Western slang. "Slang was the language of Nevada," Mark Twain explains, "the richest and the most infinitely varied and copious that had ever existed anywhere in the world, perhaps, except in the mines of California in the 'early days.' " Not until Briggs has exhausted an entire store of Western jargons, shifting easily from one to another, does Mark Twain permit the minister to understand that "Scotty" and the other townsmen want him to pronounce a eulogy at the funeral of the dead Buck Fanshaw.

"Are you the duck that runs the gospel-mill next door?" Scotty begins. Bewildered, the young minister replies that he is "the spiritual adviser of the little company of believers whose sanctuary adjoins these premises." Scotty, equally bewildered, says, "You ruther hold over me, pard. I can't call that hand. Ante and pass the buck." After another futile effort to comprehend on the minister's part, Scotty admits, "I'll have to pass . . . you've raised me out, pard . . . that last lead of yourn is too many for me—that's the idea. I can't neither trump nor follow suit." But Scotty persists, explaining that one of the boys has "passed in his checks"—that is, that he has "gone up the flume," "throwed up the sponge," in short, "kicked the bucket." And so they need a "gospel-sharp" to "jerk a little chin-music" for them. To understand Scotty

Briggs at all, the minister would need to know at least something about gin-mills, cardsharps, placer mining, poker,
whist, and the prize ring.

When the minister grasps finally that death has "scooped"
Buck Fanshaw, he has further trouble making sense of Scotty's
vigorous eulogy of his friend—"I knowed him by the
back"—"a bully boy with a glass eye," who could "lam any
galoot of his inches in America." "Just go in and toot your
horn if you don't sell a clam," Scotty urges. But when the minister wants to know whether deceased acknowledged al-
legiance to a higher power, Scotty has to answer, "All down
but nine—set 'em up in the other alley, pard. . . . Every time
you draw, you fill; but I don't seem to have any luck. Lets
have a new deal." Their final misunderstanding comes from
Briggs's admiring explanation that Buck Fanshaw "never
shook his mother," an expression that the minister of course
must take literally. Whereupon Scotty cries, "Cheese it, pard;
you've banked your ball clean outside the string," explains his
friend's devotion to his mother, and wrings the minister's
hand in friendly understanding. Again, Mark Twain draws
upon the language of reporters, of gamblers ("I knowed him
by the back"), of straights and flushes in poker, of fighting, of
bowling, of street-vending, and of pool.

"Buck Fanshaw's Funeral" is a bravura performance. Mark
Twain certainly realized that the slang would puzzle his Eastern readers and that eventually much of it would become
hopelessly dated. He saves his sketch from the fate of other work
in what Hemingway called the "ish-kabbible" school by demonstrating Scotty's ability, in the end, to translate his highly
metaphorical slang into simple English. It goes without saying
that despite certain sentimental touches in the manner of Bret
Harte, the reader sympathizes with the fairmindedness of
Buck Fanshaw and the humanity of Scotty Briggs.

Briggs's Western talk is a mixture of the slang of many indi-

vidual adventurers in "Silverland" from many nations and
localities, as Mark Twain made clear in preparing the ground
for the story; it is kaleidoscopic. The manuscript called "The
Mysterious Stranger, No. 44," set in Austria only a few decades after the beginning of printing in Europe, must in its
genesis have struck him as an opportunity to exploit his experience as a printer and his mastery of the printer's vocabulary.[12] It is an attempt to use a special vocabulary in depth, as
he had already used the language of the river pilot in "Old
Times on the Mississippi," and a number of Mississippi dialects in *Tom Sawyer* and *Huckleberry Finn*. Although he had
once warned Howells against making a printer the hero of *A
Modern Instance* on the ground that readers would be baffled
and resentful encountering so mysterious a figure—so Howells
recalls in his essay "The Country Printer" (1893)—[13] Mark
Twain created the printshop sequence in "The Mysterious
Stranger, No. 44" with gusto and skill. Here was an area of his
experience (in Hannibal and elsewhere) that he had never
treated in fiction. He had, it is true, spoken the language of
the trade to a group of printers in an address in 1886, on the
anniversary of Benjamin Franklin's birth; but these men "had
been there before." How to dramatize the complexities of the
printshop operation, in the language of printers, for a general
audience?

Mark Twain solved the problem with a fair degree of success
by setting up a conflict between, on one side, his young narrator August Feldner in alliance with the beggar-boy No. 44 (really
an angel and Satan's nephew in disguise) and, on the other,
the entire printing force. When the master of the shop accepts
the young and abused stranger as an apprentice, the experienced printers, jealous of their status and privileges, determine to deny him help and to torment him for every error he
makes in a craft wholly unknown to him. But because the
mysterious stranger can read August's mind, August out of his

own experience as printer's devil can silently convey to him exactly how to respond to the printers' commands. Thus, for the moment, August and No. 44, the industrious apprentices, defeat the mean-spirited gang of printers before they call a strike against the master just as a major order of Bibles is to be completed. And thus Mark Twain manages to construct a dramatic sequence out of the "mystery" of printing without resorting to obtrusive or patronizing explanations himself. Although the plot runs down hill when No. 44 saves the master—by creating a set of ghostly duplicate printers to complete the job by the deadline—the skills, the machinery, the delicate process of printing seem to have engaged Mark Twain's energy and imagination closely as he worked out this portion of his story. Certainly the printshop sequence is superior to almost all the actions that follow before the work collapses in a general phantasmagoria.

Under young Feldner's careful instruction, No. 44 and the reader watch the compositors "jeff for takes"—in effect "draw straws," that is, for the copy they are to set, with some of the "comps" then rapidly selecting type from the type-box and placing them in their "sticks," measuring and justifying the lines with "quads" of varying thickness, and then sliding the type onto the composing stone when the sticks are full. Galley proofs are tried, and when "outs" and "overs" (omissions and repetitions) have been corrected, the compositors make the galleys of type into pages. The pages are then locked up with "quoins" and a "sheepsfoot" (wedges and a tool for tightening them) in the "forme"—a frame to hold the heavy type metal locked together as a single unit. (Woe to No. 44, the unlucky printer's devil, if he should drop the forme, carrying it from the composing stone over to the bed of the press, and "pi" (drop into a chaotic pile of type) the pages that have taken hours of skilled labor to set.) When the forme has been gently laid on the bed of the press and the type "planed down" (the type surfaces evened out to the same plane), the type is inked, the pressman brings the tympan down on the dampened paper, and the sheet of paper receives the impression of the type pages. Later, the sheet is printed on the "verso" (reverse side), the type pages being carefully aligned to the impression on the other side of the sheet. Folded into gatherings, the sheets are then sewed, glued at the spine, and bound—to make the complete book.

To Feldner and No. 44 falls the dirty work of the printshop: making glue for the ink-balls, picking up broken type under the compositor's feet and putting it into the hell-box for melting and recasting, placing dead matter on the standing galley, washing the type before it is "distributed" (replaced in the type-box according to letter and font), and—occasionally— changing the stiff, dirty towel on which all the printers wipe their inky hands. To Feldner and No. 44 also fall the comps' traditional tricks, such as being sent for strap-oil and presumably getting the strap across the buttocks, or being pelted with a shower of quoins and types, or being derided as "bottle-assed" (after the shape of a type that has thickened in the middle from much planing down), or having to endure the sound of the comps sawing on their box-partitions with the metal rules—a raucous, farting sound of derision. Young Sam Clemens must have taken real pride in setting a clean proof. And the complex skills demanded of the printer—as implicit in the compositor's specialized vocabulary—later provided him with a dramatic sequence in an otherwise notably diffuse story.

Mark Twain knew Western slang and the jargon of several professions. He also had a strong taste for what is now known as "double-talk," [14] as any reader of his whole output will recognize. While it was naturally a talent that served him best in his lighter works, it still gives flavor to pieces otherwise boiled bland by time. At its best it is delicious (to use a word he favored) with poetic absurdities. Ballou, the simple, kind-hearted miner of *Roughing It*, suggests the author's inspiration in "Ike Partington" and sets a kind of definition:

> [Ballou's] one striking peculiarity was his Partingtonian fashion of loving and using big words *for their own sakes*, and independent of any bearing they might have upon the thought he was purposing to convey. . . . If a word was long and grand and resonant, that was sufficient to win the old man's love, and he would drop that word into the most out-of-the-way place in a sentence or a subject, and be as pleased with it as if it were perfectly luminous with meaning.[15]

It is Ballou, lost in the desert and moving in circles, who finds his plight "perfectly hydraulic" and tells his companion Ollendorff that he "did not know as much as a logarythm!"[16]

Another of Mark Twain's early ventures into double-talk—in "The Loves of Alonzo Fitz Clarence and Rosannah Ethelton" (1878), intermingled women's fashion parlance and nautical lingo, and burlesques female fiction. Rosannah wears a gown of magenta tulle, "overdress of dark bay tarlatan with scarlet satin lambrequins, corn-colored polonaise, *en panier*, looped with mother-of-pearl buttons and silver cord, and hauled aft and made fast by buff-velvet lashings."[17] So "Some Learned Fables for Good Old Boys and Girls" (1875), which satirizes the tendency of scientists to build a "mountain of demonstrated fact" out of a "spoonful of supposition," rests its conclusions on a certain Professor Snail's "perlustration and perscontation" of an "isoperimetrical protuberance."[18] So too, while Mark Twain is writing an essay on "international confraternity and biological deviation" ("Political Economy," 1870), a lightning-rod salesman persuades him that if he puts enough lightning rods on his house, the "recalcitrant and dephlogistic messenger of heaven" will be rendered harmless and "its further progress apocryphal."[19] And so a learned doctor, examining the wounded Angelo in *Those Extraordinary*

Twins (1894), "proceeded to empty himself as follows, with scientific relish—"

> . . . I concede that great care is going to be necessary here; otherwise exudation of the aesophagus is nearly sure to ensue, and this will be followed by ossification and extradition of the maxillaris superioris, which must decompose the granular surfaces of the great infusorial ganglionic system, thus obstructing the action of the posterior varioloid arteries, and precipitating compound strangulated sorosis of the valvular tissues, and ending unavoidably in the dispersion and combustion of the marsupial fluxes and the consequent embrocation of the bicuspid populo redax referendum rotulorum.[20]

Mark Twain never lost his taste for nonsense language—a taste rather like Lewis Carroll's, whose writing he admired.[21] For his children he wrote an essay on cats entirely in "Catapult," and in "No. 44, The Mysterious Stranger," a cat named Mary Florence Fortescue Baker G. Nightingale even speaks in "Christian Silence." As late as 1907, the horse of *A Horse's Tale*, learning that his new friend the Mexican Plug has had thirteen aliases, remarks admiringly: "Alias. It's a fine large word, and is in my line; it has quite a learned and cerebrospinal incandescent sound." [22]

Examples could be multiplied. One of the best appears in his letter to Howells of 13 February 1903. Howells had written his friend a letter, apparently in dead earnest but actually describing a dream in which the Clemens gardener, Sam, had rudely refused to admit him and a third friend at the Clemens gate. In an "apologetic" reply, the lord of the villa explains that upon questioning the gardener he learned his friend's identity ("a stumpy little gray man with furtive ways and an evil face") only after the gardener had repeated Howells's round curses. "He called me"—so the mythical gardener reported through Mark Twain—"a quadrilateral astronomical incandescent son of a bitch." The rhythmical beauty of these "adverbs" and the "morbid grammar" (as he puts it) suggest that his skill in "double-talk" deserves study.[23] (If the reader cares to try to improve these "adverbs" by rearranging or adding or subtracting, he will find his work cut out for him.)

It would take, in fact, a full concordance to establish the breadth and the variety of Mark Twain's vocabulary, his "Elizabethan breadth of parlance," although the Ramsay and Emberson *Lexicon* and H. L. Mencken's studies of the American language and the *Dictionary of American English* have sunk rich test-borings. But even a random search of his writings will turn up words invented for his immediate purpose, many as fine as Melville's or Dickinson's neologisms and nearly all of them useful in context. At a simple level are the new terms Mark Twain invented for imaginary countries, such as Gondour (a kind of Utopian republic) or Lingamberg or Eseldorf (Ass-ville), or that extraordinary railroad-town sequence: St. Louis, Slouchburg, Doodleville, Brimstone, Belshazzar, Cat Fish, Babylon, Bloody Run, Hail Columbia, Hark-from-the-Tomb, Napoleon, Hallelujah, and Corruptionville.[24] In the vast spaces of Captain Stormfield's heaven, brimstone is measured in kazarks (the bulk of 169 worlds such as the Wart, or the earth), and the poets Saa, Bo, and Soof, come from remote systems like Goobra and take precedence over Homer and Shakespeare.

On another level Mark Twain was fond of unusual superlatives, like "curiousest," "confoundedest," "brazenest," "ingeniousest," and "remarkablest." In a white heat of angry invention, on the subject of Bret Harte, he coined the adverbs "interiorly" and "exteriorly," the verb "filthify," and the adverb "billiardly-speaking." As he wrote Howells, "Billiardly-speaking, the President . . . scored 400 points on each, when he appointed Lowell & Taylor—but when he appointed Harte he simply pocketed his own ball." [25] Another letter to Howells had been made more "parlor-mentary" to suit Livy Clemens, his wife. Remembering a Western drinking party in honor of Artemus Ward at which a great superfluity of empty bottles accumulated, Mark Twain reported to Thomas Bailey Aldrich that Ward's speech was greeted with a "long, vociferous, poundiferous, and vitreous jingling of applause." [26] "Affeland" (old-style s's for asseland), or *Apeland* in German, is subtitled "Snivelization," a word Melville had presumably invented and Mark Twain re-invented.[27]

Perhaps Mark Twain's most famous neologism was the phrase "new deal" as he extended its meaning from poker playing or the card table to a larger, and especially a political, context. To my knowledge, the phrase first occurs in his *opera* in *Roughing It* (1872), in the comic dialogue quoted earlier between the young Eastern preacher and the Nevada old-timer Scotty Briggs. Baffled, Scotty says, "Why, you're most too many for me, you know. When you get in with your left I hunt grass every time. Every time you draw, you fill; but I don't seem to have any luck. Lets have a new deal." To the query, "How? Begin again?" he responds with relief, "That's it." [28] Mark Twain used the metaphor again to mean "a new beginning" in a letter to Howells of 12 October 1876,[29] and again in 1881, in the table of contents (Chapter XVII) of *Life on the Mississippi*. Though Howells had employed the idiom earlier—in 1881, in a general, nonpolitical context, Henry James caused his Lady Aurora, in *The Princess Casamassima* (1886) to say, "Possibly you don't know that I am one of those who believe that a great new deal is destined to take place and that it can't make things worse than they are." [30] But it was in *A Connecticut Yankee* (1889) that Mark Twain used the phrase with emphasis, and it was presumably there that a Franklin D. Roosevelt speech writer found it and helped incorporate it in the national idiom, like "the gilded age" before it.[31]

With these few illustrations I have the sense of scratching the surface only over the richest sort of mother lode. But

enough has been cited to show that Mark Twain was in love
with the language of "all trades, their gear and tackle and
trim" of the Hopkins sonnet,[32] that he spoke and wrote with a
truly Southwestern "breadth of parlance"; that he was both a
"great gabber" and gifted with the gift of tongues.

Not much more has been written in depth about Mark
Twain as a stylist than about his word strength; yet the evidence powerfully supports the argument of Ford Madox Ford
that he wrote a pure and distinguished style,[33] one of the great
styles of English literature, and it supports the central place
Richard Bridgman gives him in his pioneer study *The Colloquial Style in America* (1966). Necessarily it was a style capable
of securing for its author a great variety of effects—lyrical,
blunt, picturesque, pathetic, epic, tragic, and humorous in all
the senses of the word. This does not rule out the crude or
melodramatic or sentimental or even the dull—but nearly any
writer can achieve these, and I pass over them. It is hard to
generalize about style in the work of an author who was active
for 55 years (from 1855 to 1910), and produced news articles,
burlesques and satires, hoaxes, "personal books," domestic
comedy, plays, autobiography, travel letters, public letters,
personal letters, and persuasive writing of all sorts from en-
comium to invective. Nonetheless, after the apprentice years
Mark Twain's writing bears its own hallmarks in the various
kinds, and it is worth the effort to describe them.

Mark Twain became aware of style very early. Late in life, in
an essay explaining how he became "professionally literary,"
he observed that "one isn't a printer ten years without setting
up acres of good and bad literature, and learning—uncons-
ciously at first, consciously later—to discriminate between the
two, within his mental limitations; and meantime he is uncon-
sciously acquiring what is called a 'style.' " [34] According to
John Macy, his was an oral style, made up of "sentences amazingly finished and constructed, as if a prose style was as natu-

ral to him as breathing." [35] But if Macy and other thousands of listeners were pleased by the lucidity and wit in that offhand, colloquial delivery, they were listening to a man to whom memorization came as naturally as it did to Joseph Jefferson or any other professional actor of that day. The occasional pause while he tried for the right, the happy, word (usually finding it, of course), the apparently accidental transitions from pure fooling to serious or eloquent passages, the rhetorical balance and clarity, all stemmed from a *written* source—or from its equivalent, a limited discourse formulated so well in the mind of the speaker that he could have put it all onto paper without hesitating. When Mark Twain said, in a lecture of 1884, that from "long observation and slowly compacted experience" he learned that "the best and most telling speech is not the actual impromptu one, but the counterfeit of it," he was talking about writing as well as speaking. The "set speech," which heaves in "a little decayed grammar here, and a little wise tautology there," counterfeits embarrassment, gets the right word after a little finely acted stammering, fetches it out "with ripping effect," and then winds up firing "a parting rocket" in the way of a calculated afterthought,[36] owes something to Mark Twain the actor but more to Mark Twain the writer.

In fact, he secured nearly all these effects of the "set speech" in his dramatic writing; he was a dramatic writer who, like a playwright, tried his writing by reading it aloud. "Yarn it off as if into my sympathetic ear," advises the shrewd editor, Howells, concerning an installment of "Old Times on the Mississippi." [37] Howells means, "Write it and read it aloud and get into it all the illusion you can of your own speaking voice." Almost in response, Clemens explained to Howells that he planned to polish the speech of Aunt Rachel, narrator of "A True Story," by reading and rereading it aloud from galley proof, since she pronounced (and he would have to spell) the same word differently in differently accented parts of a sentence.[38]

From his youth, apparently, Samuel L. Clemens as printer was sensitive to every device in the typesetter's case that might clarify or preserve the sense of the words and produce the illusion of speech. He was as proud of his correct, and functional, punctuation as he was of his word-sense—and more than one printer who had the audacity to impose his rules of punctuation on his manuscript smarted for it. Anyone who has proofread copy of his dialogue knows how often he uses the apostrophe for dropped syllables in colloquial speech. The art of the pause, furthermore, as he considered it in "How to Tell a Story" was a "high and delicate art." Different effects of pause he achieved by parentheses, by square brackets, by dashes (and multiple dashes in his manuscript), and by rows of dots or ellipses shorter or longer (often regularized by printers). His use of commas, semicolons, and colons, as long as he had control over his punctuation as his own publisher, probably followed the printing-house rules in which he had grown up, so far as these marks were linked to grammatical constructs; but they also serve to mark pauses in the sentences read aloud. Few writers of the day, I suspect, produced oral compounds as Mark Twain did, usually with hyphens—compounds like "out-swear" or "talk-arastras" or "heavy-timbered" or "fire-dust" or "alkali-spider" or "harrow-teeth," [39] lengthening out to "a complacent air of 'tisn't-anything,-I-can-do-it-any-time-I-want-to," or "death-on-the-pale-horse-with-hell-following-after," and culminating in the German compounds that the Yankee rolls out when he is getting up one of his effects, like "Mekkamuselmannenmassenmenchenmoerdermohrenmuttermarmormonumentenmacher!" [40]

Still another characteristic use of type for oral effect was Mark Twain's frequent calculated italicizing of words in dialogue for accent and emphasis, and his free use of exclamation marks at high dramatic moments. Occasionally he attempts to suggest his own measured, drawn-out utterance, as when his

Conscience remarks, "I shall always address you henceforth in your o-w-n s-n-i-v-e-l-l-i-n-g d-r-a-w-l—baby!" [41] And occasionally he uses capitalization for an effect of mock-dignity, as when he writes, in 1900, "Would it not be prudent to get our Civilization tools together and see how much stock is left on hand in the way of Glass Beads and Theology, and Maxim Guns and Hymn Books, and Trade Gin and Torches of Progress" for the purpose of "Extending the Blessings of Civilization to our Brother who Sits in Darkness." [42] All these marks of punctuation and type devices are outward signs of an inner sentencing and style that we recognize as that of "Mark Twain." How functional these signs are may be tested by leaving them out of a page or two of, for example, *Adventures of Huckleberry Finn:* they are strong aids to rhythm, emphasis, and sense, and the page is less alive without them.

In what was perhaps his most illuminating piece on style, Mark Twain analyzed two passages of Howells's prose, the first a paragraph from a recent essay on Machiavelli and the second an early description of snow in Venice from *Venetian Life* (1906).[43] Though he limits himself to questions of verbal exactness, clearness, compression, and felicity of phrasing, his critique illuminates the style that both he and Henry James liked so much, and certain qualities of his own prose expression, too. When he speaks of Howells's success in finding "that elusive and shifty grain of gold, the *right word*," he is expressing his own sense that the right word produces an effect "electrically prompt," that it tastes tart and crisp. When he praises Howells for his clarity in comparing Machiavelli and Carlyle, he has in mind presumably such a phrase as "oppression without statecraft, and revolt without patriotism."

The balance and paradox reveal the training of both critic and subject in the school of Goldsmith and Pope, as well as long days of writing in printshop and newspaper offices, more often than not under competent and demanding editors. The "pemmican" quality of compression, however, was a virtue that the two writers scarcely managed to achieve every day. Sam Clemens when young had been a newspaperman and writer of travel letters, under pressure to turn out copy and meet a deadline, so that he knew how to spin out a thin story or add bulk to a subscription book by judicious borrowing. But prolix or not, he feared prolixity and dullness, as one would conclude from his refusal in early 1900 to write regularly for a humorous periodical. The temptation must have been great, for the money would have enabled him to solidify his new prosperity after having paid off his last creditors.[44] Conversely, his taste for pithy, terse expression becomes apparent in the striking Pudd'nhead Wilson maxims of the 1890s.

As for "felicity of phrasing" and "architectural felicities of construction," few writers of the nineteenth century could surpass Mark Twain. In these words he is praising Howells for qualities of prose style also decidedly his own: "easy and flowing," "unvexed by ruggednesses, clumsinesses, broken meters," "simply and [apparently] unstudied," "unconfused by cross-currents, eddies, undertows," "unadorned" yet "all adornment"—in short, a style that is "limpid" and "understandable" and, as we should say, functional. His deliberate, persistent effort to achieve a pure style unfolds in a letter addressed to Howells three decades before the essay. On reading proof of a piece Howells had edited for the *Atlantic*, he confesses his fear that he may become as slovenly a writer as Charles Francis Adams if he doesn't watch out. Then he adds:

> That is said in jest; because of course I do not seriously fear getting so bad as that. I never shall drop so far toward his & Bret Harte's level as to catch myself saying, "It (might) must have been wiser to have believed that he (could) might have accomplished it if he could have felt that he would have been supported by those who should have &c., &c., &c." [45]

His mind and eye are at work, but it is chiefly his trained ear
that enables him to parody Adams's wooden repetitions so
sharply.

What then are the prime qualities of Mark Twain's "sentencing"? Though the question cannot be answered fully without
extended analysis and illustration, one may cite immediately
his skill in managing a series of sentence elements. "Tautology
cannot scare me," he wrote in answer to a "Boston Girl" who
had criticized him for it; [46] and he seems to have meant not
only repetition of key words and words of like meaning but
also of conjunctions like "and," and of phrases and clauses as
well. For example, he cries out exasperatedly to the lightning-
rod salesman:

> Move! Use up all the material you can get your hands on, and
> when you run out of lightning-rods put up ram-rods, cam-rods,
> stair-rods, piston-rods—*anything* that will pander to your dis-
> mal appetite for artificial scenery, and bring respite to my rag-
> ing brain and healing to my lacerated soul! [47]

Rhyme, alliteration, classically balanced phrases build a rhetorical structure brought tumbling down by the double-talking
salesman's reply that he will now "hump himself." Or Mark
Twain discovers that Jim Blaine, Western miner and storyteller, in prime shape to tell his famous story,

> was tranquilly, serenely, symmetrically drunk—not a hiccup to
> mar his voice, not a cloud upon his brain thick enough to ob-
> scure his memory.[48]

Or his gentle Dick Baker explains how he had touched off a
blast in a mining shaft, forgetting that his cat was there, and
then observed, in the dead center of the erupting cloud of
smoke and rocks and dirt,

old Tom Quartz a goin' end over end, an' a snortin' an' a
sneez'n', an' a clawin' an' a reachin' for things like all possessed. But it war'nt no use, you know, it warn't no use.[49]

Or he informs us, speaking of Cooper's dialogue, that the
rules of good fiction require that

when a personage talks like an illustrated, gilt-edged, tree-calf,
hand-tooled, seven-dollar Friendship's Offering in the beginning of a paragraph, he shall not talk like a negro minstrel in
the end of it.[50]

Or, straightforwardly, "Mr. Mark Twain's" narrator, Huck
Finn, tells the reader after an adventure that he and Jim

struck for an island, and hid the raft, and sunk the skiff, and
turned in and slept like dead people.

Or the author has Tom Sawyer stride down the street "with
his mouth full of harmony and his soul full of gratitude," and
give up the whitewash brush "with reluctance in his face but
alacrity in his heart," and then remarks, of Tom's friends, that
"they came to jeer, but remained to whitewash." These examples from Tom Sawyer's *Adventures* are trite enough in humorous intent and rhetorical pattern; yet they are a stage on
the trail to Mark Twain's witty, savage "Greeting" from the
nineteenth century to the twentieth in which Christendom is
pictured as a Matron dishonored by wars

with her soul full of meanness, her pocket full of boodle, and
her mouth full of pious hypocrisies.[51]

Or we may draw again upon Jim Baker, who informs his creator that

A jay will lie, a jay will steal, a jay will deceive, a jay will betray; and four times out of five, a jay will go back on his sol-
emnest promise.[52]

Even so limited a sampling as the passages quoted reveals that
Mark Twain manipulated compound nouns, adjectives, adverbs, participles, simple verbs, prepositional phrases, and
clauses into striking series for picturesque or humorous or
purely narrative ends—usually when he was seeking a rhetorical effect, whether rising to climax or dropping into anticlimax.

Of course Mark Twain wrote direct a-rhythmical sentences
and dialogue of the plainest, simplest kind as the bread-and-
butter form of his various kinds of discourse. These sentences
are more often compound than complex; they are usually
short, their clauses are linked by "and's" and "but's" and
"for's" and "then's"; they consist of nouns and verbs predom-
inantly, and adjectives, when they occur, are striking because
they are few and warily chosen. ("As to the Adjective,"
Pudd'nhead Wilson says, "When in doubt, strike it out." [53])

How skillfully Mark Twain could combine the plain style
and the balanced style a single sentence from the opening
pages of "Old Times on the Mississippi" will illustrate.

After all these years I can picture that old time to myself now,
just as it was then: the white town drowsing in the sunshine of
a summer's morning; the streets empty, or pretty nearly so; one
or two clerks sitting in front of the Water Street stores, with
their splint-bottomed chairs tilted back against the wall, chins
on breasts, hats slouched over their faces, asleep—with shingle-
shavings enough around to show what broke them down; a
sow and a litter of pigs loafing along the sidewalk, doing a good
business in water-melon rinds and seeds; two or three lonely
little freight piles scattered about the "levee;" a pile of "skids"
on the slope of the stone-paved wharf, and the fragrant town

drunkard asleep in the shadow of them; two or three wood flats
at the head of the wharf, but nobody to listen to the peaceful
lapping of the wavelets against them; the great Mississippi, the
majestic, the magnificent Mississippi, rolling its mile-wide tide
along, shining in the sun; the dense forest away on the other
side; the "point" above the town, and the "point" below,
bounding the river-glimpse and turning it into a sort of sea,
and withal a very still and brilliant and lonely one.[54]

The whole intent and effect of this long sentence is to present
a genre picture of Hannibal (Missouri) as it lies asleep shortly
before the arrival of a steamboat transforms it momentarily
into a *moving* picture of furious activity and noise; until with
the departure of the steamboat the town sinks once again into
a dead sleep. A single sentence encompasses a single picture,
the eye of the observer moving from foreground detail to the
far distant frame. Elements of the land-and-seascape figure in
phrases of varying length, but the unifying grammatical element is the series of participles—"drowsing . . . sitting . . .
tilted . . . slouched . . . loafing . . . doing . . . scattered . . .
lapping . . . rolling . . . shining . . . turning." The one verb
following the introductory colon, in "what broke them down,"
has been dropped in as a kind of afterthought and serves only
to emphasize the sense of stasis and stillness; and the "fra-
grance" of the town drunkard disturbs the tranquility of the
scene as little as the low "lapping" of the wavelets.

This same sentence embodies one other feature of a distinguished style: its discriminating use of metaphor. The central,
unifying metaphor is that of sleep, of "drowsing." The clerks
are "broken down" in health from the exertion of whittling—a
figure extravagant but wholly in keeping. The sow and piglets
are "doing a good business" in a town almost without business. And the limitations of small-town life are vividly
pointed up by the metaphor of the great reach of the river as
an "inland sea." More than once Mark Twain deflates an ex-

travagantly rhetorical character with a remark like "Your sentiments do you honor . . . but metaphor is not your best hold." [55] The remark, itself metaphorical, may serve to suggest how persistently, self-consciously, and functionally he made use of figurative speech, both simile and metaphor. It helps also to explain why his enduring work, whether in speeches or private letters or persuasive prose, or fiction, so often strikes readers as still fresh and new. And it may serve as a new point of departure for the criticism of Mark Twain's fiction—particularly if we consider Howells's belief that the novel has its own laws of creation (mostly uninvestigated), whereas the "romance" may be understood in fair part through the older, better understood laws of poetry.

Few critics have addressed themselves to the figurative strain in Mark Twain's writings. Henry James specialists, by contrast, have noted the elegance of the metaphors in *The Ambassadors* and *The Golden Bowl*, how well on the whole they are sustained and elaborated, how effectively they define character or dramatize psychological strain. Charlotte, to illustrate, is figured to the reader as a slender silken purse filled with gold coins, and Amerigo as a Chinese pagoda without a door, around which Maggie at first wanders admiring but baffled. Similarly, the attentive reader of Howells's *Rise of Silas Lapham* will observe the protagonist with his wife "speeding" his fine Morgan mare one cold winter day and passing the other sleighs on the milldam—and discover in this characteristic action a natural metaphor of Lapham's ambition to surpass others socially and financially. And these are only two of many instances that could be adduced.

But who among the Mark Twain experts has undertaken to distinguish the nature of his figures—to determine whether they differ from the figures used by romancers, and whether they serve merely as ornament or as true weight-bearing members in his prose structures? Not more than a handful.

T. S. Eliot and Lionel Trilling have touched on the myth of the river in *Adventures of Huckleberry Finn*, and Henry Nash Smith has shown how the tough coyote and the pursuing dog form a paradigm of contrasts between the Eastern tenderfoot and the Western initiate,[56] between Sam Clemens in 1861 and Mark Twain in 1872. Following their lead, I shall propose, in the chapters to follow, that metaphor serves as a prime force in Mark Twain's writings. It may be different in kind from the metaphor of James or of Howells—and is certainly more directly drawn from the "garden of life"—but it is quite as serviceable to Mark Twain's purposes.

Again, whereas James fulfilled himself as a novelist by creating the "biographical" novel consistently rendered from an interposed "point of view," and thereby exerted a lasting formative pressure on the art of fiction, Mark Twain made his own distinct contribution to the art of fiction: the discovery, very early, of the use of masks. Browning, I believe, was James's Penelope (*pace* Ezra Pound), especially the Browning of the dramatic monologues. Now, Mark Twain discovered Browning only in 1887, long after he had evolved his own storytelling procedures; yet his skill in reading Browning's poems aloud, of interpreting them orally from a marked text and much practice, is significant as revealing a prime source of his own power as speaker/actor/writer—his astonishing use of the mask. "Mark Twain" (meaning two fathoms in riverboating argot) is the first and longest-lasting of these masks, a created character licensed to say things and to speak a kind of language that Samuel L. Clemens could not or would not. Immediately popular as public speaker and writer, Clemens-Mark Twain found that he in turn could create further narrative mask figures by first introducing them in his own formal English, and then permitting them to initiate their own dramatic monologues, in the language of the street or the mines or the river or the printshop or other rich vernaculars.

Through the Mark Twain mask, Samuel L. Clemens found that he could project his voice as genial humorist, controlled ironist, savage satirist, avowed moralist. But his great discovery was that he might then assume the role of an abused Chinaman in California, garrulous Simon Wheeler, drunken Jim Blaine, "Aunt Rachel," simple-hearted Jim Baker, Huck Finn, the ignoramus Connecticut "Yankee," August Feldner, King Leopold of the Belgians, the Czar of All the Russias—or even, as John C. Gerber says, a horse and a dog.[57] His immersion in these characters, once he had designed and adopted the right vernacular mask, tended to be intense and total. As Howells recalled it, his friend once appeared in white cowskin slippers in the drawing room of the Hartford mansion, assuming the gait and speech of a crippled old Negro slave, partly to shock his wife and make her laugh, but mostly, one suspects, out of simple creative exuberance.[58]

Where did Clemens learn the art of speaking through the vernacular mask—the art that Browning's dramatic poetry confirmed for him? Certainly he drew first on the tall tales of the Southwest (as Walter Blair, Bernard DeVoto, and Kenneth Lynn have severally shown). The tales often take the form of a "frame story," perhaps a mere anecdote, depending heavily for dramatic interest on contrasts between the formal speaker and the vernacular character. Typically an educated observer presents a backwoods vulgarian, taking a superior attitude that may be tinged with scorn or contempt, since the narrator is often a Whig gentleman and his dialect-talking subject is low white, a Democrat countryman. The attitude of superiority is anticipated in Cooper's first conception of Natty Bumppo, who is crude of manners and speech alike. The attitude is in fact common to most English and American novelists of the early nineteenth century, Melville largely excepted. It was Clemens's revolutionary step to make flat characters round, to endow his vernacular characters with humanity.

On inspection, however, a second source for his sympathetic vernacular characters may prove at least as important as his total familiarity with tall tales and the humorous literature of New England and the South. From his early youth Sam Clemens loved the Christy minstrel shows, and every "gaudy" effect that the interlocutor or his end men, Bones and Banjo, could achieve in their battle of wits. In Hannibal the Negro musical show was a new institution in the early 1840s, and as the elderly Mark Twain recalled in 1906, it "burst upon us as a glad and stunning surprise." [59] Of the dozen or more joking musicians in tall collars, sweeping swallowtails, and blackface, "Bones" and "Banjo" sat in the end chairs and bantered each other. They used a "very broad negro dialect . . . competently and with easy facility." The middleman, or interlocutor, dressed in the faultless evening costume of white society, "used a stilted, courtly, artificial, and painfully grammatical form of speech," he tells us; and of course the contrast between the minstrels and the middleman was delightfully funny.

But the minstrels were also competent popular musicians, in rudely comic songs like "Buffalo Gals" and in sentimental ditties such as "Nelly Bly." Clemens remembered the Christy minstrels with the same depth of feeling he had for the Fiske Jubilee Singers and their Negro spirituals. When, for example, August Feldner is deep in the dumps, in "No. 44, The Mysterious Stranger," Forty-Four is shrewd enough to appear before him as Bones and to restore him to himself with laughter and music. After clacking the bone castanets and cracking his heels together, "Bones" cries, "*Now* den, Misto' Johnsing, how does yo' corporsosity seem to segashuate!" He then brings tears to Feldner's eyes by singing "Way down upon de Swanee river" with "noble pathos." [60] For Mark Twain the formal-vernacular dramatic potentialities in the minstrel show of his youth were perhaps quite as great as in the humor of his day. Immediately, then, Mark Twain learned the narrative pose of the Gentleman from the humorists, especially the Southern and Southwestern humorists, and from the actors and creators of the minstrel show. More remotely, his early and enduring fondness for Cervantes's *Don Quixote* may also have stimulated his imagination in the creation of his own Don Quixotes and Sancho Panzas.

The characterization, written when he was seventeen, of the Dandy who attempts to frighten the Squatter and is badly discomfited, is probably Clemens's earliest published sketch. It is a crude effort, and crudely foreshadows the gentlemanly scorn of "Mark Twain" in Nevada for an "impudent," rival reporter, "hungry and vicious," whom he labels "The Unreliable." [61] Mark Twain's pretended disdain for "The Unreliable" was a typical journalistic jape for knowing readers, since "The Unreliable" was actually a friend on a rival newspaper in Virginia City, Clement T. Rice. By the time Clemens came to write travel letters from Hawaii, from the voyage via Panama to New York, and from the Holy Land, however, he found the Gentleman-Scoundrel contrast so useful for comic purposes that he created a wholly fictional vulgarian, Mr. Brown. In the main, Mr. Brown served Clemens as a target of rebuke for low manners and tastes; but more than once Clemens permits Brown to puncture Mark Twain's rhapsodic flights as Sentimentalist.

The limitations of the Mark Twain-Brown contrast became apparent to Clemens when he was revising the Quaker City excursion letters for book publication and an audience wider than the readers of the *Alta California*. He dropped Brown entirely, retaining only a few of his more amusing vulgarities and assigning them to other characters in the book. And by the time he was producing the Western chapters of *Roughing It*, "Old Times on the Mississippi," and *Adventures of Huckleberry Finn*, he had imagined a more complex comic pose, confronting the Tenderfoot with the Old-Timer, and had mastered a finer art. It is no accident that in these three works, together with *The Prince and the Pauper* and *The Adventures of Tom Sawyer* as children's books, Mark Twain wrote his most consistent and sustained narratives.

Chapter 2

"STARCHY"
TRAVEL BOOKS

In Roughing It, *violence,* Tenderfoot *and* Old-Timer, *the pose of slothfulness, the "altar of the golden calf."*—"Old Times on the Mississippi" *(and* Life on the Mississippi), *a "standard work" about the flush times of steamboating and about the river, "symbol of eternity." — Piloting demands courage, memory, judgment: Bixby at Hat Island. — A* Tramp Abroad. *— Jim Baker's story about the bluejays, a seamless narrative.*

It is not in the least remarkable that a sensitive boy like the young Henry James, growing up in New York and New England and Geneva, Switzerland, should begin his distinguished writing career with stories of Americans in Europe ("passionate pilgrims") and with *Transatlantic Sketches* (1875) of England, France, Italy, and the Low Countries: Henry James, Sr., affluent, a friend of Emerson, and a Swedenborgian, was resolved to give his sons a "better sensuous education" than America afforded, and this by exposing them to Europe. It is a little remarkable that an Ohio boy like William Dean Howells, whose youth of near-poverty curiously com-

pounded hard work and steady reading, should write an authentic "inside" book on Venice (1866) and follow it up with a
book of Italian travel. The key to the Italian domicile was a political one: producing a good campaign biography of Abraham
Lincoln had for its reward appointment as U.S. Consul in Venice. *But* that a Missouri scion of declassed Southern gentlefolk
should become famous for travel books—first with the immensely successful *Innocents Abroad* (1869)—is at first blush altogether surprising. On reflection, however, it comes to us
that young Sam Clemens had begun to set type at age nine,
and thus the wanderlust and freedom of the jour printer would
help account for his extensive travels and many years of European residence.

Mark Twain, Howells, and James were all responding to a
demand for travel books among American readers, as well as
fulfilling their own longing to absorb the best elements of European culture. The studies by James and Howells were issued by New England publishers and tended to reach educated, well-traveled Americans. Mark Twain's, from the first,
were bought and read and laughed over by "the belly and
members," as he put it—Americans in small towns and farms
all over the country—in part because he chose the new mass-
publisher and "subscription" publishing as a consequence of
his growing popularity on the lecture platform.

Innocents Abroad, that first travel book, proved a success
because he had learned relief and timing while turning out his
newspaper letters in the West, from Hawaii, and on the way
from San Francisco to New York by way of the Isthmus of
Panama, and because he revised carefully the newspaper letters on which the book was based. *Following the Equator* (1897)
was his last travel narrative—a largely neglected study of Aus-
tralian, South African, and especially Indian, cultures. Between them he produced the three that seem to me to be his
best: *Roughing It* (1872), "Old Times on the Mississippi"

(1875), expanded to *Life on the Mississippi* (1883), and *A Tramp Abroad* (1880).

Innocents Abroad, like most books of travel, takes its form from an itinerary, in this instance a voyage to Europe, exploration of the Mediterranean world, and the return. In general the parts of the book follow from the original travel letters to the *Alta California.* The pattern is clear and satisfying. *Roughing It,* unlike its predecessor, betrays a sharp disjunction in the final quarter, for Mark Twain was plainly no longer "roughing it" when he took ship for the Sandwich Islands and reported on the wonders of Oahu and the big island. The tone and humor of the last seventeen chapters suffer in comparison with that of the first sixty-one, and the reason is simply that, as he was rushing to fill the six hundred pages necessary to make a subscription book, "the well ran dry" and he had to fall back upon the Hawaiian travel letters written several years earlier. The break before the last quarter of *Roughing It* is thus due to the shift from the Western scene and the addition of earlier, less focused, letters. In turn both these flaws came from flagging inspiration and the pressures of subscription publishing.

Yet *Roughing It* is a much better book than *Innocents Abroad.* Mark Twain produced the bulk of it in twelve months from a single inspiration, without having to face constant deadlines. It is a vigorous, spirited work, more unified in structure and effect in its first three quarters than *Innocents.* In it Clemens was using his experience much as Melville had in *Typee* and *Omoo* and capitalizing on his striking initial success. Nothing shows more clearly that he was well on the way to becoming what James called "that queer monster, the artist" [1] than that he forged and finished the book under severe pressure. During its composition Olivia's father died; one of her close friends who was visiting her died of typhoid fever in their new home; their first child, Langdon, was born prematurely, and Livy herself became worn out from nursing. But Mark

Twain's physical and nervous energy was great. With help from his brother Orion's Western notebooks and under the stimulus of reminiscences with Joe Goodman, his editor and friend of *Territorial Enterprise* days, he wrote on with "red-hot interest." He planned to write eight hundred book pages, cut to six hundred, and turn out when finished, he said to his publisher, a "starchy book." [2] A starchy book it is.

On the primary level, *Roughing It* is a picaresque narrative filled with danger, blood, and violence. As something of a rogue, "Mark Twain" either participates in a series of adventures or witnesses them and reports them; and it goes without saying that the adventures lose little in the telling. On the first page he tells us that he would travel and have "all kinds of adventures, and may be get hanged or scalped, and have ever such a fine time" and become a hero, very rich, and "return home by sea" and talk about the marvels of the West to his admiring family and friends.[3] The tone is light—but before he leaves the West, the real Mark Twain does have his adventures. The first of these, the sound of pistol shots and blows in the night at a mail station, hints at the death of an over-talkative driver. Apocryphal or not, the mysterious violence provides the artist a lead for recounting the life of J. A. Slade, desperado, vigilante, and division agent of the Overland Mail, who killed twenty-six men in his bloody career and died on the gallows, "exhausted by tears, prayers, and lamentations" (pp. 75–96; Nat Ed 1:57–80). Almost the first scene confronting the Clemens brothers on arriving in Carson City was an argument between a Mr. Harris and a stranger, which ended when Harris rode home "with a bullet through one of his lungs, and several in his hips," the "little rivulets of blood that coursed down the horse's sides," giving the animal a "quite picturesque" look (pp. 158–59; Nat Ed 1:146).

The question of moral courage raised by the manner of Slade's death reappears in the Mark Twain account of the "stalwart ruffian called 'Arkansas,' who carried two revolvers in his belt and a bowie knife projecting from his boot, and who was always drunk and always suffering for a fight." While they were isolated for eight days at a station on high ground in the flooded Carson River, as he tells the reader, Arkansas browbeat and dominated a gang of roughs in the barroom, picking especially upon the landlord, Johnson, a "meek, well-meaning fellow" and giving him no rest. On the fourth morning, Arkansas works himself into a drunken fury and begins to shoot at the inoffensive Johnson—until "the landlord's wife suddenly appeared in the doorway and confronted the desperado with a pair of scissors! Her fury was magnificent" . . .

> With head erect and flashing eye she stood a moment and then advanced, with her weapon raised. The astonished ruffian hesitated, and then fell back a step. She followed. She backed him step by step into the middle of the bar-room, and then, while the wondering crowd closed up and gazed, she gave him such another tongue-lashing as never a cowed and shamefaced braggart got before, perhaps! As she finished and retired victorious, a roar of applause shook the house, and every man ordered "drinks for the crowd" in one and the same breath.

Arkansas's domination was broken for good; and for four days more he endured in humiliated silence "the insults the once cringing crew now constantly leveled at him" (pp. 221–26; Nat Ed 1:213–18). Mark Twain manages this intense scene in six pages, largely in the form of dialogue between Arkansas and Johnson, with only the sparest narrating of the action. He must have known how well he had managed the telling, for, even before completing *Roughing It*, he planned a Western play to consist of episodes from the book, including the "Arkansas" incident.[4]

The adventures of Mark Twain continue as he and Ballou and a Prussian whom he calls Ollendorf ford the flooded Carson River on their return to Carson City, become lost, and wander in circles during a blizzard, trying without luck to light a fire and having to spend a frightful night in the snow, "forlorn and hopeless." In the morning, to their relief—and disgust—they find that they had made camp only fifteen steps from a comfortable inn. Their "curious and absurd adventure" may have happened just as its narrator claims it did. But that he and his companions tried to light a fire by firing a pistol into a pile of twigs, or that they wept and gave up smoking, whiskey, and cards during the storm, and then shamefacedly resumed their vices the next day, may be doubted. Whatever the reality, Mark Twain's taste for burlesque weakens, or perhaps masks, the real terror he evokes of being lost in a blizzard.[5]

Mark Twain further survived the threat of drowning, with Calvin Higbie, in a rowboat on alkaline Lake Mono. He was also left "white as a sheet and as weak as a kitten and speechless" by the explosion in camp there of an old bake-oven in which some former miner had left six cans of rifle powder. (All alone, of course, he was being drawn deeper and deeper into the "flush times," the fever of gold and silver mining and of speculation in mining stocks. This fever forms—as we shall see—another leading motif in *Roughing It*.) Finally, turning reporter for the *Territorial Enterprise* of Virginia City, on his first day he wrote up a saloon killing and—so he says—thanked the murderer profusely for the column of news thus supplied (chaps. 39, 42; Nat Ed 1:39, 2, 1). This burlesque account parallels the earlier paragraph on the "picturesque" shooting of Harris, and introduces three sardonic chapters (48–50) on murder in Virginia City and the West.

Mark Twain notes that the first twenty-six graves in the Virginia City cemetery were "occupied by *murdered* men." He explains how the "long-tailed heroes of the revolver"—desperadoes, gamblers, saloon-keepers—held more than equal status with lawyers, editors, and bankers, because each had "killed his man." He cites examples and quotes extracts from the *Enterprise* to show how deputy marshals might be killers in office and how, in new countries, "murders breed murders." Then, against this drum roll of shots and unpunished slaughter, he counterpoises a "scrap of history" from the life of Captain Ned Blakely (Captain Edgar Wakeman in reality), a warmhearted, hard-headed sailing captain based in San Francisco. In this story—related often in dramatic form—Captain Blakely has arrested a bully in the lawless Chincha Islands who while ashore had killed his Negro mate before a half-dozen witnesses. Under persuasion, Blakely had agreed to the motions of a trial, but had hung the murderer with his own hands after reading him four chapters of the Bible. These stories of killings are recounted coolly and ironically, but the author states his purpose openly enough. "I desire to tamper with the jury law," he declares, "to put a premium on intelligence and character, and close the jury box against idiots, blacklegs, and people who do not read newspapers" (chaps. 48–50; Nat Ed 2:7–9). In this context his original dedication seems the more pointed: "TO THE LATE CAIN THIS BOOK IS DEDICATED . . . in that it was his misfortune to live in a dark age that knew not the beneficent insanity plea." [6]

The sustained motif of violence and adventure in *Roughing It* ends in anticlimax, after Mark Twain's months in Hawaii and his first success as a lecturer in San Francisco. His final adventure is a practical joke. On the divide between Virginia City and Gold City, six masked men rough up the journalist and his lecture agent and take their money and their watches. Only a few hours later he learns that the robbers had all been his friends, with other friends listening in the darkness to the whole proceeding, and that his agent had been in on the joke (chap. 89; Nat Ed 2:38). Despite the lively and amusing dialogue that Mark Twain reports as having taken place between him and his robber friends, one senses that even after five years the author was not much amused by the memory.

The pose of tenderfoot ignorance, as will appear, underlies and unifies the Western chapters of *Roughing It*. A pose of one-half utter, feckless laziness and the other half speculative gold fever serves the author equally well in patterning his book on the West and providing a consistent mask for "Mark Twain" the narrator. There is an implication in this pose—rather deep hidden but insistent—that luck is for the lucky, who are few, and that work and a vocation are for the many, of whom Mark Twain counted himself one. Thus, in my judgment, the theme of *The Gilded Age* (1873) was already forming in his mind in *Roughing It*, and *Roughing It* means almost the opposite of what Van Wyck Brooks took it to mean—a glorification of the get-rich-quick spirit. His miner friend Jim Gillis, according to biographer A. B. Paine, always declared, "If Sam had got that pocket [of gold nuggets] he would have remained a pocket-miner to the end of his days, like me." [7] But Gillis was wrong, for he had no notion of the power of Clemens's drives, or his ingrained belief that money must be earned, or the extent of his commitment to writing. Van Wyck Brooks was too often taken in by the Mark Twain mask. Howells speaks with authority when he observes of Clemens that "You were all there for him, but he was not all there for you." [8]

This pose of slothfulness is open and constant, whereas the implication that work is the normal and proper lot of most men may be read only in the constant, fruitless search of "Mark Twain" for wealth, and his pointedly absurd adventures as a prospector-speculator. This search begins when he and Johnny K—— lay out a timber claim on the shores of Lake Tahoe, Johnny of course doing most of the work. They become landowners, possessed of some three hundred acres of dense yellow-pine forest. They lose their property when their carelessly tended campfire sets the forest ablaze. By and by Mark

Twain is "smitten by the silver fever," and he and three partners push two hundred miles over to Unionville, in the Humboldt country. He finds a "deposit of shining yellow scales" in a shallow rivulet, and thinks to overwhelm his partners with gold ore worth two thousand dollars a ton, only to learn from Ballou, the old-timer, that he has found "fool's gold" (iron pyrites). When Ballou discovers a quartz outcropping with signs of gold and silver in it, they stake out a claim for the "Monarch of the Mountains" mine. But a week of digging and blasting, first a shaft and then a tunnel, is enough to discourage them, and they "resign." As the camp fills up with people, they take up new claims, trade "feet" with others, acquire part ownership in dozens of claims—and cannot pay their butcher and grocer bills. The whole scene was "a beggars' revel," says Mark Twain.[9]

His next venture, with Ballou and Ollendorf, came close to being his last, for they were caught on horseback in a blizzard in which a Swede and two drovers died. Reaching the Esmeralda mines, in which they owned "feet" and had been paying assessments, they found that the owners had been living on the assessments and that the claims were worthless. Esmeralda, in short, proved to be another Humboldt. When his money ran short, and flour reached a dollar a pound, Mark Twain tells us, he went to work as a laborer in a quartz mill at ten dollars a week and board. At the end of the first week of heavy labor, he asked for a raise, and was fired—he says (chaps. 30–33, 35–36; Nat Ed 1, ibid.), though the truth is probably that at the time he was learning quartz milling in anticipation of running his own mine and mill—in the golden future.

The pattern continues, a little wilder at each turn. A certain Mr. Whiteman had inherited a map locating a cement mine near Mono Lake in which "lumps of virgin gold were as thick . . . as raisins in a slice of fruit cake." Mark Twain the writer, looking back, spoke of the map as a curse. So, when the new Don Quixote and his partner, Calvin Higbie, learn through a friend that Whiteman is in town, disguised, they leave in great secrecy at midnight and reach the lake a few hours later, only to observe the "rest of the population" filing over the divide in a long procession and drifting down to the lake shore (chap. 37; Nat Ed 1, ibid.).

The climax of Mark Twain's "slothful, valueless, heedless career," as he called it in recollection, occurs when the Wide West mine in the Esmeralda district "strikes it rich." Examining and puzzling over a fresh specimen of the new, very valuable Wide West "rock," Higbie concludes that it is not the "rock" that had been extracted during the weeks before. By sliding down the shaft at night and searching carefully, he discovers that a "blind lead" crosses the Wide West vein, diagonally. That same night Higbie and Mark Twain take the foreman of the Wide West company into partnership—the procedure was lawful and precedented—put up the notice of their claim to the blind lead, and revel in the certainty of future wealth. All they need do to make their claim total is to work their new property within ten days. If they do not, anyone who chose might seize it.

The sequel, as Mark Twain relates it, is as gripping as the discovery and claim. Called away to nurse Capt. John Nye, a friend who lay seriously ill, he left a note for Higbie. Higbie had gone after that "thrice accursed cement" on notice from Whiteman, and had left a note for his partner:—"Don't fail to do the work before the ten days expire," throwing it through a broken window pane in his haste. The foreman had been called to California on a matter of life and death. When Mark Twain and Higbie reached the town, they met at the cabin, found the unread notes, and learned that they were ruined, because fourteen townsmen had "relocated the blind lead" the moment the ten-day period had elapsed. A few months later they discovered that the new company and the Wide West had consolidated and that one of the fourteen men had sold out his share of the combined companies for $90,000 in gold. So Mark Twain could claim, "I was absolutely and unquestionably worth a million dollars, once, for ten days." Higbie, he adds, after ten subsequent years of hard work had managed to get together twenty-five hundred dollars, and intended to "go into the fruit business in a modest way" (chaps. 40–41; Nat Ed 1, ibid.).

Concluding his account, Mark Twain admitted that it "reads like a wild fancy sketch" but insisted that it was really a "true history," with abundant proof of its veracity. That he nursed Captain Nye for a time is true; that he forfeited holdings in the Wide West mine through neglect while Higbie was searching for the cement "plum cake" is also true; but that he lost a great fortune in consequence seems highly dubious, on Paine's testimony. In this key episode the skilled storyteller unobtrusively heightens and transmutes his experience.[10]

This same storytelling flair operates in the account of how Mark Twain came to write for the *Territorial Enterprise:* he had tried "various vocations," he stated, and "amounted to less than nothing in each"—though five of the vocations are imaginary. More, he had been a very slow compositor—though evidence abounds that he had been both fast and accurate. Finally, he confesses that he, a poor and disappointed miner, could never go back home to be snubbed, whereas he still believed that he could make money in mining. "I was scared into being a city editor," he wryly avows (pp. 292–95; Nat Ed 2:1–4). In actual fact he deliberated for some time before he took the position on the *Enterprise,* and he minimized his experience as a writer.

As a reporter for this flourishing newspaper (the "Mark Twain" pseudonym appeared for the first time on his stories), he achieved almost instant distinction, and his salary soon

jumped from twenty-five to forty dollars per week. Reveling in
the flush times of the mining communities, he recounted how
reporters received "feet" of mining stock for writing up new
claims and new mines on any terms, and how friend would
present to friend twenty-five feet of a stock worth twenty-five
dollars per foot, as though it were a cigar. It was thus, he
wrote, that he accumulated half a trunkful of mining-stock cer-
tificates, while his pockets filled up with twenty-dollar gold
pieces. At the same time, looking backward, he exposed the
ways in which mines might be "salted" with richer ore or
even melted silver coins, and how assayers might lie, for a
price. Simultaneously, without editorial comment he informed
the reader of Joseph Goodman's high standards and editorial
independence, the real prosperity of his newspaper, and the
solid returns to owners and drivers of the great freighting
firms that brought flour and timber and mining supplies over
from Sacramento to the mining towns (chaps. 44–45; Nat Ed
2:3–4).

Leaving Nevada for California, Mark Twain notes humorously that he wanted a change, for he had in Goodman's
absence penned enough "bitter personalities" in the *Enterprise*
to bring Goodman six challenges to duel on his return. But he
did not as yet repress his yen for sudden wealth. Dan De
Quille promised him the opportunity to go back East and sell a
rich silver mine for a "princely sum." It was the "blind lead
come again" (p. 402; Nat Ed 2:118). Then, after a period of
butterfly idleness in cordial San Francisco, "out went the bottom and everything and everybody went to ruin and destruction!" He threw his worthless stocks away. He missed the
long-awaited opportunity to go East by failing to read a note at
his desk and thus just missing his steamer at the wharf; and a
few months later he learned that the entrepreneurs with whom
he was to go to New York City had sold the silver mine for
three million dollars. It was the "blind lead" still once more.

Whereupon, he tells us, he lost heart, neglected his duties as a reporter, was discharged, and fell into utter poverty. One final venture into pocket-mining in Tuolumne County with "an old friend of mine" and a certain Dick Baker of Dead-Horse Gulch left him "centless as the last rose of summer" and "too mean and lazy" to get another newspaper job in San Francisco.

After noting his five hard months of daily correspondence from San Francisco to the *Enterprise*, and describing at length his "half a year's luxurious vagrancy" writing letters from the Sandwich Islands for the *Sacramento Union*, Mark Twain concludes with a flourish. Though he feared failure for his first public lecture in San Francisco, he achieved an explosive success by forming his friends into a claque. "All the papers were kind in the morning; my appetite returned; I had abundance of money," he wrote. "All's well that ends well." [11] The last apparent self-revelation comes in the MORAL of *Roughing It:* "If you are 'no account,' go away from home, and then you will *have* to work" (p. 570; Nat Ed 2:304). So Sam Clemens maintains the Mark Twain mask of good-for-nothing laziness to the very end, and caps the rags-to-riches motif with the episode of his "first" great success as a humorous and eloquent speaker. The real moral so little insisted upon lies in Mark Twain's escape from victimization at the "altar of the golden calf" (p. 415; Nat Ed 2: 132) or the "California sudden-riches disease" [12] into his true vocation of lecturing and writing.

Closely linked to the double pattern of violent adventure and wild dreams of sudden riches in *Roughing It* is the tenderfoot's gradual initiation into the life of Washoe and his evolution into an old-timer (as Henry Nash Smith and John C. Gerber have shown [13]). Mark Twain writing the book was the experienced old-timer remembering and creating a younger, innocent narrator for particular ends, as the original title, "Innocents at Home," attests. Tenderfoot Mark Twain informs the reader in the first chapter that he proposed to stay in Nevada

some three months. Old-timer Mark Twain admits ruefully-
humorously that he stayed seven years—and thus casually re-
assures the reader who might wonder what Clemens was
doing during the Civil War that he had been in the West.

The distinction is maintained throughout the book. The
Syrian camel who choked to death on one of Mark Twain's
sentences in a manuscript, the anecdote of the coconut-eating
cat that Eckert tells in Bangkok, and the comparison of Kilauea
and Haleakala to Vesuvius, though they have their immediate
charm, indicate that the writer of the book is not his un-
traveled innocent self. The fable of the foolish (Eastern) dog
with a good opinion of his strength and speed pursuing the
uncatchable (Western) coyote is a fine paradigm (in Smith's el-
egant interpretation) of the persistent tenderfoot / old-timer
conflict. The coyote of course vanishes in a burst of speed and
leaves the dog exhausted, alone—and enlightened. One thinks
of Simon Suggs' pawky saying, "It's good to be shifty in a new
country." [14] The conflict is made explicit in a passage when
Mark Twain recalls "afterward" how the proud and blessed
"FORTY-NINER" pitied, looked down upon, and ridiculed the
"emigrant" as a low, inferior creature. The conflict turns into
action when the travelers' poor pistols and poorer aim are
demonstrated; when a "sociable heifer" invites the Clemens
brothers to "lay over for a couple of days" in her town of Cottonwood and they fearfully refuse; when Mark Twain buys a
"Genuine Mexican Plug," believing that he has bought a
horse; when he mistakes mica and iron pyrites for gold; and
when again, as Smith has observed, he undergoes a kind of
initiation in the blizzard.

The artist Mark Twain had several reasons for developing
his contrast of Eastern and Western types—which ended in the
tenderfoot's becoming acclimated and accepted. As "Mark
Twain" he had already experimented with the comic poses of
the Sufferer and the Simpleton (as Gerber has called them),

but the mask—or persona or pose—of the tenderfoot promised larger results. It enabled him, first, to present the rich and strange elements of Nevada life without intrusive explanation—and the risk of seeming patronizing or superior. Second, it gave free rein to his passion for elucidating the skills and knowledges of the West, indeed, every sort of frontier *expertise*. Thus, only once in *Roughing It* did he find it necessary to add a note explaining mining terminology: at the end of Dick Baker's dramatic monologue about his cat, Tom Quartz. Third, it permitted him to write a simplified, fictionalized history of the mining boom and to analyze Western character from the perspective of an expert who learned the hard way.

In my belief, however, Mark Twain dropped the mask of the tenderfoot narrator well before he had finished the book, and for good reasons. The dichotomy plainly implies Western superiority as well as Western difference. Whatever he may have felt at the time in Nevada and California, he was about to move to Hartford, Connecticut, when he was writing *Roughing It*, and he could not accept the Western view unreservedly. The weapons he tells us he carried are symptomatic. As a tenderfoot he went West carrying a "pitiful little Smith & Wesson's seven-shooter, which carried a ball like a homoeopathic pill." In the West, when he was a miner, he carried the "universal navy revolver" slung to his belt, though he wore it only "in deference to popular sentiment." But on taking the job of city editor in Virginia City, he discarded the revolver for good, even though the other editors and all the printers carried guns.[15] That is, even before he left the West he was not wholeheartedly of the West because he was recognizing its limitations.

Mark Twain's tribute to the "driving, vigorous, restless population" of the California camps is well known: "a *curious* population," he calls it, "no women, no children, no gray and stooping veterans,—none but erect, bright-eyed, quick-moving, strong-handed young giants" (p. 415; Nat Ed 2:132). They were generous, like the men of Gold Hill, who auctioned one floursack over and over again to support the U.S. Sanitary Commission during the Civil War. They were self-reliant, like Joe Goodman; they were spirited and enduring, like the pony rider racing fifty miles in every kind of weather through "the blackness of darkness." Like Buck Fanshaw and Capt. Ned Blakely they practiced rough justice. But they also persecuted the Chinese and condoned endless murder, and—Mark Twain concludes his rhetorical summary, "Where are they now?" Scattered, decrepit, shot or stabbed in street frays, many of them gone, they were sacrificed on the "altar of the golden calf," like the Swede who died in the blizzard, or the "mendicant 'Blucher,' " or Calvin Higbie, who dropped mining only after working hard at it for ten fruitless years (*Roughing It* is dedicated to Higbie).

The book is, finally, a splendid anthology of anecdotes and tales. These vary in quality and relevance, but the best of them—and there are many good ones—are finely wrought, firmly based in character, and in some manner related to the motifs of violent adventure, or the lazy man striking it rich, or the greenhorn's initiation. In the area of "plot" movement, these fictional nodes make for the same variety of pace that Mark Twain sought to maintain in his lectures—by alternating between vernacular humor and quite formal eloquent description or "useful" information. At the level of anecdote, Mark Twain points up the difference between the immense mile-wide Mississippi and the rivers of Nevada by explaining that "One of the pleasantest and most invigorating exercises one can contrive is to run and jump across the Humboldt river till he is overheated, and then drink it dry" (p. 203; Nat Ed 1:194). Or he contrasts the terrible heat of Fort Yuma with the endless winter of Mono Lake by noting the tradition, attributed to John Phenix, that once when a very wicked soldier died at Fort

Yuma, he "of course, went straight to the hottest corner of per-
dition—and the next day he *telegraphed back for his blankets*"
(p. 412; Nat Ed 2:129). Or he makes vivid the power of the
daily wind in Virginia City by distinguishing its contents in
levels, thus:

> . . . hats, chickens and parasols sailing in the remote heavens;
> blankets, tin signs, sage-brush and shingles a shade lower;
> door-mats and buffalo robes lower still; shovels and coal scut-
> tles on the next grade; glass doors, cats and little children on the
> next; disrupted lumber yards, light buggies and wheelbarrows
> on the next; and down only thirty or forty feet above ground
> was a scurrying storm of emigrating roofs and vacant lots. (P.
> 160; Nat Ed, 2:147)

One of the liveliest anecdotes concerns the "Brigade" of
New York office-seekers-turned-surveyors who assemble in
their boarding house a menagerie of tarantulas under tumblers, and who enjoy stirring them up in their glass prisons.
The emprisoned hairy spiders, big as saucers, were "starchy"
and "proud," according to the narrator, and would "take up a
straw and pick their teeth like a member of Congress." But the
tables are turned when at midnight a Washoe Zephyr blows a
stable roof into the side of the boarding house and knocks
over all the tumblers. The "creeping, bloody-minded tarantulas" route the Eastern tenderfeet and drive them into panic
(pp. 164–67; Nat Ed 1:151–54). Here Mark Twain employs effectively the pattern of tables-turned in a single sharp reversal;
it is, however, less effective in the victory of mild-mannered
Williams over the blustering Admiral, for the reason that the
second episode has almost no context, whereas the tarantulas,
the "wickedest-looking desperadoes the animal world can fur-
nish," belong naturally to the same world as the sorry-looking
coyote who persistently and decisively fools the inexperienced
dog. They enlarge the fable of tenderfoot and old-timer.[16]

Whether at the level of the tall tale, the short sketch in which the narrator is "sold," or the animal fable, *Roughing It* is especially rich. These stories may be lifted from their context and enjoyed for themselves; yet each of them gains from the matrix and enhances the matrix. The stories in order concern Bemis and the buffalo (and, as a kind of pendant, Eckert and the coconut-eating cat); Brigham Young and his wives; the Mexican Plug; General Buncombe and Judge Roop; Buck Fanshaw's funeral; Capt. Ned Blakely as a judge, Western-style; Jim Blaine and his grandfather's old ram; Dick Baker's astronautical cat, Tom Quartz; Williams *vs.* the "Admiral"; Simon Erickson, William Beazeley, Horace Greeley and the turnips; and "Markiss." [17] The last three sketches are inferior in themselves and neither gain from nor contribute to their Hawaiian setting. The Admiral, first presented as a kind of Ned Blakeley, in his defeat degenerates into a blustering hypocrite. "Markiss" is an irritably told tall tale. The attempt to read and decipher Greeley's letter about growing turnips is a momentarily amusing piece of verbal idiocy, but no more. The three stories are all part of Mark Twain's effort to expand his book to subscription-volume length.

Jim Blaine's free-wheeling attempt to tell about his grandfather's ram, for all that it ends with a tall-tale anticlimax as he falls asleep, has more grounding in character. Listening to the drunken Blaine, waiting for a point that never comes, Mark Twain and the reader are "sold." Now, while the "sell" story is in fact a simple if not crude form, Mark Twain could manage it effectively. Thus, in an elaborate fake trial staged by Judge Roop and certain old-timers, General Buncombe tries to defend in court the rights of a farmer whose ranch had been buried ten feet deep by another man's ranch in a landslide— and of course loses the case. Rather better is Mark Twain's tale of how he had been "sold" a genuine Mexican plug; that is, a worthless bucking bronco. His brother confidently tried the brute after it had "shed" Mark Twain and some others, and had to report that on his trip to the Capitol "he had been in the air so much he felt as if he had made the trip on a comet." This "fancy sketch," belongs to an old tradition in American humor of racing, swapping, buying, and selling horses, including Faulkner's "Spotted Horses." A passenger on the mail coach, Bemis by name, had earlier prepared the way for the initiation of Mark Twain and of General Buncombe by means of *his* tall tale of a buffalo hunt. With great reluctance and a perfectly straight face, he had revealed how a wounded buffalo bull drove his horse mad, pursued horse and rider to a tree, overtaking dogs and jackass rabbits and coyotes on the way, and began to climb the tree after him. But Bemis survived the ordeal: he lowered a coil of his lariat over the climbing bull's head, fired his "comprehensive" Allen revolver in the bull's face, and left the beast dangling in the air and going into convulsions (chap. 7; Nat Ed 1:7).

It is implicit in Mark Twain's pose of artlessness that he should introduce the tale of Capt. Ned Blakeley's love of "simple, straightforward justice" as a "digression." Actually, as we have seen, Blakeley's hanging the murderer of his black mate, after reluctantly agreeing to a trial, forms the appropriate climax for Mark Twain's treatment of "blood and carnage," of murder condoned, and of the non-functioning jury law in the West. Scotty Briggs's dialogue with the Eastern minister as they arrange for Buck Fanshaw's funeral charms the reader with its "pemmican" vernacular and poetic idiom, but it also voices the same motif of violence and justice, for Fanshaw would have peace, even if he had to send fourteen men home on shutters to manage it.

Mark Twain's mounting skill in managing a point of view is everywhere apparent in the tall tale about Brigham Young's troubles with his many wives. He is reporting what "a Gentile by the name of Johnson" remembers about his conversation

with Brigham Young at breakfast "in the hennery". As one
might expect, Young's troubles in domestic economy, with
competing wives and children, increase in absurdity. But
Clemens-Mark Twain-Johnson moves almost imperceptibly
from indirect-discourse narrative, to occasionally repeating
what Young says, to a four-page dramatic monologue by
Young, *crescendo*. The absurdities become twice as absurd as
the illusion of reality increases in the speaking voice. The art
is scarcely apparent until the mask-Mark Twain pricks the
balloon, saying, "Some instinct or other made me set this
Johnson down as unreliable" (chap. 15; Nat Ed, 1, ibid.). It is
the very art that Christopher Newman, hero of Henry James's
novel *The American*, had witnessed and learned to emulate.
"He had sat," James tells us, "with western humorists in circles around cast-iron stoves and had seen tall stories grow
taller without toppling over, and his imagination had learnt
the trick of building straight and high." [18]

Roughing It is surely, as Louis J. Budd has pronounced it,
Mark Twain's "sunniest book." It is outstanding among the
"personal books," brimming with anecdotes and stories that
the narrator projects through the masks of feckless laziness
and tenderfoot ignorance and of disillusioned knowledge as
well. It exposes the fear and venality that are the prime motives for murderous violence on the frontier. It concludes by
demonstrating that the gold-hungry dream-of-success that
so filled the hearts of miner-speculators in Nevada and California was almost purely illusory. The revelation is all the
more credible—and dramatic—because Mark Twain *younger*
shared in the dream so fully, and even more persistently
than Mark Twain *older* reveals. *Roughing It* is also what its
author predicted it would be, a high-spirited, "starchy"
book. It thrilled him through and through even as he wrote,
Clemens recalled, "to think of the life, the gladness and the
wild sense of freedom that used to make the blood dance in

my veins on those fine overland mornings!" (RI, p. 48; Nat Ed 1:31). He was filled with the excitement of encountering a new land that would prove at least as forbidding as it was beautiful, and a new generation of men nearly all of whom were lost but who would have laughed the idea to scorn if they had been told so. In this work Mark Twain reconciled two of his deepest motives as a writer: to tell an engrossing story and to record and interpret a phase of American history.

Although, like *Adventures of Huckleberry Finn* (1885), *Roughing It* (1872) sags toward the end, the work concludes brilliantly: the narrator finds his vocation in lecturing and writings. *Life on the Mississippi* (1883), which is sixty chapters long, and also a subscription book, suffers from some of the same disjunctures in the last two-thirds of the work, and in the final three chapters and four appendixes runs downhill to a flat conclusion. Yet, once again, taken as a whole—or perhaps taken at its best—*Life on the Mississippi* is what Mark Twain maintained he was going to make it, a superior book of autobiography and history. The first third, roughly, comprising the *Atlantic Monthly* installments (1875), constitutes the longest, most closely planned and finely wrought unit in the whole body of the "personal books." Thus, the early "Old Times on the Mississippi" papers, with the three succeeding chapters that complete the piloting sequence, may best be considered as a distinct sequence within the much looser structure of the book that Mark Twain was to write seven years later. The idea of using the "matter of the Mississippi" had lain long in Mark Twain's consciousness. As early as 1866 he had written his mother that he intended to get at such a book. In 1871 he wrote his wife Livy that he wished to spend "2 months on the river & take notes, & I bet you I will make a standard work." [19] The minister Joseph Twichell's enthusiasm for this "virgin subject," so right to "hurl into a magazine," was matched by that of Howells, whose uncles had been Ohio

River pilots. Mark Twain produced the seven "Old Times" papers from memory for the *Atlantic;* and in 1882 he went back to the river with his publisher, James R. Osgood, and a stenographer, Roswell Phelps, to take notes for the book.

"Old Times" is a work of genius, stimulated by Mark Twain's memory and imagination and channeled by his sensitivity at every point in the writing to the sophisticated *Atlantic* audience and to the most perceptive critic of the day, his friend Howells. He was on his mettle. He was being paid at a higher rate than any contributor to the *Atlantic* had ever been paid before. He could trust the intelligence of his readers in that they "don't require a 'humorist' to paint himself striped & stand on his head every fifteen minutes." [20] He worked very hard both composing and revising, under such shrewd advice as that of Howells in urging him to write colloquial narrative.[21] The "Old Times" sequence is the heart of *Life on the Mississippi,* and most of the succeeding chapters are linked to it as if by veins and arteries. To switch the metaphor, the essential tie between the first third and the remaining two-thirds is Mark Twain's rendering of change on the river—both growth and decay—between the pre-Civil War years and the early 1880s. Yet by 1875 Mark Twain had already set the prime motifs of the work, remembering his boyhood ambition to go on the river and its fulfillment in morning freshness when he became a pilot in the flush times before the Civil War.

The "voice" of Mark Twain in "Old Times on the Mississippi" carefully modulates somewhere between boyhood and late 'teens, though in fact Sam Clemens was nearly twenty-two when he went on the river as a cub. This means that the narrative is filtered through the sensibility of an ignorant and rather lazy youngster, though young Clemens could actually steer anything on the Mississippi smaller than a steamboat, and already knew a great deal about steamboating. The reasons for the mask are many; but the most important were to establish, by contrast with the "cub's" ignorance, the astonishing knowledge and skill of pilots like Mr. B—— (Horace Bixby), Mr. W., Mr. X., even Capt. Isaiah Sellers and Mr. Brown, and to provide dramatic means by which *Atlantic* readers, most of them ignorant of piloting and the West, could be informed and made to feel superior to the informer by the chance to laugh at his "leather-headedness." In short, the cub is initiated into the mystery of piloting, matures in slow stages, and after achieving freedom and power, leaves the river at the moment of collapse of steamboating's "flush times." [22] Mark Twain combined private and public experience to produce a thrilling story of a vanished past.

The "education" of Mark Twain, the ignorant cub pilot, occurs on a kind of graph through a series of emotional ups and downs, from joy to utter discouragement, from the illusion of knowledge and growing confidence to utter humiliation and sheer funk. This is very much the pattern of Stephen Crane's *The Red Badge of Courage,* and it is little wonder that Crane valued *Life on the Mississippi* above the other Mark Twain books, even *Huckleberry Finn.* At the very outset the "fledgling" is humiliated by a steamboat mate who bursts into nonplused profanity when the young passenger offers to help him.[23] Then, on being accepted by Horace Bixby as his cub for a five-hundred-dollar fee, the cub is flayed for his cowardice his first time at the wheel for failing to shave the anchored steamships at New Orleans closely enough. Only a little later he is jeered at as a veritable babe-in-arms for failing to realize that he might not sleep the night through, but must stand his watch, four hours off and four on (chap. 6).

The cub suffers humiliation, despairs, matures in knowledge, and occasionally is able to stand back and summarize what he has learned or has yet to learn in the future. It culminates in a final lesson "pretty hardly learned." With the crew's help Mr. B—— plots to undermine the cub's confidence one

day after he has become a "good steersman" and is "brim full
of self-conceit." B—— turns the steamboat over to his cub at a
crossing that the cub *knows* to be deep and easy. The captain
and crew uneasily assemble on the hurricane deck. The cub
fearfully calls for soundings from the leadsmen, is given false
answers that signify rapidly shoaling water, and in panic
"backs" the engines and brings the ship to a standstill—in the
middle of a "bottomless" crossing. Overwhelmed by a storm
of "humiliating laughter," he realizes the trick played on him
and feels "meaner than the meanest man in human history"
(chap. 13).

This crowning humiliation, which resembles certain *rites de
passage* required for entering manhood among primitive
tribes, essentially frees the cub Mark Twain from his depen-
dence on B——, who now says to him, "You shouldn't have
allowed me or anybody else to shake your confidence," and
adds: "When you get into a dangerous place, don't turn coward. That isn't going to help matters any." The humiliating incident also repeats the psychological figure of each learning
episode. In each, Mr. B——erupts in red-hot profanity at the
beginner's blunders, but then patiently, "ever so gently," explains or demonstrates to his cub the particular new skill demanded. The developing relation between Mark Twain and
Mr. B—— forms a fine, subtle strain in the "plot" of "Old
Times." Mark Twain's first reactions to Mr. B——'s instructions are that his mentor cannot be serious, or that he wants to
be "entertaining." He then becomes resentful, incredulous,
and deeply discouraged, in turn. Gradually monologue
changes to dialogue, and B——'s manner shifts from quick
anger to mild sarcasm to confidence-instilling reassurance, to
full subtle explanation, and to the admission at last concerning
the difference between a wind-reef and a bluff-reef (safety and
disaster): "I can't tell you. . . . By and by you will just naturally *know* one from the other" (p. 118; Nat Ed, p. 77).

This stumbling education in signs and portents and skills is solidly supported by a recurrent metaphor of schooling. When B—— questions Mark Twain concerning the names of points and finds that he doesn't know them, the cub was "down at the foot again," and his all-but-final "lesson" is a lesson in "water-reading"—learning surface signs on the water, that is, "as if it were a book." The figure is developed thus:

> The face of the water, in time, became a wonderful book—a book that was a dead language to the uneducated passenger, but which told its mind to me without reserve. . . . And it was not a book to be read once and thrown aside, for it had a new story to tell every day. Throughout the long twelve hundred miles there was never a page that was void of interest, never one that you could leave unread without loss, never one that you would want to skip, thinking you could find higher enjoyment in some other thing. There never was so wonderful a book written by man. . . . (P. 118; Nat Ed, p. 77)

He elaborates the figure by speaking of an *"italicized* passage"—a "legend of the largest capitals, with a string of shouting exclamation points at the end," and he concludes, "When I had mastered the language of this water and had come to know every trifling feature . . . as familiarly as I knew the letters of the alphabet, I had made a valuable acquisition. But I had lost something, too." At this point, the "Cub Pilot's Education" is "nearly completed."

These passages are from the third "Old Times" paper, which tells of the changing shape of the river and the "face of the water," so beautiful to a cub or a passenger—potentially so menacing to the experienced pilot. Mark Twain's characterization of the Mississippi bears comparison with Joseph Conrad's contrasting portraits of the Atlantic and the Pacific oceans, in *The Mirror of the Sea*, but is, ultimately, the more subtle. Though given to personification, he rarely speaks of the river as "he" or "she." Instead, from the beginning, he introduces occasional hints that the river is a Protean force, a power of nature equivocally benevolent and sinister. It is from the first "the great Mississippi, the majestic, the magnificent Mississippi," which forms a "sort of sea" along the Hannibal reach: still, brilliant, and lonely. The river changes its shape continually, and it looks different in starlight, gray mist, pitch-dark, and different kinds of moonlight. Its face bears "long slanting lines" (dangerous bluff reefs), wind reefs (harmless but deceptive stirrings of the surface), fine lines ribbed like a fan (little reefs forming), slick greasy-looking places (shoal water), and faint dimples (hideous marks of submerged rocks and wrecks). The river is a "fisher" and a potential "killer of steamboats": one victim for every mile in the two hundred miles between St. Louis and Cairo alone. The experienced pilot looks on its face as if he were a doctor reading the "lovely flush in a beauty's cheek" and noting the "break" that ripples over some deadly disease, a sign and symbol of "hidden decay." So it becomes to the experienced eye the "fickle Mississippi," a "villainous" river, with a complexion ranging from fine to muddy.

When Mark Twain reread his "Old Times" essays and expanded them at the end of his five-thousand-mile journey, he developed the metaphor of the river as a Protean, superhuman force: what T. S. Eliot was to call a "dark brown god." He opened his *Life on the Mississippi* with a prefatory metaphor, the Mississippi basin as "The Body of the Nation," and implied throughout the book that the river is its spirit, destroyer, and preserver. The "remarkable river" he then defined by citing the reactions of various European travelers on the river. Capt. Basil Hall found "grandeur." Mrs. Trollope saw another Bolgia of Dante's Hell at the river's mouth and found the scene "utterly desolate." Hon. Charles Augustus Murray at St. Louis beheld "might and majesty." Captain Marryat, R.N., recalled a century of unmitigated crime on the "turbulent and bloodstained Mississippi," and considered the desolating torrent "a great common sewer," a veritable "devil." Alexander Mackay, conversely, looked upon the Mississippi with "reverence." All these tourists, Mark Twain concludes, "remark upon the deep, brooding loneliness and desolation of the vast river." He himself recalls the "lonesome Mississippi" as a "blank, watery solitude . . . still the same, night after night and day after day— majestic, unchanging sameness of serenity, repose, tranquillity, lethargy, vacancy,—symbol of eternity, realization of the heaven pictured by priest and prophet" (chap. 27). For Thoreau, drifting during a sultry day on Walden Pond, "A boatman stretched on the deck of his craft and dallying with the noon would be as apt an emblem of eternity . . . as the serpent with his tail in his mouth." [24] For Mark Twain the river spirit of his youth lived in an atmosphere less euphoric: that peaceful-desolate Sunday solitude that occurs again and again in his writings.

The older Mark Twain observes admiringly that the Government's snag-boats are "pulling the river's teeth," and that the West Point engineers believe they can "fetter and handcuff that river." But, he adds, prophetically,

> One who knows the Mississippi will promptly aver—not aloud, but to himself—that ten thousand River Commissions, with the mines of the world at their back, cannot tame that lawless stream, cannot curb it or confine it, cannot say to it, Go here, or Go there, and make it obey; cannot save a shore which it has sentenced; cannot bar its path with an obstruction which it will not tear down, dance over, and laugh at. (P. 302; Nat Ed, p. 234)

Melville had asked, "Will the Whale Survive?" Mark Twain puts his query into the mouth of Uncle Mumford, "What does Ecclesiastes vii, 13 say?" expecting the reader to know the answer: "Consider the work of God: for who can make that straight that he hath made crooked."

There is then a sense in which this untamable river is a mythical force, a never-to-be-trusted divinity. In a truer sense, perhaps, the river is a neutral natural force against which the pilot pits his energies and, for the most part, triumphs. So, in the character of the men who master its secrets but respect its power lies the essential drama of the "Old Times" chapters and the entire work. The qualities demanded of the pilot, as Mark Twain informs the reader, are memory, courage, and judgment. A good memory and a "calm, cool courage that no peril can shake" can be acquired, though only through total commitment. Judgment is "a matter of brains," and a precondition for success in piloting. Mark Twain's devotion to his subject and his art may be measured by the fact that nearly every action in the "Old Times" sequence bears directly on questions of memory, courage, and judgment (chap. 13).

"I think a pilot's memory is about the most wonderful thing in the world," says Mark Twain—but it is wonderful, he adds, only because it is trained and disciplined and eventually becomes unconscious. By contrast, the pilot Mr. J—— in "Old Times" (Mr. Brown in *Life on the Mississippi*) suffers from the great misfortune of being imprisoned in his memory, unselectively, like the remarkable, interminable Jim Blaine of *Roughing It*. The fearful demands put at first upon a cub's memory are, naturally, the subject of the first chapters.

Courage, though it can be learned, as he insists, is a higher quality, one flowing from the code of captain and pilot forbidding either to leave the steamboat until every person aboard is safely away from it. The best example of courageous action is the manner of Henry Clemens's death. When the *Pennsylvania*'s boilers blew up through all the decks of the ship, Sam's younger brother, a lowly "mud-clerk," had been flung into the water. Even though he was badly scalded by steam and not far from shore, he swam back to the *Pennsylvania* to help save the injured, fainted on reaching the wood-flat used for rescuing the passengers, and died of his injuries six days later in an improvised hospital in Memphis (chap. 20). Mark Twain mentions also the honorable death of a pilot he had known, one whose boat caught fire and who had remained at the wheel until he could beach it. He was the last man ashore, clothing in flames, and died of his injuries a few hours later (chap. 49). Perhaps because the narrative role of "fledgling" made it necessary to exaggerate his fears and moments of panic, Mark Twain permits himself to record one moment of his own courage while he was a cub. When a certain bullying pilot, Mr. Brown, had falsely accused his brother Henry of dereliction to duty and of lying, Sam, defending his brother from physical attack, administered a beating to Brown. As he recalled, he had expected to be tried for his mutinous act, on a steamboat under way, but the Captain, in private, commended him for the act, and then warned him never to mention the incident publicly.

Judgment is the third and highest characteristic of the qualified pilot, arising as it must out of innate intelligence, memory, and courage. One extravagant illustration of such judgment, developed from one of Mark Twain's own experiences, is the story of Mr. X, a fine pilot and a somnabulist, who relieved his partner George Ealer in the pilothouse on a black night. After taking the passenger packet through a blind, tangled crossing, in low water, Mr. X had left the pilothouse empty, to return to bed, the wheel untended; he had been asleep the whole time (chap. 11). An earlier, parallel account of Mr. Bixby's exploit at Hat Island in the "upper river" is thoroughly credible and immensely dramatic, epitomizing as it does the knowledge, courage, and judgment of a superior pilot. The audience for the "daring deed" is Mark Twain the "cub" and the narrator, together with eight or ten pilots going down to "look at the river" between trips—that is, to update their knowledge of the upper river at low water. The dramatic necessity is for Bixby to make the "intricate and dangerous" Hat Island crossing before nightfall, the river below it as far south as Cairo being relatively open and easy. Mr. Bixby's partner had already delayed the steamboat by grounding it; if the "river inspectors" failed to reach Cairo that night, their boats at St. Louis would all be delayed. (One further bit of essential knowledge for the landlubber reader is that pilots almost never ran downstream, at night, in low water, for the boat in such conditions was too easily helpless "with a stiff current pushing behind her.")

In the last hour before sunset the burden of suppressed excitement grows, while the pilots are all gathered in the pilothouse behind Bixby, watches in hand, until one of them observes, "Well yonder's Hat Island—and we can't make it." But as the disappointed pilots are about to leave the pilothouse, "one who had his hand on the door-knob and had turned it, waited, then presently took away his hand and let the knob turn back again." (This gesture is what "makes the emotion" in Hemingway's phrase.) With nods of admiration, wordlessly, insensibly, the others "drew together behind Mr. Bixby" while the sky darkened into night. Bixby, calm and easy in the midst of growing tension, calls for soundings, slows the steamer down, and puts it over the first reef in the "utterly invisible tracks." Then he stops the engines altogether and the boat drifts into the "blacker gloom" and the "deeper shadow" marking the head of Hat Island. Meanwhile, he "stood by his wheel, silent, intent as a cat, and all the pilots stood shoulder to shoulder at his back." One of them whispers, "She'll not make it," while the leadsmen's cries reveal that the water is growing shoal and shoaler. Bixby warns his engineer; the ship touches bottom, and then instantly

> Mr. Bixby set a lot of bells ringing, shouted through the tube, "*Now*, let her have it—every ounce you've got!" then to his

partner, "Put her hard down! snatch her! snatch her!" The boat rasped and ground her way through the sand, hung upon the apex of disaster a single tremendous instant moment, and then over she went! And such a shout as went up at Mr. Bixby's back never loosened the roof of a pilothouse before!

Mark Twain measures Bixby's full stature by explaining to the reader the precision needed to thread the blind reefs, shave the head of the island and brush into the overhanging foliage, and at one place pass "within arm's reach of a sunken and invisible wreck" that would kill the quarter-million-dollar steamboat and take "maybe a hundred and fifty human lives into the bargain" (chap. 7).

In these concentrated few pages Mark Twain constructed a tale as fine as any of Cooper before him or Conrad after. The passage from day to darkness and the pressure of time, the image of the pilot releasing the turned doorknob as he discovers Bixby's determination to run the crossing in the dark, the sense of solidarity among the pilots as they gather "shoulder to shoulder" behind him, the oppressive silence broken by the great shout of triumph: all these evoke a wonderful compliment, whispered in awe to himself, from one of Bixby's guests: "By the Shadow of Death, but he's a lightning pilot!" The phrase invokes the perilous passage of Psalm 23. Seeing through the dark like a cat, passing through the "deeper shadow" of Hat Island, brushing with death at the sunken wreck, Bixby is indeed made to seem a child of the fire and of light.[25]

The absolute power of the Bixbys, granted them for their ability to outwit so formidable an adversary as the Mississippi, had for its corollary—so Mark Twain tells the reader—absolute freedom. "A pilot in those days," he asserts, "was the only unfettered and entirely independent human being that lived in the earth," freer than kings and parliaments and editors and clergymen—and freer than writers. Because they possessed "boundless authority," leisure, high wages, and pride in their craft, it was little wonder that they and their mates and crews should feel to the full their "official rank and dignity" (chap. 14).

Mark Twain "loved the profession" and "took a measureless pride in it." Rather surprisingly, he takes equal pleasure, near the end of the "Old Times" papers, in detailing the slow growth and eventual monopoly of the Pilots' Benevolent Association. (He also maintained membership in the printer's union all his life and plainly believed in craft unions, even though he became a reckless entrepreneur in book publishing and typesetting machinery.) The effect of his brief historical excursus on the pilots' guild is curious. The dominant motive of the pilots was self-interest—the preservation and increase of their high wages and status. On the other hand, Mark Twain argues, the benefits to members and their families were matched at once by an increase in safety and efficiency in steamboating, due to the admirable communication system created by the pilots' association. Where a pilot earlier had to run a shoal area that he himself saw only once or twice a month, he now had a hundred sharp eyes "to tell him how to run it." No wonder, as Mark Twain remarks, that insurance underwriters came to support the Association, whose member pilots could make more trips and with much greater safety to passengers and cargo than non-association pilots (chaps. 14, 15).

But, just as the "flush times" on the mining frontier ended almost overnight, so the expanding railroads, the Civil War, a defalcating treasurer, and the appearance of the tugboat ended the "flush times" of steamboating, and the Association and the "noble science of piloting" became at once "things of the dead and pathetic past!" (pp. 191–92; Nat Ed, pp. 141–42).

When Mark Twain expanded the "Old Times" series, so compact and single in motive and effect, he had to find a larger principle to accommodate the new material he had gathered on his river trip of 1882. At the outset he seems to have intended a brief "physical history," a brief account of exploration, and a glimpse of early commerce in keelboats, broadhorns, and rafts, to be followed by substantial accounts of the "flush times" and the "comparatively tranquil" present epoch. While this pattern is discernible in the published book, it is disproportionate and weak, and no more coherent, really, than the chronological sequence of his five-thousand-mile trip from St. Louis to the Gulf and back up to the head of navigation at St. Paul and Minneapolis.

Mark Twain found a much stronger organizing principle in the striking contrasts to be observed between the river and the towns of his childhood and piloting days, and the Mississippi Valley in 1882. The principle sometimes fails him, as his materials on new industry, new libraries and public buildings, and increased population tend to run to poor journalism and fall into sheer dullness. The strength of the principle is that it permitted him legitimate poetic celebration of the precious and irrecoverable past—his own variation on the ancient theme of *ubi sunt*. It provided links to the matter of "Old Times." It allowed a partially de-Southernized Southerner the chance to analyze the pre-War feudal South, note the South's present advantages, and satirize its present backwardness. Preeminently, it stimulated memories of his boyhood and youth, in Hannibal and on the river. In this last connection, *Life on the Mississippi* may be regarded as a rich mine for episodes and characters in *Adventures of Huckleberry Finn* (as Walter Blair has shown). Here it has been my chief purpose to reveal how fine a chain of gold links Mark Twain wrought in the seven papers of "Old Times on the Mississippi."

> Hard upon the beech oar
> She moves too slow,
> All the way to Shawneetown
> Long while ago.[26]

In *A Tramp Abroad* (1880), written and published in the interim between "Old Times on the Mississippi" and *Life on the Mississippi*, Mark Twain once again assumes the stance and the language of the feckless lazy man, pretending to his reader that he is a walker and hiker in Germany, Switzerland, and northern Italy, but revealing that he does his walking by train and carriage and his climbing by telescope. Interspersed among the accounts of places and people encountered are a number of German legends (at least one of them manufactured) by our author in the spirit of "Rip Van Winkle"; quoted records of mountain climbing disasters, by such classic writers as Edward Whymper (made more vivid by Mark Twain's absurd stories of his own climbing); and a chapter sequence in which he makes a raft trip down the Neckar to Heidelberg.

The raft trip is notable for its peaceful beauty, and a storm on the Neckar in which the sea is running inches high, the water shoals to two feet, and the log raft springs a leak! The captain, a mariner for forty years on the Neckar, says that he had never seen a storm to "make a man's cheek blanch and his pulses stop" like this one. This fine bit of burlesque is Mark Twain's German version of the American ballad of the "raging E-ri-e Canawl." [27]

A second linking between Germany and America, "Baker's Blue-Jay Yarn" (as it is entered in the table of contents) burlesques German legends with a tall tale of American character and setting. Simple contrast or simple confession of irrelevance had sufficed Mark Twain earlier, when he had introduced Western anecdotes into the Mediterranean world of *Innocents Abroad*, or a few foreign experiences into *Roughing It*. But in "Baker's Blue-Jay Yarn" he faced up to the problem of relating a purely American story in a German setting, and he solved it by building a delicate but strong bridge between the two. To print the yarn without the bridge leading to it in the preceding chapter, as some anthologists have done, is to ignore much of the high art with which Mark Twain built his tall tale higher and higher without letting it "topple over" (pp. 31–42; Nat Ed 1:12–22).

Mark Twain the writer begins by working up an atmosphere of "German legends and fairy tales," much as Irving might have done. Lost in the deep silent twilight of the Neckar woods one afternoon, as he recalls, he fell into "a train of dreamy thought about animals which talk," rather artificially invoking his fancy and getting his spirit "in tune with the place." His mood "to enjoy the supernatural" is sharply broken into by a raven uttering a harsh croak over his head. He begins to feel like an intruder. The raven, eyeing him, croaks again—a croak "with a distinctly insulting expression about it," as if to say, "in raven, 'Well, what do *you* want here?' " A second raven answers the call of the first, and the two, side by side on a limb, "discussed me as freely and offensively as two great naturalists might discuss a new kind of bug,"—and in a language he cannot understand, though he is certain that some of it was not used in church. But when the two ravens "called in another friend," Mark Twain is forced to leave, and the ravens crane their necks and laugh, like any "low white people." As he admits,

> They were nothing but ravens—I knew that,—what they thought about me could be a matter of no consequence,—and yet when even a raven shouts after you, "What a hat!" "O, pull down your vest!" and that sort of thing, it hurts you and humiliates you, and there is no getting around it with fine reasoning and pretty arguments. (Pp. 32–35; Nat Ed, 1:13–15)

In two pages Mark Twain has thus set a stage "peculiarly meet for the occasion" of his humiliation, and has transformed the ravens from croaking birds, to adversaries who "bandy words in raven," to experts in the Western American art of slangy insult. The bridge is now completed. Mark Twain may now appropriately generalize, "Animals talk to each other, of course," and add that he never knew but one man who could understand them. The columned forest-aisles of Germany dissolve into the hills of a lonely corner of California among woods and mountains, from which the last miner but one— Jim Baker—had moved seven years before. The half-credulous, half-sophisticated "Mark Twain" can now slip the mask of Baker over his own, and turn from formal to vernacular narration.

The character of Jim Baker emerges in a few light, swift strokes. He is a middle-aged, simple-hearted miner, too deeply ashamed of his failure in the West to go back to the States after thirteen years. He has studied the beasts and the birds—his only neighbors—so closely that he fully believes he knows their tongues. He talks to himself. Yet if he is a little touched because of his long exile, he is touched as poets are. He is a St. Francis of the Sierras.

Two sentences at the end of the last bridge-paragraph report indirectly Baker's assertion to Mark Twain that bluejays are the best-educated and best talkers among birds and beasts— and then Baker becomes the narrator himself directly quoted, and Mark Twain disappears. Now, according to Baker, a bluejay has more moods and feelings than other creatures, and is unsurpassed by any in putting them into language: language variegated, faultless in grammar, and "bristling with metaphor." Cats of course use good grammar, Baker admits, but when they get excited "you'll hear grammar that will give you the lockjaw." A bluejay, even if he has feathers and "don't belong to no church," is "just as much a human as you be," because he will steal, deceive, betray, go back on his promise, outswear cats and "any gentleman" in the mines, out-scold anything human or divine, cry, laugh, feel shame, reason, plan and discuss, and realize "when he is an ass just as well as you do" (pp. 36–37; Nat Ed, 1:16–17).

Baker's preamble to his yarn, for all its touches of poetry and satire, demonstrates his total commitment to the bluejay world, and induces in the reader a comparably strong illusion of a little world where rascally tall-talking bluejays behave and speak like human beings. So it happens, when a bluejay lights on an abandoned cabin roof one Sunday morning as Baker is taking the morning sun, cocks his head at a knothole, drops an acorn from his mouth, and says, "Hello, I reckon I've struck something," that the reader is so immersed in the story already that he is quite unconscious of the complex narrative technique at work: from Clemens to "Mark Twain" to Jim Baker (via the German ravens) to bluejays to *a* bluejay. Conrad's narration at several removes in *Chance* (composed thirty years later—with a technical virtuosity that even Henry James found a little overwhelming) is scarcely more intricate than Clemens's management of his material.[28]

The essential drama of the bluejay, the acorns, and an unfillable knothole in a cabin roof now is voiced in dramatic monologue and dialogue:

> [Bluejay]:
> "It looks like a hole, it's located like a hole,—blamed if I don't believe it *is* a hole!" . . .
>
> "O, no, this ain't no fat thing, I reckon! If I ain't in luck!—why it's a perfectly elegant hole!" . . .
>
> "Why I didn't hear it fall!" . . .
>
> "Well, it's too many for *me*, that's certain; must be a mighty long hole; however, I ain't got no time to fool around here, I got to 'tend to business; I reckon it's all right—chance it, anyway!" . . .
>
> "Consound it, I don't seem to understand this thing, no way; however, I'll tackle her again." . . .
>
> "Well, *I* never struck no such a hole as this, before; I'm of the opinion it's a totally new kind of a hole." . . .

"Well, you're a long hole, and a deep hole, and a mighty sin-
gular hole altogether—but I've started in to fill you, and I'm
d——d if I *don't* fill you, if it takes a hundred years!" . . .

"*Now* I guess I've got the bulge on you by this time!" . . .

"I've shoveled acorns enough in there to keep the family
thirty years, and if I can see a sign of one of 'em, I wish I may
land in a museum with a belly full of sawdust in two minutes!" . . .

[To another jay]:
"Now yonder's the hole, and if you don't believe me, go and
look for yourself." . . .

[Second jay]:
"How many did you say you put in there?"

"Not any less than two tons." . . .

[Old jay]:
"Come here! . . . Come here, everybody; hang'd if this fool
hasn't been trying to fill up a house with acorns!"

(Pp. 39–41; Nat Ed, 1:18–22)

This verbal framework Jim Baker clothes with actions and ges-
tures singularly appropriate to the bright blue and white hy-
peractive Western bluejay and to human character as Baker has
known it in the mines, with the super-addition of "bristling
metaphor" in Mark Twain's happiest vein. So, the first time
the jay looks into the knothole, he shuts one eye and puts the
other to the hole "like a possum looking down a jug" and
winks his wings with gratification. The second time, after
dropping an acorn into the hole he tilts his head back with
"the heavenliest smile on his face"—a smile that fades gradually out of his countenance "like breath off'n a razor" when he
cannot hear the acorn hit bottom. He scratches the back of his
head with his right foot, fails again, cusses himself "black in
the face," and after two hours of heaving acorns comes
"a-drooping down . . . sweating like an ice-pitcher," drops

another acorn in, and looks once again. This time he leans his back "agin the chimbly," and his torrential swearing that ensues makes profanity in the mines seem "only just the rudiments" to Baker.

Other jays, hearing the first jay "doing his devotions," begin to assemble (as the ravens had), and soon the whole region " 'peared to have a blue flush about it" as an entire congress of jays peer into the hole and deliver themselves of thoroughly human opinions, "jawing and disputing and ripping and cussing." When the old jay peers into the half-open cabin door and dispels the mystery, the whole congress investigates, laughs, and guffaws over the absurd contract for an hour. Like human beings, observes Baker, bluejays have a sense of humor, though an owl visiting the famous spot from Nova Scotia failed to see the point or to find anything funny in the situation. Mark Twain seems to be suggesting, as he would say many years later in "A Fable," that "you can find in a text whatever you bring, if you will stand between it and the mirror of your imagination." [29] In short, "Baker's Blue-jay Yarn" is a triumph because of its seamless narrative development, its easy passage through formal opening into a vernacular tale of real elegance, and its transmuting the atmosphere of German legend into the air of Western myth. It is the high point of *A Tramp Abroad*.

Chapter 3

────◆·◆────

SHORT FICTIONS

"Jim Smiley and His Jumping Frog," Mother Utterback and Jimmy Finn, the bloated old hag from Five Points. — "A True Story" and Aunt Rachel as black heroine, in the vernacular. — Domestic comedy with the McWilliamses, including their burglar alarm. — "The Invalid's Story." "Captain Stormfield's Visit to Heaven" and its inspiration: a "heaven on a liberal plan." — "The Man That Corrupted Hadleyburg": "lead us into temptation." — A fairy tale, "The Five Boons of Life."

From the emphasis we have given to particular episodes in *Roughing It* and *A Tramp Abroad* perhaps the reader will begin to conclude that Mark Twain achieved his very best—almost flawless—writing in many of the short sketches. This is not to argue that formally flawed books, like *Roughing It* and *Life on the Mississippi,* or, to anticipate, *Adventures of Huckleberry Finn,* may not be good, or even great, books. Nor is it to deny that "Old Times on the Mississippi" and *The Adventures of Tom Sawyer* are finely sustained longer works. It is, I think, simply to acknowledge that his talent, his span of attention and concentration perhaps, worked best and most unremittingly in relatively short pieces of writing. This chapter will deal with the finest, as I see them, of the short stories and short novels—fictions in which Mark Twain, like the realist he was, concentrated on elements of character and the real speech of living men and women.

Aside from a journalistic scoop on the survivors of the burning of the clipper ship *Hornet*, which appeared in the Sacramento *Union* for 19 July 1866, and reappeared in *Harper's Magazine*, the first Mark Twain story to be read nationally was "Jim Smiley and His Jumping Frog," published in the New York *Saturday Press*, 18 November 1865. It was widely reprinted—and it made many people laugh. Of the various kinds of humorous stories Mark Twain learned to tell, two are especially notable. The first is the vernacular character's tedious free-association tale that never comes to a point, like Jim Blaine's drunken spiel about his grandfather's old ram (1872) or like Mark Twain's own "A Medieval Romance" (1890).[1] The second is the vernacular tale that is only *apparently* long-winded and pointless, and ends with a true "snapper."

"The Celebrated Jumping Frog of Calaveras County,"[2] as the author later titled it, is of this second kind. It is a frame story, in which narrator Mark Twain, speaking formally and a touch legalistically, asks earnest, sincere, "fat and bald-headed" Simon Wheeler about a friend's friend, the Reverend Leonidas W. Smiley (p. 8; CSS, p. 1). The stage is set for Wheeler's "interminable" analysis of a certain Jim Smiley's passion for wagering on his menagerie of animals, and his losing a forty-dollar bet to a passing stranger in a mock-Homeric contest between his own trained jumping frog and an "amature" frog from the swamp. The crux of the tale comes when Smiley leaves the stranger alone to go find a second frog, so that the stranger has a chance to fill Jim Smiley's trained frog with quail-shot. The reader can swallow this absurdity only because the entire first half of the story, as Wheeler drones it out, is devoted to Smiley's gambling compulsion. Smiley will bet on a horse-race, or a dog-fight, or a cat-fight, or a chicken-fight, or even on the speed of a straddle-bug, or *even* whether the parson's wife, who lay ill, would live or die (pp. 10–11; CSS, p. 2). Warming to his task, Wheeler then explains how Jim Smiley's mare, a sorry-looking nag, would always fetch up at the end of the race a neck ahead; and how Smiley's ornery looking bull-pup, named Andrew Jackson, would always beat other dogs by an unshakeable grip on a hind leg—until the day that Andrew Jackson is set against a dog without any hind legs, gets "shucked out bad," and limps off to die, broken-hearted (pp. 11–13; CSS, pp. 2–3).

Wheeler's narration, while loosely strung together with "ands" and "buts," is only irrelevant at first glance. As the reader is led closer and closer to the bet on the highly trained frog Dan'l Webster, the animals (set in a careful order) become more and more human in their behavior, culminating in the "genius" and perseverance of Andrew Jackson—and the gifted, modest, straightforward (and wide-mouthed) Dan'l Webster. Dan'l could whirl through the air "like a doughnut" and come down flat-footed like a cat. He could catch a fly on the counter, and drop to the floor "as solid as a gob of mud." And when he tries to jump, filled with bird-shot, he "give a heave, and hysted up his shoulders—so—like a Frenchman."

Mark Twain's metaphors help to make these creatures characters in a fable. Above all, Jim Smiley—the reader grows convinced—will do *anything* to set up a bet, even to catching a frog for a stranger to enter into a contest with. Smiley learns how his frog has been "anchored out" by the stranger (now gone), because it looks "mighty baggy" and weighs "five pound." This rare undeserved defeat with his jumping frog has been suggested by the unfair defeat of Andrew Jackson. Then, when Simon Wheeler begins another tale, about a cow, the gentlemanly Mark Twain leaves, finding the "history of the enterprising vagabond *Jim* Smiley" enough (pp. 18–19; CSS, pp. 5–6); and the frame of the story is complete. Although its author later called "Jim Smiley and His Jumping Frog" a "villainous backwoods sketch," [3] the piece is in fact a constantly engaging Aesopian fable, one resting on the character of the compulsive bettor—in this case Jim Smiley. The idea for the tale came from an Arkansas anecdote called "Frogs Shot Without Powder," appearing in *The Spirit of the Times* ten years earlier.[4] But what is mere backwoods " 'cuteness" in the original is transformed into mock-heroic drama in the "Jumping Frog."

The Mark Twain talent for drawing "vagabond" or low-life characters is adumbrated in a number of fine vignettes leading up to Jim Smiley. In January 1866 he remembered for *Golden Era* readers a kindly steamboat captain, Ed Montgomery, who often bought green wood from old Mother Utterback below Grand Gulf, Mississippi, simply because she was poor and the mother of six gawky "gals." At second hand, Mark Twain reproduced her encounter with the captain and a group of lady passengers in her dirt-floored cabin, thus:

"Good morning, Captain Montgomery!" said she with many a bustling bow and flourish; "Good morning, Captain Montgomery; good morning, ladies all; how de do, Captain Montgomery—how de do—how de do? Sakes alive, it 'pears to me it's ben years sense I seed you. Fly around, gals, fly around! you Bess, you slut, highst yoself off'n that candle-box and give it to the lady. How *have* you ben, Captain Montgomery?—make yoself at home, ladies all—you 'Liza Jane, stan' out of the way—move yoself! Thar's the jug, help yoself, Captain Montgomery; take that cob out and make yoself free, Captain Montgomery—and ladies all. You Sal, you hussy, git up f'm thar this minit, and take some exercise! for the land's sake, ain't you got no sense at all?—settin' thar on that cold rock and you jes' ben married last night, and your pores all open!" [5]

This is recognizably the writer who boasted, "Tautology cannot scare me,"—especially in reporting how people talk.

The picture "By a Native Historian" of Jimmy Finn undergoing attempted reform by the temperance people of Hannibal (1867) makes fun of both the town drunkard and the reform element. "He got remorseful about the loss of his liberty," the "Historian" recalls, and "then he got melancholy from thinking about it so much; and after that, he got drunk. He got awfully drunk in the chief citizen's house, and the next morning that house was as if the swine had tarried in it." Though Finn reformed once more, he recanted, sold his body for a quart of whiskey, drank it all at one sitting, and died, leaving the town more bored than ever.[6] The portrait (1867) of "a bloated old hag" from the Five Points, in jail with him in New York City, is rather different in effect. Mark Twain had tried, idiotically, to break up a street fight and had been jailed over night. The old woman's husband had "drifted off somewhere," and so she had taken up with another man; she had had a little boy—but it took all her time to get drunk and stay drunk, so he starved or froze one winter night, she didn't know which. But it was a "d——d good thing for him," she said, "because he'd have had a miserable rough time of it if he'd a lived." Mark Twain gave her a cigar—and she offered to divide her smuggled-in bottle of gin with him.[7]

Mother Utterback and the bloated hag from the Five Points are realized in no more than a few hundred words very largely through their own language. By the time the artist conceived and composed "A True Story, Repeated Word for Word as I Heard It" for the *Atlantic* in 1874, he had passed through his apprenticeship and could bring to bear on Aunty Cord's telling of certain great events in her life his knowledge of the formal-colloquial frame story, the potential of the vernacular for effects of pathos as well as humor, and certain small but effective actions performed as though on the stage.

The immediate inspiration for this first Mark Twain piece to be published in the prestigious *Atlantic Monthly* was the history of Auntie Cord, the cook at Quarry Farm in Elmira, who had been "in slavery more than forty years." [8] As he explained to Howells, he had first *told* the yarn to John Hay and some others; they had liked it; he then decided to *write* it. As for his repeating the tale "Word for Word as I Heard It," this can scarcely be literally true. He said, "I have not altered the old colored woman's story except to begin it at the beginning, instead of the middle, as she did—& traveled both ways." [9] The intent of the subtitle is plainly to claim the status of history rather than fiction for the story, and perhaps to warn the reader not to expect humor as its central feature.

The illusion of biography or private history is created at once by the subtitle and by the unusual reference to the "I" introducer of the tale as "Misto C——"; yet the creative or fictive touch appears immediately in the renaming of the real Auntie Cord as "Aunt Rachel." What echoes resonated in the name "Rachel" for Clemens—as for Melville: "Lamentation & bitter weeping; Rachel weeping for her children refused to be comforted for her children, because they were not." [10]

The stout cook, Aunt Rachel, so jolly, so fond of laughter, so willing to be chaffed, suddenly turns sober at the thoughtless question from "Misto C——": "How is it that you've lived sixty years and never had any trouble?" Her answer to the question, "Has I had any trouble?" is in effect the drama and the story. [11] She begins by telling of her relative happiness, in slavery in Virginia, with her husband and their seven children, her little Henry's scarring his head and wrist, and her boast (like her mother's) that she is a Marylander, "one o' de ole Blue Hen's Chickens" (p. 592). She then recounts her pain and misery as her family is sold at auction in Richmond, and her fierce resistance when her youngest is taken from her, and his whispering to her that he will run away and work and buy her free-

dom. With the opening of the Civil War Aunt Rachel becomes
cook for a group of Union officers in a big headquarters house,
and often asks them about her son, just as (she learns later) he
has been searching for her, while servant to a Union colonel.
This managing of essential fact in their twenty-two year sepa-
ration leads of course to the long-delayed and very moving
recognition of mother and son. Henry is part of a *"nigger* ridg-
ment" on guard at headquarters, and at a dancing party in her
big kitchen overhears her scold the laughing young black dan-
cers: "I wa'n't bawn in de mash to be fool' by trash! I's one o'
de old Blue Hen's Chickens, *I* is!" He cannot sleep thereafter.
And when he returns to the kitchen early in the morning,
Aunt Rachel looks into his face, finds the scars on wrist and
forehead, and cries, "If you an't my Henry, what is you doin'
wid dis welt on yo' wris' an' dat sk-yar on yo' forehead? De
Lord God ob heaven be praise', I got my own ag'in!" Aunt
Rachel then returns to the original question, saying "Oh no,
Misto C——, *I* hain't had no trouble. An' no *joy!*" (pp.
593–94).

The transformation of Aunt Rachel from conventional Negro
cook and servant to a pathetic and intensely individualized
heroine takes place quickly. When the yarn begins, she is
seated at twilight on the porch steps of the farmhouse below
her employers, as befits a servant. Then (as she warms to her
story) she had gradually risen, and "now she towered above
us, black against the stars." At the end, she re-enacts the discovery of her son's identity with intense physical immediacy,
and pushes back the hair and the sleeve of "Misto C——" just
as, she says, she had done with Henry (p. 594). The whole
sketch is thus rendered dramatic through its dialogue and its
slight but revelatory actions. A final dimension, like the name
Rachel, emerges in parallels to an old spiritual that was surely
in Clemens's mind when he was writing the story—"Nobody
Knows deh Trouble I've Seen." The singer mourns, "Some-

times I'm up, sometimes I'm down / Oh, yes, Lord / Sometimes my head's bowed to the ground / Oh, yes, Lord," voic-
ing directly what Aunt Rachel feels in reviewing *her* troubles.
The conclusion of the spiritual, too—"Glory, Hallelujah"—is a
cry of acceptance very close to Aunt Rachel's quiet, under-
stated assertion, "*I* hain't had no trouble. An' no *joy!*" (p. 594).
The Hartford housemaid Katy Leary testified that one moonlight night at the Charles Dudley Warner house, "Mr. Clemens" sang spirituals and became lost in his singing:

> He put his two hands up to his head, just as though all the sor-
> row of them negroes was upon him; and then he begun to sing,
> "Nobody Knows the Trouble I Got, Nobody Knows but Jesus."
> That was one of them negro spirituals songs, and when he
> come to the end, to the Glory Halleluiah, he gave a great
> shout—just like the negroes do—he shouted out the Glory,
> Glory, Halleluiah! [12]

Aunt Rachel gains stature by association with the biblical
Rachel and the anonymous singer of "Nobody Knows deh
Trouble I've Seen." Yet she is unsentimentally drawn, a recognizably flawed human being, in that she is proud of her Mary-
land ancestry and contemptuous of slaves who are "trash"
because they were "bawn in the mash"—that is, in the cattle-
food bin of a barn. She naïvely thinks of her boy Henry as still
a child rather than the grown man he has become. She suffers
and is angered by the laughter of the "spruce young nigger"
and the "yaller wench" who find her red turban funny. But
she knows what she is *for*—she is a cook—and she is as courageous as she is loving, beating the auctioneer's men over the
head with her chain when they take Henry forcibly·from her.

Recognition of the quality of Mark Twain's story came immediately from the Civil War veteran and writer, J. W. De
Forest. Shortly after the tale appeared, the author of *Miss Ra-
venel's Conversion from Secession to Loyalty* (1867) wrote to

Howells: "By the way, tell Mark Twain to try pathos now &
then. His 'True Story,'—the story of the old negress,—was a
really great thing, amazingly natural & humorous, & touching
even to the drawing of tears." [13] What his editor thought of it
is implicit in the fact that the *Atlantic* sent the author twenty
dollars a page for it—the highest rate ever paid to any of its
contributors. [14]

Clemens wrote Howells that he need not pay heavily for
"A True Story" since, as he felt, the sketch was "rather out of
[his] line." What was very much in his line was domestic farce
drawn with apparent immediacy from the Clemens home life
in Hartford. Mark Twain especially liked novel gadgets; and
just as Howells liked to entangle his characters in elevators
and talking machines and parlor cars and sleeping cars, so
Samuel Clemens of Hartford drew laughs from his and Olivia's
involvements with burglar alarms and telephones. A represen-
tative sequence consists of "Experience of the McWilliamses
with the Membraneous Croup" (1875), "Mrs. McWilliams and
the Lightning" (1880), and "The McWilliamses and the Burglar
Alarm" (1882). [15]

The framing for all three pieces is the same. As they travel
together by train, Mortimer McWilliams recounts to "Mr.
Twain" a recent experience, usually involving his wife Caro-
line—or Evangeline. For purposes of the genre of farce, Caro-
line-Evangeline McWilliams is subject to absurd whims and
fears. In the first sketch she and her husband suffer a sleepless
night of farcical acts and fearful talk over their small daughter's
case of "membraneous croup," until the arrival of the doctor,
who cures the child's "fatal" cough by taking a small sliver of
pine wood from her throat. The second piece dramatizes
Evangeline McWilliams's fear of lightning, the folklore of what
draws lightning and what prevents it, and presents the spec-
tacle of Mortimer McWilliams reading aloud German instructions that he does not fully understand for saving one's life in
thunderstorms. The presumed storm turns out to be the flash

of cannon and the rumble of cannon fire at the news of Garfield's nomination for the presidency.

The funniest of the three stories concerns McWilliams's explanation for not going "one single cent on burglar alarms." [16] The first burglar, encountering McWilliams early one morning in the McWilliams house, loquaciously apologizes for smoking and for failing to ring the first-floor burglar alarm—since he came through the second-story window. So the burglar-alarm salesman is called back from New York and adds alarms to the second and then the third floors, charging three hundred dollars each time; and by this time the "annunciator" has forty-seven tags on it. The only problem is that the cook opens the kitchen (back) door at five every morning; and the "first effect of that frightful gong is to hurl you across the house, and slam you against the wall, and then curl you up, and squirm you like a spider on a stove lid" (p. 318). (One time the gong wakes even a dead stranger in the McWilliams house.) The expert fixes it so that opening the kitchen door turns *off* the alarm; so of course burglars walk in at night and fill all the spare beds. McWilliams and his coachman, awakened by the sound of the gong, fire shotguns at each other, cripple a nurse, and take off all of McWilliams's back hair. It had been a false alarm. By now the narrator begins to disconnect particular rooms from the annunciator, and in time *all* the rooms are disconnected and the whole machine goes out of service. The burglars walk in one night shortly thereafter and carry off the burglar alarm, "every hide and hair of it"—"they just cleaned her out, bag and baggage" (p. 322). McWilliams tries once more, putting in at "prodigious" cost a new system governed by a "new patent clock." Yet it is not long before the clock perversely puts the alarm on in the daytime and turns it off at night. "Now," says McWilliams,

> there is the history of that burglar alarm—everything just as it happened; nothing extenuated, and naught set down in malice. Yes, sir,—and when I had slept nine years with burglars, and

maintained an expensive burglar alarm the whole time, for their
protection, not mine, and at my sole cost—for not a d——d cent
could I ever get *them* to contribute—I just said to Mrs. McWilliams that I had had enough of that kind of pie; so with her full
consent I took the whole thing out and traded it off for a dog,
and shot the dog. (Pp. 323–24)

And he bids Mark Twain goodbye as he leaves the train.

The McWilliamses are a wealthy couple living in New England, refined people living in a refined society, whatever one
may infer about Mortimer McWilliams's tendency to farcical
exaggeration. Their creator, however, had a strong taste for
every sort of literary effect, including scatological humor as
gamey as Jonathan Swift's. Most devoted readers of Mark
Twain have somewhere encountered "1601, Conversation as it
was by the Social Fireside in the Time of the Tudors," in one
of its many private printings, and have been amused in one
degree or another by the investigation into the identity of the
"stinker" with which it opens, and the sexual anecdotes that
follow. But "1601" is formless and even mild compared to
"The Invalid's Story," Mark Twain's invention of a dying narrator whose health was destroyed when he accompanied the
decaying corpse of a friend in a heated baggage car—the coffin
being actually a box of rifles with a package of Limberger
cheese resting on it. The story gains momentum from the effort of the expressman Thompson and the narrator, to modify
the stench first with carbolic acid and then by burning a pile
of chicken feathers, dried apples, leaf tobacco, rags, old shoes,
sulfur, and assafoetida near the coffin.

The piece secures its effect almost entirely from the vernacular understatement employed by Thompson in describing the
unmodifiable, original, "sublime" smell. "It ain't no use. We
can't buck agin *him*. He just utilizes everything we put up to
modify him with, and gives it his own flavor and plays it back
on us." [17] Originally omitted from "Some Rambling Notes of

an Idle Excursion" (probably on Howells's advice), the sketch was restored in *The Stolen White Elephant* (1882), yet never popularly reprinted thereafter.[18] Whatever Howells's qualms about the *Atlantic* audience, and the author's own doubts, it is a capital tale of its kind.

"Captain Stormfield's Visit to Heaven" exists in three forms: a manuscript from the early 1870s with later additions and notebook entries, not all of them published; the middle chapters, which Mark Twain himself published after his wife's death as "Extracts from Captain Stormfield's Visit to Heaven," in *Harper's* in December 1907 and January 1908 and then in a Christmas gift book; and a second, fuller version published in 1952 as Part I of *Report from Paradise*.[19] It is unique among the Mark Twain stories in that he conceived the idea as early as 1886 and tinkered with the story almost to the time of his death; and it is a work of high imagination and vivid satire as well.

The Mark Twain *aficionado* will recognize Captain Stormfield almost at once. He is Capt. Hurricane Jones in "Rambling Notes of an Idle Excursion" (1877), Capt. Ned Blakely of *Roughing It* (1872), who demands and gets frontier justice for the murder of his Negro mate, and Captain Waxman, who tells about the fabulous rats that left a doomed ship (still earlier, in an *Alta California* letter).[20] In real life he was Capt. Edgar (Ned) Wakeman, on whose steamship Mark Twain sailed to New York via the Isthmus of Panama in 1866, and with whom he again took passage when returning to California in 1868: a "portly, hearty, jolly, boisterous, good-natured sailor," a superior ship's captain, an expert interpreter of the Bible, and a yarn-spinner to rival Mark Twain himself.[21] It was on this second voyage that the Captain told his passenger of a visit he had made to heaven, his dream shading into reality as he had told it to many listeners in succession. Not long thereafter Mark Twain put the story germ on paper; and this was the be-

ginning of his lifelong preoccupation with "Captain Stormfield" (p. xii). The dream visit fell in with another persistent
interest of ex-Presbyterian Samuel Clemens: again and again
in his writing he turned to heaven and hell, Adam and Eve,
Satan and the Saviour, and the doctrines of election and predestination, although he had been in full revolt against all
such since his adolescence.

In 1906 Mark Twain recalled writing down Captain Wakeman's experiences in heaven in "the first quarter of 1868, I
think" (p. xii). This coincided with his reading—along with
any number of his contemporaries—of Elizabeth Stuart Phelps
Ward's novel *The Gates Ajar* (1868): he had turned the story, he
says, into a burlesque of a book that had "imagined a mean
little ten-cent heaven about the size of Rhode Island—a heaven
large enough to accommodate about a tenth of one per cent of
the Christian billions who had died in the past nineteen centuries. I raised the limit." [22] Before he was through, that is, he
was admitting pagans and measuring *his* heaven in light-
years.

But *Gates Ajar* nonetheless meant much more to Mark Twain
than a target for ridicule. Elizabeth Phelps, who had lost her
lover in the Civil War, felt some of the same current of religious revolt that stirred in Clemens himself. The intellectual
core of her novel, as distinguished from the strong emotional-
sentimental strain, involves a fresh view of what heaven must
be like. It protests any literal exegesis of *Revelation*, and of
harps, choirs, the throne, robes, pearly gates, jewels, unend-
ing light, total exposure of the soul, idleness, solemnity—
a place where "Sabbaths have no end." It is also aware of the
speculation that the people who have lived and died would
cover the earth twice over—or at least the state of Pennsylvania! For her part, Elizabeth Phelps, through the dialogue between the heroine and a sensitive aunt, proposes the possibil-
ity that heaven may be very much like the earth made

spiritual. Perhaps the sun is the heaven of each system as Isaac Taylor had speculated. Though skeletons will surely not draw on their skins at the day of judgment, nor will human ashes be reconstituted, the human form divine will persist. If there are no days, there will be succession of time. People will be busy there. If there are harpists, there will be pianists (a suggestion that surely shocked the orthodox among Mrs. Ward's readers). Who is to say that heaven will not have the animals in it?— Martin Luther thought that it might. Strikingly, heaven may be a place for those who failed on earth, and intellectual rank in heaven must bear some proportion to goodness. Above all, heaven will provide for talk, and for fun, and for books, and for food, and for the renewal of human love. How pleasant it will be, the heroine conjectures, to meet and perhaps even to shake the hand of David, or Paul, or Cowper, or President Lincoln, or Mrs. Browning. [23]

The tone of Elizabeth Phelps's story is idealistic, consolatory, and often sentimental. But she read widely and was open to ideas, and plainly in *The Gates Ajar* she furnished Mark Twain more stimuli for events and ideas in "Captain Stormfield" than he was aware of or ever acknowledged.

Another real person furnished the prime satiric target of "Captain Stormfield." The Reverend Mr. T. DeWitt Talmage, minister of Brooklyn's Central Presbyterian Church, had observed in *The Independent* in 1870 that if all the churches were free and admitted working men, the uncommon people would be made sick by the bad smells of the common, so that he, Talmage, would have no part of this work of evangelization. This snobbery was just Mark Twain's meat. In reaction he wrote a very sharp piece for the *Galaxy*, calling it "About Smells" (May 1870). If laboring men from all the countries of the world—and this would include St. Matthew, Benjamin Franklin, the Twelve Apostles, and the Son of the Carpenter himself—are to be found in heaven, he asks, where will Mr. Talmage go? [24]

Elizabeth Phelps's bright young heroine had asked skeptically enough, "How can untold millions of us 'lie in Abraham's bosom'?" [25] Talmage (so Captain Stormfield reports) avows in his sermons that the first thing he will do when he gets to heaven is to "fling his arms around Abraham, Isaac and Jacob, and kiss them and weep on them." But with sixty thousand people arriving every day, the patriarchs would "be tired out and as wet as muskrats all the time." [26] No, says Stormfield, Mr. Talmage's endearments will be declined, with thanks.

In the longer printed version edited from manuscript by Dixon Wecter, "Captain Stormfield's Visit to Heaven" is really unfinished, like the other two versions; but most readers will feel content with the work as it stands, for it ends with a characteristic grand torchlight procession to celebrate the arrival in heaven of a "hard lot," a barkeeper from New Jersey. In the first quarter, a dramatic monologue addressed to the reader, Captain Eli Stormfield of San Francisco at his death whizzes off into outer space and through the sun, moving at 186,000 miles a second, as in a dream. Being sociable, Stormfield is glad to meet Solomon Goldstein, a Jew from Chatham Street, New York. At first patronizing, misreading Goldstein's motive for crying, Stormfield is desolated to learn that the Jew is weeping for his dead daughter, whom he expects never to see again, since Stormfield has persuaded him that both he and the Jew are bound for hell. A second "blur of light" closes up to them, one Bailey from Oshkosh, a shrewd Republican who had saved his ticket by pairing off with a Democrat before committing suicide out of disappointed love. This burlesque figure is followed by Sam, a "cheerful good-natured cuss" who had been a slave nearly half his life. Sam too is distressed by Stormfield's certainty that he is on his way to hell, and out of kindness gives him his pipe and tobacco. The Jew, the suicide, and the Negro, traveling sociably along together (pp. 7–16), prepare the reader for a heaven that accommodates Eskimos, Tartars, Chinese, Mexicans, English, Arabs (very few white people), not to speak of a certain "sky-blue man with seven heads," from other universes (pp. 33–34, 25). The first narrative quarter concludes with a splendid race between Stormfield and a continent-sized comet. Stormfield in effect is winning the race—until he makes the mistake of thumbing his nose at the rival captain. The rival captain lightens ship by throwing overboard eighteen hundred thousand billion quintillion kazarks of brimstone—a kazark is the bulk of one hundred sixty-nine worlds—and soon disappears beyond Stormfield into the blackness of outer space (pp. 18–22).

The last three-quarters of the narrative are spieled off to "Peters" by Captain Stormfield, so that there is a listener for the storyteller; but Peters never responds, and Mark Twain manages his story of Stormfield in heaven mostly through dialogue between the captain and the head clerk, then a "nice old gent" named Sam, and finally bald-headed Sandy McWilliams. The ground for all this portion is simply a series of discoveries as to the true nature of the afterlife, all of them reversals of the conventional and expected.

The first blow to Stormfield's vanity is that the busy head clerk cannot identify San Francisco or the United States or the earth on the map of universes, which is as big as Rhode Island; and when the underclerk does find it, it is under the name of the Wart. The comet race, that is, had lasted long enough to divert Stormfield to a heavenly gate billions of leagues from the right one (pp. 24–27). This branch of heaven has no earthlings or harps or hymn-books in it; and heaven is both inconceivably large and immensely varied—as varied as its inhabitants. On reaching the corner of heaven for people from his own universe, Captain Stormfield is awarded "A harp and a hymn-book, pair of wings and a halo, size 13," by a Pi-Ute Injun gatekeeper whom he had known in Tulare County.[27] But it takes him only half a day of trying to fly and singing the only song he knows to discover from a new acquaintance, Sam, that heaven is *not* a haven of rest for "warbling ignoramuses" but just the "busiest place you ever heard of," where nothing harmless and reasonable is refused anybody. Heaven, Sam explains, has pain and suffering; but they do not last and they do not kill; without them, there could be no happiness. Above all, though the heavenly denizen must earn a thing to enjoy it, in heaven "you can choose your own occupation": the shoemaker with the soul of a poet will in heaven be a poet (pp. 34–42).

Stormfield's education proceeds in heavenly discourse with the New Jersey angel, Sandy McWilliams. One picks his age after experiment, usually at the "place where his mind was last at its best," and one's intellect grows sharper in heaven, Sandy explains. The ideas are realized in the episode of a middle-aged, gray-haired mother's finding her child, who in twenty-seven years has grown into a philosopher, and learning to her sorrow that they have almost nothing in common any longer. They will come together, "but not this year, and not next," Sandy predicts. Pain and suffering, in short, are their lot, but not forever (pp. 43–53).

One of the unexpected and striking features of the hereafter, Captain Stormfield learns, is that it is a *kingdom*, where the prophets and patriarchs are deeply revered and are seen only on the rarest and greatest occasions. Just as there are paradoxes and discrepancies in Samuel Clemens's earlier views about caste and class ("Does the race of man love a lord?" Yes, and so in some fashion does Mark Twain), so they reappear in Stormfield's story. Sandy reveals how the heavenly inhabitants—apparently including himself—are awe-struck before the prophets and patriarchs. He makes it obvious, however, that earthly royalty take low status, and that heavenly justice prevails for the "mute inglorious Miltons" if not all the Pudd'nhead Wilsons of the earth; that the aristocracy of heaven is an *aristoi* of talent, not of rank or riches (pp. 63–66).

The drama and fun of this view take form in a series of characters, real and imagined. The Reverend Talmage of Brooklyn is here immortalized as a man who will never come near Abraham's bosom, or Jacob's or Isaac's either, though he had fully expected to weep there. The prophets, among them Homer and Shakespeare, take precedence over the patriarchs. Yet Billings, a tailor from Tennessee, whose poetry no one would print and who was ridden on a rail by his neighbors before his death, ranks above Homer and Shakespeare. More, the poets Saa, Bo, and Soof, from three different and remote systems, are known *throughout* heaven, as Homer, Shakespeare, and Billings are not. A certain Absalom Jones from the Boston back country, though he died obscure, was a greater military genius than Napoleon. Also, the sausage maker of Hoboken, Duffer by name, who fed the poor unobtrusively all his life, was greeted in heaven as Sir Richard Duffer, Baronet. Such, McWilliams tells Stormfield, is heavenly justice (pp. 67–80). In sum, Stormfield's heaven is a heaven on a liberal plan whose king, mentioned only once in reverence by the head clerk as the savior of uncounted worlds (p. 26), is like the Widow Douglas's Providence—generous and forgiving.

The work is touched by sentimentality and burlesque, but never more than briefly. It fails of any conventional ending. Yet it is surely one of Mark Twain's works of humane feeling and high imagination. One might in fact conclude that the tone of "Captain Stormfield's Visit to Heaven" is close to that of *Adventures of Huckleberry Finn*. Except for two "voyage" chapters written in 1901, it was complete in the early 1880s; so that, with the exception of the incomplete, totally different "Chronicle of Young Satan" (1897), never again was Mark Twain to write fiction so well.

What then of "The Man That Corrupted Hadleyburg," which was published in *Harper's* for December 1899, a short novel

comparable in length to the 23,000-word "Captain Stormfield"? With its weaknesses on its head (and they are real, I
believe), the Hadleyburg tale is built around a complicated
and subtle plot, and a whole town full of vigorously sketched
characters surrounding one couple portrayed in depth, the
Richardses. The form of narration is what Howells called the
"historical" (as opposed to the biographical and autobiographical). The novelist, that is, behaves as though he were an
historian, moving from narrative summary to letters to soliloquy to dramatic occasion just as he sees fit.[28] The genre is the
tale of revenge, like Poe's "Cask of Amontillado," expanded
with constant satiric exposure of the "the unco guid" leading
citizens of Hadleyburg, that exceptionally honest and upright
town. So far as the reader has followed sympathetically the
plight of the Richards couple, the effect of the story is wrench-
ing pathos; yet it is equally an effect of high moral comedy, in
that the citizens of Hadleyburg have learned to reject their
former motto, "Lead us not into temptation," and to follow
their new one, "Lead us into temptation" (p. 83). They recognize, in short, that a "fugitive and cloister'd virtue" cannot
compare to virtue tried and hardened through resistance to
temptation.

The givens of the story are two. First, Hadleyburg is famous
for its honesty, though the town is actually "honest, narrow,
self-righteous and stingy." Second, a big, mysterious stranger
passing through suffers a deep offense from the town (its nature never specified) and becomes bitter and revengeful.
Wishing to corrupt the entire body of leading citizens, the
stranger in retaliation leaves a sack of gold coins, $40,000
worth, to be claimed by the inhabitant who can demonstrate
that he once gave the stranger twenty dollars in charity. The
demonstration is to be made by the claimant's repeating the
remark which he made at the time to the stranger. Verification
of the remark is to be made by a letter in the sack.

Edward Richards and his wife Mary receive the money from the stranger and pass it on, as instructed, to the Rev. Mr. Burgess, who will in public receive any claim to the sack, and test the claim by the letter (pp. 1–21). It is essential to the development of Mark Twain's story that Richards should be a genuinely honest person suffering from poverty in old age as an overworked bank clerk. Similarly, the Reverend Burgess has to be the most hated person in town, a minister without a congregation, whom the town had universally condemned for an act he did not commit—the act again unspecified. Richards, who could have saved Burgess, had been afraid to testify to his innocence; and had in fact only managed to warn the minister privately of the intent of many townspeople to ride him out on a rail. Still a third person, Barclay Goodson, now dead, is essential to the plot, for he was the only person in town who was charitable enough to give a stranger twenty dollars, and he too had been hated by the town for his low opinion of it.

The Richards couple, like the other "quality" townspeople, rack their brains to imagine what the stranger's remark could have been. Then a second letter, signed "Stephenson" by a second stranger, who is of course actually the original, reveals to the Richardses that Goodson had made the remark and he the writer had overheard it; that Goodson had told him Richards had done him a great service once (that is, he *thought* it was Richards); and hence that Richards deserved the sack of gold. The crucial remark, "Stephenson" reports, is this: "You are far from being a bad man: go, and reform" (p. 26).

The Richards's deep pleasure in learning the key to the treasure is, however, undermined by Richards' inability to remember what service he had performed for Goodson. Eventually, rationalizing, Richards gathers together a dim recollection that he had saved Goodson from marrying a "very sweet and pretty girl" who "carried a teaspoonful of negro blood in her veins." This fantasizing about the evidence, this wishful

thinking, is marked by the compounded ironies that character-
ize Mark Twain's treatment of race elsewhere. It is followed by
the disclosure that all the nineteen principal citizens of Hadleyburg receive the same letter—and that subsequently each of
them manages to get his claim into the hands of the former
minister. And they all begin to spend the $40,000 in antici-
pation (pp. 27–34).

All this leads up to the *scène à faire* of the novel. The townspeople gather in the town hall: the nineteen principal citizens,
the town satirist Jack Halliday, the tanner, the hatter, the saddler, and the Reverend Mr. Burgess in the chair, with the national press well represented. Apparently the generosity of a
Hadleyburg citizen is to be rewarded; actually Hadleyburg's
honesty and good reputation are on trial. When Burgess reads
the first letter with the key sentence, both Billson and Wilson
stand up as Burgess reads the writer's name, and both claim
the money, to the townspeople's bewilderment. When Burgess
reads the first of two letters enclosed in the sack, both claim-
ants stand revealed as "dishonest blatherskites." The
stranger's key remark in full was: "Go, and reform—or, mark
my words—some day, for your sins, you will die and go to
hell or Hadleyburg—TRY AND MAKE IT THE FORMER" (p.
47). This sentiment and the revelation of Billson and Wilson's
crookedness are greeted by a tempest of laughter from the audience. But when the banker Pinkerton's letter is read aloud
and then the claims of the other leading citizens, the laughter
turns into roaring humor and a satirical song about the "Incor-
ruptibles" of Hadleyburg, based on a tune from the "Mikado."
Richards, meanwhile, seeking to confess his guilt among the
others, had been denied the floor by Burgess. After reading
eighteen of the letters, the minister fumbles in his pocket,
then reports that he has read them all. Richards and his wife
are saved. A second letter from the mysterious stranger reveals
how fully he has hoaxed the town and explains how he wished

to injure them all in their vanity. And when Burgess opens the sack, the coins are discovered to be only gilded disks of lead (p. 65).

When the saddler proposes that Jack Halliday auction off the lead coins and the town award the money to their "*one* clean man left," Edward Richards, they agree with enthusiasm and run the bidding up to over $1,200. At this point an interested stranger—"Stephenson," the original stranger—outbids the others, and asks the town's consent to stamp upon the face of the lead coins the names of the eighteen citizens. He will sell them and guarantee a check to the Richards couple for $10,000. One of the townspeople pays face value for the lead coins—in order to stamp his opponent's name on them all and defeat him in a crucial election with railroad money involved. The Richardses receive the entire $40,000 in checks made out by Stephenson to the "Bearer," and Stephenson writes to Richards:

> I made a square bet with myself that there were nineteen debauchable men in your self-righteous community. I have lost. Take the whole pot, you are entitled to it. (P. 76)

A note from Burgess follows:

> You saved me, in a difficult time. I saved you last night. It was at cost of a lie, but I made the sacrifice freely, and out of a grateful heart. None in this village knows so well as I know how brave and good and noble you are. At bottom you cannot respect me, knowing as you do of that matter of which I am accused, and by the general voice condemned; but . . . I am a grateful man. . . . (Pp. 76–77)

Under this double blow and the suspicions engendered thereafter by their guilt feelings, the Richards couple begin to break down, and Richards, with his hypersensitive conscience and delusions of persecution, destroys the checks. Physically and

mentally exhausted, Richards confesses the whole truth about
the sack, how Burgess saved him from disgrace, and his cowardice in failing to clear Burgess years before. He dies forgiving Burgess wholeheartedly for, as he thinks, repenting and
exposing him as he deserved, unaware that "once more he had
done poor Burgess a wrong" (p. 83). On this note of irony and
pity Mark Twain concludes the "corruption" of Hadleyburg's
top nineteen citizens, lightening the conclusion, however,
with the implications of Hadleyburg's change of mottoes.

It is a mixed end to a mixed story. The stranger never learns,
apparently, that he *had* corrupted Hadleyburg totally. In this
respect Mark Twain outdoes his Calvinist forebears, who believed that perhaps one out of ten thousand souls might be
saved. Here, of the nineteen leading citizens at any rate, *none*
is "saved." On the other hand, the remarkable town-hall
drama is pervaded by laughter and by a lilting tune. The house
is in a roaring humor, and for Mark Twain humor mostly
means freedom. What young Satan, of "The Chronicle of
Young Satan," argues so eloquently in talk with the boys of
that tale is made dramatic here: laughter is the one power possessed by man that is strong enough to blow shams apart.
Music is a power coequal with laughter, though Mark Twain
cannot so vividly demonstrate its use. Paradoxically, a suf-
ficiency of money and vanity seem as invariably powerful in
turn-of-the-century Hadleyburg as the doctrine of predestination a century or two before among New England Cal-
vinists. But the power of grace in laughter is equally unquali-
fied. In this story at least, Mark Twain makes them both vital,
equal principles of his plot.

There are soft spots in that plot, as even the most believing
reader will discover. The motivation of the stranger, *alias* Stephenson, in corrupting Hadleyburg is never disclosed, and
perhaps it need not be; it is an initial condition for what happens, and presumably the town is capable of giving deep of-

fense, especially to a foreigner. But what the Rev. Mr. Burgess had purportedly done to make the townspeople prepare to ride him on a rail is never disclosed, either. One can of course argue that the supposed act—of which he is innocent—may be *imagined* by readers more luridly than if it had been named; but two such mysterious acts in a single short novel are one too many. One wonders also how it happens that a minister without a congregation, the most hated man in town, is permitted to chair the town meeting, even though the mysterious benefactor had so requested.

Flaws aside, "The Man That Corrupted Hadleyburg" is Mark Twain's last major published fiction, and its popularity among anthologists and readers is deserved. How widely its reputation has spread is subtly touched on in the motion picture "High Noon." This intense Western film of 1952 depicts a town corrupted by fear of three desperadoes who return to the town to kill the sheriff who had sent them to jail. Following a single camera shot of two of the killers at the railroad station waiting for the noon train, the camera pans up to the signboard reading "Hadleyville."

A final memorable piece of short fiction, "The Five Boons of Life" (1902),[29] is given the form of the fairy story, and narrated in an intense style that approaches but never falls over into blank verse. The personae of the small drama are simply the good fairy with her basket of gifts—Fame, Love, Riches, Pleasure, Death—and the youth. "Choose wisely," she admonishes him, "for only one of them is valuable." The youth chooses Pleasure; but over the years his pleasures disappoint and mock him. ("With follies light as the feather / Doth Youth to man befall.") The fairy appears again. The man considers long, and chooses Love. After many, many years, he loses the last of those he loves, and he curses Love from his heart. The fairy now warns him to choose warily, for only one of the three remaining gifts has any value; and the man selects

Fame. When the good fairy returns, she reads his mind: his
name had filled the world for a little while—then came envy,
detraction, calumny, hate, persecution, derision, and finally
pity. He is as bitter as he is miserable. ("Then evils gather together, / There wants not one of them all— / Wrath, envy,
discord, strife.") "Choose yet again," the fairy tells him. In a
long burst of deluded enthusiasm the man selects wealth and
power, since (he believes) riches will buy contentment and esteem. But in three short years the man is poor and hungry and
in rags. The gifts he had chosen were in truth Pain, Grief,
Shame, and Poverty. Now he implores the good fairy to
bring him "dreamless and enduring sleep." But the fairy, when
asked by a child to choose for it, had given the child Death.
("Thy portion esteem I highest, / Who wast not ever begot; /
Thine next, being born who diest / And straightway again art
not.") When the man asks what is left for him, the fairy responds, with pity, "the wanton insult of Old Age." (". . . seal-
ing the sum of trouble / Doth tottering Age draw nigh, / Whom
friends and kinsfolk fly, / Age, upon whom redouble / All
sorrows under the sky.")

The running gloss I have introduced parenthetically from a
chorus in the Oedipus Coloneus of Sophocles [30] may serve to
illuminate the classic sentiment as well as the classic economy
of the fable. It goes without saying that the cameo fairy story
speaks through the indirection of its art for Clemens himself.
Earlier he had asserted that "pity is for the living, envy is for
the dead." In a very late letter he characterized death as "the
most precious of all the gifts this life has for us." [31]

Chapter 4

◆◆

THE
"BOY BOOKS"

The Adventures of Tom Sawyer, *its drama and pathos.* — Adventures of Huckleberry Finn, *in the "autobiographical" form.* — *Growth of understanding between Huck and Jim.* — *The dark underside of the narrative.* — *The novel as comedy.* — *Verbal fun, burlesque, satire, false pathos, irony, pathos.* — *Mark Twain's letter defending his "abused child."*

Critics and plain readers and not-so-plain readers alike have tended to agree that the best of the Mark Twain *romances* deal with "the matter of Hannibal," as Henry Nash Smith has called it. Or, if we may expand the scope of the phrase a little, the action of these superior romances arises from the life of Petersburg (the fictional Hannibal) and of lesser towns on the Mississippi, and the consciousness of a "bad boy" and a river-rat and a Negro slave.

Two fictions more limited in scope than *Adventures of Huckleberry Finn* followed the promise of its title that *more* adventures might be forthcoming: *The Tragedy of Pudd'nhead Wilson*

in 1894 and *Tom Sawyer* in 1896. The first is a melodrama set
once again in a re-created Hannibal permeated with the meta-
physics of black skin-white skin difference. It presents a
"black" heroine, Roxana, who is fifteen-sixteenths white,
who in independence and vigor looks back to Aunt Rachel and
forward to William Faulkner's Dilsey. The second isolates Tom
and Huck and Jim on an air-raft-balloon voyage from Missouri
to the Sahara Desert and back. Their three-cornered debates
over crusades, map colors, time zones, "ornithologers," fleas,
mirages, tariffs, indemnities, metaphors, and the currents of
the upper air make *Tom Sawyer Abroad* the brightest, most
continually entertaining of the fictions about the three friends.
But it is easy to let one's sense of the greater comedy overwhelm that of the lesser, so that the ideal reading order, governed by one's increasing appreciation and the works' breadth
and even length, might be *Tom Sawyer Abroad, Tom Sawyer,
Pudd'nhead Wilson,* and *Huckleberry Finn.*

The Adventures of Tom Sawyer (1876), the first of the Hannibal romances, is a most ingeniously plotted narrative. Four
distinct lines of action are revealed in it, according to Walter
Blair's formulation. Tom's changing relation to Becky Thatcher
and its culmination in his finding a way out of McDougal's
cave is one such line. Another is Tom's relation to his Aunt
Polly: his running away with Joe Harper and Huck Finn to
Jackson's Island and his triumphant emergence at his own funeral. The third involves Tom, and Huck, with the sinister
Injun Joe; Tom's testifying for Muff Potter, terrified, in the
murder trial; and their release from terror only when Injun Joe
dies of starvation in the cave. The discovery of hidden treasure
by Injun Joe, as Tom and Huck in hiding witness the event,
and its recovery by the boys in the cave, forms the final plot
line, linked closely to the Injun Joe sequence.[1] All four plots
are pulled together and resolved by the events taking place in

the cave and the disclosures at the party of leading townspeople immediately following.

However ingeniously plotted in multiple actions like J. F. Cooper's, *The Adventures of Tom Sawyer* is still a fiction limited by the fictional conventions of its time—inevitably perhaps, since it was only Mark Twain's second novel. (His first had been a sprawling collaboration with Charles Dudley Warner, *The Gilded Age* of 1873). It was never quite clear to the writer whether he was producing a story for children or a story about children for adults as well. In the end he tried to make it both, and with a large degree of success. But whenever the narrator spoke to the adult reader about his young characters he tended to weaken these parts of the book; whereas in the strong episodes he presented the boys' actions—both overt and psychological—dramatically, without editorial comment.

The test for this assertion is simple. Are the memorable pages of the book rendered dramatically? Every reader will think of particular passages, but a consensus surely exists. Tom's "conning" his friends into performing a whitewashing chore for him and then rewarding him for it comes at once to mind, though it truly says more about Tom's artistic and rhetorical skill than it illustrates Mark Twain's editorial comment on the difference between Work and Play. Similarly the boys' revelation of the treasure to the townspeople makes a satisfying scene, though it is a wholly conventional novelistic "distribution of prizes." Decidedly more memorable is the frightening experience endured by Tom and Becky when lost in the cave, watching their last candle flicker out and losing their sense of time in the "horror of utter darkness," before Tom reaches the end of his kite-string and glimpses a far-off speck—by day-and-night chance—of daylight. Earlier, Tom (and Huck, too, to a lesser degree) had suffered continual crises of anxiety over their secret knowledge that Injun Joe rather than the harmless drunk Muff Potter had murdered the doctor in the graveyard. Injun Joe's ferocity is the cause of their terror; and Huck suffers like Tom before he brings himself to reveal Injun Joe's threat to disfigure the Widow Douglass. Testifying in court only compounds Tom's fear. "Tom's days were days of splendor and exultation to him, but his nights were seasons of horror," the narrator reveals; and "poor, Huck was in the same state of wretchedness and terror." [2] Thus, in his deepening concern for Becky's survival, and in his decision to save Muff Potter and expose himself to Injun Joe's ferocity, Tom Sawyer undergoes a genuine trial by fire; he matures under strong pressure.

Fears of starvation and of mutilation and death are not, however, the strongest emotions Mark Twain elicited from Tom's adventures. His strongest scene in the novel elicits true pathos, from Aunt Polly's suspicion that Tom has lied to her once again: her struggle of conscience over testing Tom's assertion, and her discovery that he had told her the truth. Tom confesses to his aunt that when he had come home secretly that night, in the middle of his runaway pirating, he had written her a note on bark to tell her that he and Huck and Joe really were not drowned, but then had put it back in his jacket when the splendid theatricality of reappearing at their own funeral occurred to him. And he had kissed his aunt while she slept, "Because" he says, "I loved you so, and you laid there moaning and I was so sorry." Aunt Polly's crisis of conscience then flares up as she gets Tom's jacket out of the closet after he has gone. "No, I don't dare," she says to herself. "Poor boy, I reckon he's lied about it—but it's a blessed, blessed lie. . . ."

> She put the jacket away, and stood by musing a minute. Twice she put out her hand to take the garment again, and twice she refrained. Once more she ventured, and this time she fortified herself with the thought: "It's a good lie—it's a good lie—I won't let it grieve me." So she sought the jacket pocket. A

moment later she was reading Tom's piece of bark through flowing tears and saying: "I could forgive the boy, now, if he'd committed a million sins!" [3]

Mark Twain the man had a super-subtle conscience, and the corresponding power in his art to give a final turn to the moral screw. Aunt Polly discovers Tom's moral gain after she has doubted his truthfulness: this bears the true Mark Twain hallmark.

The links between *The Adventures of Tom Sawyer* and *Adventures of Huckleberry Finn* (*Tom Sawyer's Comrade*) are real and obvious enough, from the reappearance of Tom and Huck (their importance mostly reversed) to Mark Twain's intent to write a sequel and eventually to publish the two narratives in one volume. The differences, however, are striking: the introduction of Jim, one of the fullest of Mark Twain's characterizations of Negro slaves; the emergence of Huckleberry Finn from the shadow thrown by Tom; and a varied series of frescoes of life along the Mississippi river and its "sivilization." Above all, Mark Twain has found the right narrative mode for his epic comedy. He had built the story of Tom Sawyer by laying dramatic incidents together with the mortar of summary, generalization, and editorial comment—Mark Twain as author-mason. Now he drops "Mark Twain" after the first paragraph of the tale, and dares to take on the delicate task of telling the story, in the vernacular, through the eyes and sensibility of a river-rat, who is *the central figure of the book, the hero, as well as the "I" narrator.*

An astonishing amount of writer's and printer's ink has been put to paper mostly to condemn—and occasionally to justify—the "frame" structure of *Huckleberry Finn*—that is, the opening and closing chapters, where the focus is on Tom Sawyer's antics, and Huck in Tom's presence returns to his status of a satellite character. But that spiritual heir of Mark Twain, J. D. Salinger, through Holden Caulfield, provides one good

explanation for the framing. Holden does not like Hemingway's *A Farewell to Arms* because Frederic Henry emerges as
an egotist and a prig, telling his own story as hero.[4] Mark
Twain was surely aware of this danger, and skirted it effectively by keeping Huck in the background at both the opening
and the close of his own story. In truth, the "romance" of
Huck Finn's picaresque adventures begins and ends under a
thoroughly absurd fictional convention. The poor white
youngster who in the Tom Sawyer novel could not even read
and had to be shown how to write his own initials, is now
after a few months of schooling the composer of a long letter to
the reader.[5] He addresses that reader orally—for it is a *speaking*
letter, dictated or tape-recorded as it were—and ingratiatingly
in the first paragraph; and he confides his plans to the reader
in the last paragraph and signs his communication "Yours
truly / Huck Finn" to conclude the work. But the absurdity of
the form is glimpsed only momentarily as the reader enters
into and emerges from the imaginary world of the story, and it
vanishes entirely while he is inside that world. The skill, that
is, with which Clemens speaks through the double mask of
"Mark Twain" and that of his vernacular-voiced adolescent is
all but flawless. It is all the more baffling, then, that when
Howells, in his magisterial "Novel-Reading and Novel-Writing," distinguished the basic forms as "autobiographical,"
"biographical," and "historical," he failed to name *Adventures
of Huckleberry Finn* as a capital example of the "autobiographical" form, since he recognized clearly enough that
Henry James was the master of the "biographical" novel.[6]

Of the many critical ways into *Adventures of Huckleberry
Finn*, three seem particularly rewarding: the growth of understanding and friendship between Huck and Jim, along with
Tom's ambiguous role in this development; the dark underside of the narrative; and the total character of the work as
comedy.

To give the reader of a novel a sense of a character's "bottom nature" (as Gertrude Stein called it) is a prime ambition of the novelist; and it is difficult enough to conceive of a life-like, complex figure and then to reveal that character gradually and persuasively, facet by facet. But the novelist's greatest accomplishment is surely not merely to reveal "bottom nature" gradually but at the same time to show by outer action or inner conflict-and-resolution a real change in character. The change may be a change in knowing, or in hoping or despairing, or in comprehending through sympathy, and it may move downward or upward; but it is finally, in the very largest meaning of the word, moral. These novelistic principles or goals—if such they are—may at least be inferred with abundant evidence from the growing friendship between Huck Finn and Jim—a poor white youth and a slave. That growth—inconceivable for a well-brought-up boy like Tom Sawyer—is accented by occasional reminders of Huck's status as a lonely orphan and by the massive, scarcely visible, yet omnipresent force of slavery throughout the work.

It is one of the conditions of Huck's ability to accept a slave as a friend that he cannot (presumably) remember his illiterate mother and that early in the story he loses Pap, the father who is no father. He is hungry more often than not, and he is often lonely. At the very beginning, with Miss Watson "pecking" at him, he feels "so lonesome I most wished I was dead" (chap. 1), though he does find her convenient to cite as a relative who might be sacrificed as "family" (chap. 2). Huck escapes from his Pap not only because Pap often beat him but also because it was "dreadful lonesome" locked up in the Illinois cabin (chap. 6). But when Huck finds Jim, also a fugitive, on Jackson's Island, he is glad to see him and is lonely no longer (chap. 8).

"Home" for the orphan and the fugitive slave is first the cave on the island (chap. 9), and thereafter, with increasing

conviction, the little section of a lumber-raft that Jim rebuilds
to make comfortable. Huck says he is "mighty glad to see
home again" after being caught on the big lumber-raft. Even
though he comes to like the Grangerford family ("dead ones
and all"), when Buck Grangerford is killed in the feud he is
"powerful glad" to see Jim again. Jim hugs him in relief that
he has escaped, and they agree that "there warn't no home
like a raft, after all" (chap. 15). Even in the midst of the "lonesomeness of the river," its "solid lonesomeness," Huck concludes, "it's lovely to live on a raft" (chap. 19). Huck's keeping
"peace in the family" on the raft after rescuing the King and
the Duke from an angry mob is by contrast ironic enough. But
his discovery that Jim is often "low and homesick" and lonesome for his wife and children is a true revelation. It also anticipates the selling and breaking up of the black family, the
slaves of Peter Wilks, by the fraudulent heirs, the King and the
Duke, and the grief that the deed causes Mary Jane Wilks and
her sisters. Huck and Jim constitute therefore a true family,
even a "community of saints," as Lionel Trilling has suggested,[7] on their primitive floating home.

   But this is a status they must both achieve, the major effort
having to be made by Huckleberry Finn. In their very first encounter, Tom Sawyer plays a characteristic trick on the sleeping Jim, taking his hat from his head and hanging it on a limb.
Jim's accounting for the event as the work of witches, his con-
sulting the hair-ball to predict Huck's future with Pap, his
knowledge of signs—including the bit of folklore that a hairy
breast means future wealth, and even the boom-and-bust anecdote he tells about his bank and his speculation, reveal a
good deal about a superstitious slave who "knowed most everything" about signs, who yet has the courage to run away
when his mistress talks of selling him "down to Orleans" for
"a big stack o' money" (chap. 8).

   Jim's escape has in some sense been predicted by Pap Finn's

outrageous diatribe against a "free nigger" from Ohio who appears in Petersburg wearing broadcloth and carries a gold watch and chain, who "could talk all kinds of languages," who could even vote, and who could not be sold by the "guvment" until he had been in the state six months (chap. 6). Yet at this point the difference between the free Negro and Jim is great.

When Huck re-encounters Jim on Jackson's Island, both are fugitives, Huck from both his mistress Miss Watson's kind of "sivilization" and Pap Finn's murderous moods, and Jim from slavery—specifically from the threat of slavery in the plantation South, "down the river." Huck, even at the risk of becoming known as a "low-down Abolitionist," twice promises Jim that he will not tell on him. But even after they are well established in the cave (and Jim has spared Huck the knowledge that the corpse in the floating house is Pap Finn's), Huck is enough like Tom Sawyer to play a trick on Jim. He kills a rattlesnake on their flooded ridge and coils him up "ever so natural" on Jim's blankets for "fun," but when Jim flings himself down on the blanket, the snake's mate is there, and bites him. Jim recovers by drinking heavily of Pap's whiskey, eating a piece of the dead snake roasted, and wearing the rattles on his wrist. He believes that handling snake-skin brings bad luck. Huck, however, quietly gets rid of the dead snakes, and never lets Jim know that he had played so dangerous a trick on him.

Wanting to learn what is going on, Huck stops at the cabin of Mrs. Judith Loftus over the river and learns that a reward of $300 for capturing Jim has stirred up the townspeople, including her husband, who plans to search the island after midnight. Mrs. Loftus, so kind to Huck, reminds him, and the reader, that "three hundred dollars is a power of money." So it is that Huck and Jim push off that night with raft and canoe on their journey to freedom.

After the adventure of the wrecked steamboat *Sir Walter Scott*, they plan to sell the raft and take a steamboat up the

Ohio from Cairo, into the free states. But a fog separates them, Huck in the canoe and Jim on the raft; Huck wishes "the fool would think to beat a tin pan"; and then they are further separated by a big island and then they run still separated through a nest of towheads. Tired and lonely, Huck tries to take a cat nap, sleeps, wakes to a clear night and starlight, and finally finds the raft again all "littered up with leaves and branches and dirt" from the rough trip through the towheads, with Jim sitting asleep exhausted, holding the steering oar. After waking Jim, who is profoundly glad that Huck has survived, Huck now pretends that he has been asleep on the raft all the time and that Jim must have been drunk or dreaming. Though he is incredulous of a dream that could be so filled with anxiety for Huck and so tiring, Jim recounts what had happened and "interprets" it as a warning from providence. But as the dawn light grows, Huck points to the leaves and rubbish on the raft and asks what *they* stand for. When Jim, who is "the easiest nigger to laugh that ever was" (chap. 20), gets the reality untangled from the dream, he says, unsmiling:

> What do dey stan' for? I's gwyne to tell you. When I got all wore out wid work, en wid de callin' for you, en went to sleep, my heart wuz mos' broke bekase you wuz los', an I didn' k'yer no mo' what become er me en de raf'. En when I wake up en fine you back agin, all safe en soun', de tears come en I could a got down on my knees en kiss' yo' foot I's so thankful. En all you wuz thinkin 'bout wuz how you could make a fool uv ole Jim wid a lie. Dat truck dah is *trash;* en trash is what people is dat puts dirt on de head er dey fren's en makes 'em ashamed. (Chap. 15)

Huck feels mean; and after a sharp struggle of conscience he humbles himself to a nigger, as he says, "but I done it, and I warn't ever sorry for it afterwards, neither." He did Jim no more "mean tricks," he tells the reader; and in fact he does not.

The effect of Jim's rebuke and of the entire episode is produced with fine dramatic and verbal art. Jim's understanding of what his "dream" means epitomizes much of the action of the entire novel. Thus, the towheads stand for quarrelsome people and mean folks; the current is a man who will try to help them; but if they persist quietly they will "get out of the fog and into the big clear river, which was the free states."

Jim's dream has the quality of a Negro spiritual, or of a revival hymn about Beulah land. The heart of his rebuke centered in the word "trash." Huck had observed earlier the "old dead brush and trash" that hung over the banks of the towheads; Jim looks at the trash on the raft, then at Huck, and back at the trash again. Distinctions between "nigger Jim" and "white trash" Huck Finn (who is surely Irish) count as nothing in the realm of friendship. A striking earlier analogue, if not the source for this giant step in the friendship between Jim and Huck, is Tom Sawyer's recital to his Aunt Polly, as though he had dreamed it, of everything he had overheard during the night he had returned from Jackson's Island, and her rebuke to him for making a dream-joke out of what had made her heart so sore.[8]

A further sharp turn of the screw of conscience occurs as the voyagers draw nearer to Cairo. Huck has been learning. Now Jim is becoming "all over trembly and feverish to be so close to freedom"; he keeps talking about how he will save all his earnings when he is free and buy his wife; and they will then work to buy their two children; and if their master will not sell them they will even get an Abolitionist to *steal* the children for them. Violating the commandment "Thou shalt not steal" *and* the Fugitive Slave Law as well makes Huck's blood run cold, and his conscience drives him to take the canoe with the intent to "tell on" Jim to the first person he meets ashore. But he feels sick at the idea—and is saved the trip when two armed men in a skiff come along hunting for five runaway slaves.

Huck lets conscience go, and tells the slave-hunters that the man in the wigwam on the raft is white, and is his father. When they insist on seeing for themselves, Huck "confesses" that Pap is sick and that other people have refused to help them. The men conclude that "Pap" has smallpox, advise Huck how to fool other people at the next town, and even float two twenty-dollar gold pieces down to him on a board—their *conscience* money. Jim, meanwhile, has been clinging to the raft, ready to "shove for sho' " if he must, or to return if the men go away. "Give a nigger an inch and he'll take an ell," Huck moralizes (chap. 16). The effect of a taste of freedom on Jim, Huck finds, is astonishing, enspiriting, electrifying.

The joint adventure of Huck and Jim is now at an end. They have missed Cairo. They lose their canoe. Huck is taken in by the Grangerfords, and Jim remains in the swamp off-stage, cared for by the Grangerford slaves. Then, when Huck finds another canoe and rescues the King and Duke from a mob, he and Jim become in effect prisoners of "royalty." The two con men strike the reader at first as sympathetic, rather Falstaffian, rascals; but the true measure of the King is that, even though a slave has just saved him from tar and feathers and a mob, in the end he will sell Jim, another slave, for "forty dirty dollars." In the second half of the novel, Mark Twain plans primarily to illustrate life in small towns along the Mississippi, though he is careful not to let Jim drop wholly out of sight.

The next stage in the developing relation of Huck and Jim marks a new perception of Jim's humanity on Huck's part and a new revelation, by Jim, of his own "leather-headedness." This stage is effectively prepared for in Huck's explanation to Jim of "the orneriness of kings" (especially "Sollermun," who proposed to cut a child in two) and the mystery of why *their* king "do *smell* so," like other rapscallion kings in history. The broad satire gives way to pure pathos when Jim confesses to Huck how much he misses his wife and children "away up

yonder," "Po' little 'Lizabeth! po' little Johnny!" He admits to
Huck that one time after his little girl had recovered from
scarlet fever, he had sent her sprawling with a slap to the side
of her head when she had failed to shut the door at his command. But the child had not heard the door slammed to by the
wind, nor could she hear her father shout directly behind her.
"Oh Huck," Jim confesses, "I bust out a-cryin' en grab her up
in my arms, en say, 'Oh, de po' little thing! De Lord God
Amighty fogive po' ole Jim, kaze he never gwyne to fogive
hisself as long's he live!' Oh, she was plumb deef en dumb,
Huck, plumb deef en dumb—en I'd ben a-treat'n' her so!"
Huck has learned that Jim loves his "people" as much as white
folks do theirs. Jim reveals with passionate self-reproach that
he too belongs to the "damned human race" (chap. 23).

During the entire Wilks episode Jim is again invisible, as he
had been throughout the Grangerford-Shepherdson feud. But
the human reality of Negro slaves, as well as the King's towering greed, is revealed when the King, playing the part of the
dead Peter Wilks's brother, sells the slave mother down the
river and the two sons up to Memphis. The Wilks sisters and
the slave family hang around each others' necks and cry incon-
solably, and Mary Jane Wilks is bitter. The deed makes Huck
sick—but he can stand it, knowing as he does that the sale is
fraudulent and that the slave family will soon return to the
Wilks girls and be reunited.

The culminating event follows the exposure of the King and
the Duke, and the King's selling of Jim, as he had always been
ready to, with the long-prepared fraudulent handbill. This is
an event wholly interior to Huck, a decision fully as dramatic
as Isabel Archer's on that night-long vigil in *The Portrait of a
Lady*. Huck faces social disgrace in Petersburg and, as he
imagines it, the everlasting fire of hell for stealing. He writes a
letter to Miss Watson revealing Jim's whereabouts, and this
eases his conscience for the moment; but then he remembers

all the times Jim had befriended him in all their time on the river together, so that he hesitates, knowing that he will have to decide, forever, between right and wrong. The sinful decision, to tear up the letter and "*go* to hell," Huck then compounds by a second—to violate the Seventh Commandment and steal Jim out of slavery *again*. The antislavery poet James Russell Lowell treated the same choice with high rhetoric in "The Present Crisis":

Once to every man and nation comes the moment to decide,
In the strife of Truth with Falsehood, for the good or evil side;
Some great cause, God's new Messiah, offering each the bloom or
    blight,
Parts the goats upon the left hand, and the sheep upon the right,
And the choice goes by forever 'twixt that darkness and that light.

.   .   .   .

Careless seems the great Avenger; history's pages but record
One death-grapple in the darkness 'twixt old systems and the Word;
Truth forever on the scaffold, Wrong forever on the throne,—
Yet that scaffold sways the future, and, behind the dim unknown,
Standeth God within the shadow, keeping watch above his own.[9]

Huck's decision to "go the whole hog" and to "take up wickedness again" is a single fictional act realized in the vernacular, and at least as impressive as the choice Lowell visualized so formally in such an august setting.

With the reappearance of Tom Sawyer, Jim's full humanity retreats once again under the mask of a superstitious slave who is willing to go along with the white boy's bookish plans for imprisonment and escape, Dumas-style. Similarly, Huck in the company of Tom is mostly Huck as he was in the opening chapters—an admiring, mostly willing accessory to Tom's antics. But the issue of slavery still crops up in these burlesque chapters, even though the reader may have guessed that Tom can "help" Jim escape only because he knows that Jim is already free by Miss Watson's will.

Thus, when Aunt Sally Phelps greets Huck (believing him to be Tom) he observes "a little nigger girl and two little nigger boys, without anything on but tow-linen shirts," who "hung on to their mother's gown, and peeped out from behind her at me, bashful" and then, behind "Aunt" Sally, "comes her little white children, acting the same way the little niggers was doing" (chap. 32). Soon after, Uncle Silas tells his wife that before breakfast he has been studying Acts 17—wherein one may find the assertion that God "hath made of one blood all nations of men" (17:26). Both Aunt Sally and Uncle Silas are kind to Jim, who is imprisoned in a shed from which he could escape any time he chose. The Phelpses are genuinely kind people. Yet such is the unconscious weight of the "peculiar institution" upon them that Huck can explain his steamboat's delay on the river this way and Aunt Sally can reply, thus:

> "It warn't the grounding—that didn't keep us back but a little. We blowed out a cylinder-head."
> "Good gracious! anybody hurt?"
> "No'm. Killed a nigger."
> "Well, it's lucky; because sometimes people do get hurt."
> (Chap. 32)

This vignette, so matter-of-fact in the telling, would do Jonathan Swift credit. Aunt Sally's response says something sharp about a paradox in one strain of Southern character—just as it does about "Tom Sawyer's" laconic explanation. But wily Huck is of course lying: he is not Tom Sawyer, there had been no explosion, and no one was hurt. The presumption is strong that he is simply telling an immediately acceptable lie—with some scarcely visible managing from Mark Twain.

One further pattern of comment on slavery lends a subtly sa-

tirical glow to Tom's efforts to free Jim. Tom, naturally, will
have no part in Huck's direct plan to free Jim: he is certain that
they can find a way "twice as long" (chap. 34). In the "best
authorities," according to Tom, it takes prisoners "weeks and
weeks and weeks" to dig out, and it took one prisoner "thirty-
seven year" to escape from the "Castle Deef." Though Tom
recognizes that they will have to release Jim before very long,
he thinks that by rights it ought to take a couple of years.
Huck is willing to "let on" that they were at it "a hundred and
fifty year" (chap. 35), so long as they get Jim out directly. But
Tom pursues his fantasy. After an evening of digging so that
their hands "looked like they'd been chawed," Tom is in high
spirits.

> He said it was the best fun he ever had in his life, and the most
> intellectual; and said if he only could see his way to it we
> would keep it up all the rest of our lives and leave Jim to our
> children to get out; for he believed Jim would come to like it
> better and better the more he got used to it. He said that in that
> way it could be strung out to as much as eighty year, and
> would be the best time on record. And he said it would make
> us all celebrated that had a hand in it. (Chap. 36)

The emblematic climax of this "gradualist" motif appears in
Jim's coat of arms as Tom works it out. His description concludes with "a runaway nigger, *sable*, with his bundle over his
shoulder on a bar sinister: and a couple of gules for sup-
porters, which is you and me; motto, *Maggiore fretta, minore
atto*. Got it out of a book—means, the more haste, the less
speed."

Aside from the burlesque of heraldry, the image and the
paragraph together satirize the pre-Civil War view that slaves
are content in slavery, and that slavery will come to fade away
in time, at some later day in a later generation. As for making
those people "celebrated that had a hand in it," Mark Twain
had already attacked the plantation slave-owner in *Life on the*

Mississippi. Apparently this pattern of delay is also by implication a protest of the treatment of Negro citizens, North and South, in the middle 1880s, slavery by this date being a metaphor for the discrimination and the denial of civil rights that George Washington Cable, Mark Twain's partner on the 1884 lecture circuit, protested so vigorously in "The Freedman's Case in Equity" (1885).[10]

The developing understanding, respect, and indeed love between Jim and Huck is a prime source of continuity and interest throughout the novel, but with more concentration in the first half. With the appearance of the King and the Duke in the second half and with Jim often out of the action, the work focuses in on "royalty's" fleecing of gullible citizens in Pokeville, Bricksville, Pikesville, and other little towns down the river. The tone the King takes—"Cuss the doctor. What do we k'yer for *him?* Hain't we got all the fools in town on our side? and ain't that a big enough majority in any town?" (chap. 26)—is not far from that of Melville's Mississippi novel, *The Confidence Man* (1857). But those who fleece and even those who are fleeced in *Adventures of Huckleberry Finn* produce a two-faceted effect: "Human beings *can* be awful cruel to one another" (chap. 33), observes Huck when the rapscallion King and Duke are ridden on a rail, tarred and feathered.[11] "It was enough to make a body ashamed of the human race" (chap. 24). This continual drama of foolish and ferocious citizens in action—"the damned human race"—we may consider a second major motif in *Huckleberry Finn.*

This phrase, which fell from the author's lips so often during the last decade of his life, is a curse deriving ultimately from the thorniest of the five thorny points of Calvinism, the concept of original sin; and it is a generalization. The maxim, "Man is part angel, part rat; mainly rat" is his concise version of the generalization.[12] More specifically, in Huck Finn's *Adventures* an astonishing number of characters act from greed, or sexual hypocrisy, or fear and hatred of Negro slaves, or vanity and "histeronic" exhibitionism, or a taste for violence, or "mullet-headedness," or cowardice, or courage-in-the-mob-only, or outright sadism. What characters, then, in this great comic novel appear to deserve damnation for their actions?

Exhibit A must be Pap Finn, whether drunk or sober. His face is "a tree-toad white, a fish-belly white"—a total lack of color that seemed so sickening and so frightening to Ishmael in *Moby-Dick*. This outer aspect is a true measure of Pap's interior meanness. Though he is often funny, he is more offensive than funny, and finally he is more vicious even than offensive. Only Huck's agility and wit save him from being stabbed to death by Pap in the grip of *delirium tremens;* and, appropriately enough, Pap soon dies of a stab in the back by fellow deadbeats and robbers. Pap's diatribe against the educated free Negro from Ohio provides the author with the pretext for a brilliant cadenza of irony and humor (chap. 6), but Pap's prime trait is not racism but violence, predictive of violence to come.

The "gang of murderers" whom Huck encounters on the derelict steamboat *Sir Walter Scott* are thieves who are falling out even as Huck first overhears them. Two of the three have bound Jim Turner hand and foot, and Bill threatens to shoot him in the head, because Turner has in the past always claimed a bigger share of the loot by threatening to turn state's evidence. Besides, Turner has killed a man in the same way; and he would have killed *them* to get all the pickings from the dead steamboat. But Jake Packard, apparently wishing to spare Turner, stops Bill from the act, and Turner blubbers out his gratitude. Out of hearing of the bound killer, Jake explains to his partner that Turner will be drowned when the wreck breaks up in an hour of two, so that he "won't have nobody to blame for it but his own self" (chap. 12).

Because their raft has broken loose, Huck and Jim are about to be left on the wreck themselves with the bound murderer. But Mark Twain has an ultimate refinement to make in the way of crime and punishment. When Jake and Bill climb into their skiff, Bill remembers that Turner still has his share of the cash, and they turn back to the stateroom to "go through him." At this point Jim and Huck shove off in the robbers' skiff. Because Huck thinks "how dreadful it was, even for murderers, to be in such a fix," he cons a steam ferryboat man from the next small town into going out to the wreck to save them. But the wreck breaks up as it slides off the rock, and all three murderers are drowned. It is in character of course for the two rapscallions to decide to let the river do their killing for them; and to find death themselves in their last cruel act. Despite the gap of centuries between them, the steamboat episode (chaps. 12–13) is much of a piece with Chaucer's "Pardoner's Tale" of three robbers who search for, and find, death.

Pap and the *Sir Walter Scott* thieves are low-life types. The two men in the skiff who are out searching for five runaway slaves are perhaps small farmers, deathly afraid of smallpox but possessed of enough conscience to give Huck forty dollars in gold. The feuding Grangerfords and Shepherdsons are quality folk, however, and Saul and Rachel Grangerford are kind to Huck and considerate in every family relationship. Buck Grangerford, who is close to Huck in age (thirteen or fourteen), becomes his special friend. The social life they lead, with a "stack of people" gathering from all around, staying five or six days, and having dances and picnics and balls, is a pleasant life, and Huck considers them "a handsome lot of quality." They are churchgoers and, apparently, men and women of principle. But the Colonel calls for guns when Huck knocks at their door at night; the men bring guns when they visit the hospitable Grangerfords; and when the feuding families attend the same church, they keep their guns between their knees or standing against the wall while they listen to a sermon on brotherly love.

Huck gets his first taste of the feud when Buck fires at Harney Shepherdson from ambush and Harney covers Buck twice with his rifle but holds fire. Harney is in love with Sophia Grangerford and elopes with her, and the young couple run away and survive. Huck's second experience is nearly his last, for the elopement sets the feud violently ablaze again, and he is forced to witness the last act from the fork of a cottonwood tree where he is hiding. Outnumbered by Shepherdsons, Buck and his nineteen-year-old cousin Joe attempt to revenge the death of Colonel Grangerford and Buck's two older brothers. While they are attempting an escape by swimming wounded down the river, the Shepherdson men run along the bank firing and yelling, "Kill them, kill them!" Later Huck drags the two bodies ashore, sick at heart and crying a little, because Buck had been "mighty good to him." It is small wonder that for weeks and months Huck suffers nightmares and cannot get shut of them. He has witnessed "gentlefolk" conducting a miniature war, the original cause of which has long been forgotten. He has also witnessed the crumbling of Christian principle, of any sense of fair play, of regard for the young or respect for the old. Small wonder too that he and Jim, who had been sure Huck was killed, are "powerful glad" to be back on the raft again, free and easy and comfortable.

The town of Bricksville is especially rich in human beings who can be and are "awful cruel to one another." There are the town loafers, a country-man named Boggs in for his "monthly drunk," a lanky man with a cane, the "gentleman" Colonel Sherburn, keeper of the biggest store in town, the King and the Duke, and all the "Arkansaw lunkheads" who come to see the King caper in "The Royal Nonesuch" because the handbills read in large letters, "LADIES AND CHILDREN NOT ADMITTED."

Huck introduces the town to the reader with sketches of a "mighty ornery lot" of tobacco-chewing loafers, who like to sick the dogs on a sow and her piglets, or put turpentine on a stray dog and set fire to him, or tie a tin pan to his tail and watch him run himself to death. It is a circus day and a weekend, and the town is crowded with families from the country. Among them is Boggs, a periodic drunkard, who is good-natured and harmless drunk or sober but blusters and threatens people when he is drunk. When Boggs blackguards Colonel Sherburn and threatens to kill him, Sherburn gives him until one o'clock to leave town. When the hour comes, Boggs's daughter and his friends are still trying to get him away, but it is too late; Sherburn fires both barrels of his pistol into the drunken man's chest. Boggs dies in the drugstore with a large Bible under his head and another on his breast, while his gentle sixteen-year-old daughter wails and cries.

Whatever the reader's understanding of Sherburn's pride in his name or of a code that sanctions warning and then "execution," his attention is immediately drawn to the big crowd around the drugstore, squirming and pushing and shoving to get a look at the dead Boggs. For their benefit a long, lanky man in a big white fur stovepipe hat, holding a cane, re-enacts the killing.

> [He] marked out the places on the ground where Boggs stood, and where Sherburn stood, and the people following him around from one place to t'other and watching everything he done, and bobbing their heads to show they understood, and stooping a little and resting their hands on their thighs to watch him mark the places on the ground with his cane; and then he stood up straight and stiff where Sherburn had stood, frowning and having his hat-brim down over his eyes, and sung out,

"Boggs!" and then fetched his cane down slow to a level, and says "Bang!" staggered backwards, says "Bang!" again, and fell down flat on his back. The people that had seen the thing said he done it perfect; said it was just exactly the way it all happened. Then as much as a dozen people got out their bottles and treated him.

One is reminded of the obliging undertaker at Peter Wilks's funeral, later in the story. When the grieving mourners are distracted by a dog barking and growling in the cellar, he goes there to stop the racket, then returns and in a coarse whisper explains, *"He had a rat!"* One remembers also the crowds in Nathanael West's *The Day of the Locust* who go out to the airport on the chance of seeing a plane crash. Certainly the loafers who are made "happy all over" by a dog fight form a part of this avid crowd, for they all respond at once to Buck Harkness's demand that Sherburn ought to be lynched.

The townspeople, now a lynch-mob carrying clotheslines, swarm over Sherburn's fence, then stop dead still when Sherburn steps onto his front-porch roof with a double-barreled gun (probably a shotgun) in his hand. The tongue-lashing Sherburn administers before he drives them away by cocking the gun comprises perhaps the only episode in the novel in which the reader gets the sense that Mark Twain's mask has inadvertently dropped to disclose the features of Samuel Clemens. One thinks of the creator of so many mob scenes as well as of the chapters (in *Life on the Mississippi*) on violence in the North and feudal South, who planned a book on lynching and wrote "The United States of Lyncherdom." [13] Sherburn's speech is nonetheless in character for a man who has just killed a fellow man, serene and secure in a false code of personal honor. The townspeople, he tells them, have enough courage to tar and feather "poor friendless cast-out women that come along here," but they brought only half a man with them (Buck Harkness), and they are all of them cowards. If they intend to lynch him, he continues, they will have to come in the dark and wear masks and bring a *man* along. The people successfully defied by Sherburn are the same people whom the King and the Duke "sell" two nights in a row with their short, indecent skit—and by whom they become $465 richer. (On the third night the rapscallions light out just before the performance, and leave the crowd holding the bag—their unused rotten eggs and dead cats and decayed cabbages.)

If, as has been asserted, Pap Finn leads the procession of exemplary members of "the damned human race" in *Huckleberry Finn*, the King and the Duke surely bring up the rear. In something like the way that the Grangerfords and Shepherdsons take on darker and darker traits as their feud is renewed, so the King and the Duke show themselves more and more unscrupulous, greedy, and vicious as they move down the river with Huck and Jim under their control. One measure of their baseness is their decision to stay on in the Wilks's town in order to sell off the Wilks girls' slaves. They are not satisfied with dead Peter's $6,000 in gold. But like Jake Packard and Bill on the *Walter Scott*, they discover that "overreaching don't pay," and are lucky to escape sleeping in their cravats, as the Duke puts it. The last drop of the King's meanness is disclosed when Huck learns from the Duke that the King has sold Jim for forty dollars, in a long-contemplated act of treachery.

The growth of understanding between Huck and Jim, and the dark streak of human cruelty and perversity realized in the King and the Duke and others, are the two strong strands out of many that, twisted together, form the fabric of *Huckleberry Finn*. And yet the developing image of a "community of saints" on the piece of lumber-raft and the frequent exposure of damnable characters (in Bricksville, for example) together come nowhere near describing adequately the real content of the novel or the feeling with which most readers remember it. A third strand—perhaps the indispensable third—is the *humor* generated by the story: the elements infused in it from the first page onward by way of keeping the work a comedy.

Many years later the author observed that "we grant God the possession of all the qualities of mind except the one that keeps the others healthy; that watches over their dignity; that focuses their vision true—humor." [14] The implications of this definition for *Huckleberry Finn* are plain. Because it is a true comedy, its humor will run deep as well as shallow, the depths shaded by pathos on the one hand and by satire on the other. The satire, on feuding (and war), on pumped-up grief and "obituary eloquence" (the "Ode to Stephen Dowling Botts, Dec'd"), on the gilt of the gilded age ("royalty" as entrepreneurial types), and on slavery (Tom's protracted "rescue" of Jim), derives also from a sardonic view of the institutions of "snivelization" and of human nature. Nonetheless, Jim *is* freed from chattel slavery at the end of the story; and, by a simple adaptation of the frontier myth, Huck will remain free by lighting out for the Territory, westward. If, in short, the concluding chapters dominated by Tom Sawyer tend to be shallow in their humor and to distort the frame, they still belong to the humorous plot of the story.

What is funny in *Huckleberry Finn?* A great deal more than the reader remembers if (in defiance of Mark Twain's opening instructions) he is concentrating on the serious elements of the novel. That "more" covers a dazzling display of humor, from purely verbal wit and farce to burlesque to sharp satire to comedy growing out of character and of behavior.

Huck Finn's verbal humor is often a pure delight—as, for example, when Huck and Jim talk about "borrowing" (Pap Finn's word) a chicken or melons or new corn (chap. 12), but are uneasy because the Widow Douglas has said that borrowing was just a soft name for stealing, and so they decide to stop borrowing crab apples and "p'simmons" (inedible and unripe fruit) and save the euphemism and their conscience. Or as Huck observes that when Tom Sawyer arrives at the Phelps house, he "lifts his hat ever so gracious and dainty, like it was the lid of a box that had butterflies asleep in it and he didn't want to disturb them"—a figure wonderfully appropriate to a boy in his store clothes who values the style of a greeting. Or when Aunt Sally "hot and red and cross" at the breakfast table cracks the children's heads with her thimble because she cannot find Silas's shirt, and Huck records his consternation in these words:

> My heart fell down amongst my lungs and livers and things, and a hard piece of corn-crust started down my throat after it and got met on the road with a cough and was shot across the table and took one of the children in the eye and curled him up like a fishing-worm, and let a cry out of him the size of a war-whoop, and Tom he turned kinder blue around the gills. . . .

The passage is as rich in metaphor as it is filled with action piled on action. "Putrified" for "petrified" (Aunt Sally), "balditude" for "baldness" (the King), "orgies" for "obsequies" (the King), "diseased" for "deceased" (the King), even "sivilize" for "civilize" (Huck all along) are kinds of word play that add to the humor of the style.

Often the humor arises from situation. Huck has just slid a chunk of corn pone and a hunk of butter from the Phelps's cellar cupboard into that ragged straw hat of his and clapped the hat onto his head when Aunt Sally discovers that he is up during the middle of the night. When the butter melts and runs down his forehead, Aunt Sally cries, "He's got the brain fever as shore as you're born, and they're oozing out!" (chap. 40) before she learns that Huck was only raiding the pantry. More seriously, Jim is frightened by the apparition of Huck's ghost just at daylight on Jackson's Island before Huck recounts how he "got killed" (chap. 8)—a situation prefiguring Tom Sawyer's fright on meeting Huck at the Phelps farm:

"Don't you play nothing on me, because I wouldn't on you. Honest Injun, now, you ain't a ghost?" (chap. 33). Aunt Sally's distraught state of mind and the boys' belief in haunts and ghosts make such situations possible.

The humor of burlesque is dominant after Tom Sawyer reappears and takes over (chaps. 34–42), such as in the final sequence, in which Tom creates a burlesque coat of arms for Jim, with the terms of heraldry absurdly mangled. Yet even earlier, burlesque figures frequently in the narrative. Huck's description of the Grangerford house and the relics of Emmeline Grangerford, dead at fifteen, is especially memorable for the way in which these "frescoes of the past" are presented. It *is* a nice house with a lot of style, as Huck maintains, specifying the big clean fireplace, the room of Emmeline kept trim and unchanged by her mother, who sewed and read her Bible there, the little piano on which the young ladies accompanied themselves singing "The Last Link is Broken," and the good cooking—"just bushels of it" (chap. 17). But the lovingly detailed bits of local color also permit the narrator touches of burlesque that are "delicious," as he might say.

The center-table book *Pilgrim's Progress*—that key work in American culture—is "about a man that left his family it didn't say why," and in it Huck finds statements "interesting, but tough." Emmeline's funerary drawings are fully described and the caption of each is given: "Shall I Never See Thee More Alas," "I Shall Never Hear Thy Sweet Chirrup More Alas," and "And Art Thou Gone Yes Thou Art Gone Alas." The pictures prepare the reader for the remarkable "Ode to Stephen Dowling Botts, Dec'd," a poem of "obituary eloquence" whose quality is suggested by the rhymes "shots," "spots," and "knots" for Botts. Perhaps the height of the burlesque is achieved when Emmeline fails just once to produce a poem for a deceased neighbor, because "she hung fire on a rhyme for the dead person's name, which was Whistler." The point is that the chiming mantel clock, the chalk birds, the oilcloth table cover from Philadelphia, the books and pictures, and above all Huck's *liking* all that family, "dead ones and all," provide a real and attractive setting for the burlesque pictures and the "Ode."

The camp-meeting in the Pokeville backwoods, where a preacher has worked the crowd up with his singing and preaching and where converts are coming up to the mourners' bench "just crazy and wild," is a fit setting for the King's pious spiel. A pirate in the Indian Ocean for thirty years, he tells them, he has suffered a change of heart and now intends to return to "turn the pirates into the true path" (chap. 20). The burlesque of "missionarying" is successful only because it is brief. Much the same may be said of the burlesque Hamlet's soliloquy, which the Duke "learns" the King—a traditional mishmash of well-known lines from the popular Shakespeare plays delivered with excessive feeling. As Huck observes, the Duke "howled, and spread around, and swelled up his chest, and just knocked the spots out of any acting ever *I* see before" (chap. 21)—a "part to tear a cat in" indeed.

Adventures of Huckleberry Finn is shot through with the humor of irony, verbal and dramatic, as is illustrated in the playlet-debate between Huck and Jim on the topics of Solomon and the children, kingship, and the French language in chapter 14. The chapter derives from the books on royalty Huck had found in the loot from the wrecked steamboat, and it looks forward to Jim's mourning for his wife and children and the boarding of the raft by the Duke and Dauphin. But it is also a chapter of pure fun. Huck has reason and logic behind him in explaining to Jim how Solomon determined the real mother of the disputed child and why Jim would not be able to understand French. Yet Jim triumphs in both arguments. "Sollermun" foolishly thought he could " 'spute 'bout a whole chile wid a half a chile"—proof, Jim argues, that he didn't know enough "to come in out'n de rain"; and the *"real p'int"* was in Sollermun's upbringing. If he had had only two children (like Jim) instead of about five million, he wouldn't have been "waseful o' chilen." As for the debate on the language of cats and cows and men, it takes the form of Socratic dialogue, Huck and Jim in turn interrogating each other. The snapper follows when Jim makes Huck admit that a Frenchman is a man, and then asks, *"Well,* den! Dad blame it, why doan' he *talk* like a man? You answer me *dat!"*

The raftsmen's chapter (16) is rarely included as a proper part of *Adventures of Huckleberry Finn* inasmuch as it had been lifted out of the unfinished manuscript and used as part of Chapter 2 of *Life on the Mississippi.* But if it is regarded as a true part of the *Adventures,* it adds to the story the wildly poetic boasting of a couple of "ring-tailed roarers," and a tall tale about Dick Allbright and his baby following him on the river in a "ha'nted bar'l." The humor of the two heel-cracking boasters who appear to be just about ready to annihilate each other is humor of character as well, since a "little black-whiskered chap" who is tired of their boasting thrashes both of them for a "couple of chicken-livered cowards" (chap. 16).

The deep relation of humor and pathos evident in "A True Story" emerges at least twice in *Huckleberry Finn.* When the runaway Jim tells Huck that Balum had given his ten cents to the poor expecting to get it back a hundred times over—so the preacher had told him—Jim observes that he would be glad to have his ten cents back and call it square. When Huck reminds Jim that the sign of hairy arms and a hairy breast means future wealth, Jim answers that he is rich now, because he owns himself and he is worth eight hundred dollars. As for Huck, pathos and humor arise from his unusual capacity for "understanding and forgiveness," as Lionel Trilling has defined the trait of empathy,[15] and the occasion is the country circus preceding "The Royal Nonesuch."

Huck is enchanted by the bareback riders and the ever-so-witty clown. Then a "drunk man" tries to get into the bareback act, and the crowd laughs at him and threatens him, until the ringmaster persuades the crowd to let the drunk try to ride just once. When the drunk, his heels flying at each jump, clings to the running horse's neck, the crowd laughs till the tears roll down. "It warn't funny to me, though," Huck recalls; "I was all of a tremble to see his danger." Astonishingly, the drunk rises to a standing position on the circling horse's back and throws off layer after layer of outer clothing till "there he was, slim and handsome, and dressed the gaudiest and prettiest you ever saw" before he bows and skips off to the dressing room. The ringmaster Huck feels pity for, too, because he believes that the man had been humiliated by one of his own performers without realizing it. Huck's obtuseness here is a function of his good-heartedness, and both shine out against the mob spirit of the audience. The "drunk" performer, the "innocent" ringmaster, the potentially mob-violent audience, and Huck the naïve reporter: their interactions compound the ironies and humor and pathos simultaneously. The circus scene, one of the finest dramatic scenes in the novel, follows immediately upon Colonel Sherburn's defiance of the lynch mob (chap. 22). The circus audience was presumably composed for the great part of the same people who wanted to hang Sherburn but who changed their minds under his contemptuous denunciation and pointed shotgun.

The most persistent strain of humor in Mark Twain's masterpiece is not pathos-humor, however, but false pathos. Consider. First Pap Finn reforms, shakes hands with people, and swears he has started on a new life; then he gets drunk and turns the judge's spare room into a pigsty (chap. 6). The King appeals to the "dear people" of Pokeville camp-meeting and "that dear preacher there, the truest friend a pirate ever had," breaks into tears, kisses the prettiest girls while swabbing his eyes, and carries away eighty-seven dollars and seventy-five cents along with a three-gallon jug of whiskey (chap. 20). The Duke works on the sympathies of the Wilks family friends by playing deaf and dumb (whereas Jim's four-year-old daughter was left really "deef and dumb" from scarlet fever); and he goes a "goo-gooing around, happy and satisfied, like a jug that's googling out buttermilk" (chap. 29). But it is pre-eminently the King who "leaks" tears, who slobbers out a speech "all full of tears and flapdoodle," "soul-butter and hog-wash," and who at the auction of the Wilks girls' slaves looks his "level piousest" and chips in a little Scripture now and then "or a little goody-goody saying of some kind." Even Huck Finn's stories improvised for Mrs. Judith Loftus, or the men in the skiff, or Aunt Sally are touched by the same falsely-pathetic diction that characterizes the palaver of the Duke and the King. The con men's appeal for sympathy is "sickening" to Huck, however; and funny as it is, it bespeaks their rapacity. All such attempts to gull people through "confidence" and sympathy are satirically edged; and the key to the satire lies in the sickly-sweet, exaggerated language.

How different from the calculatedly false speech of such rap-scallions is the talk of Aunt Sally Phelps, and the "clack" of farmers and farmer's wives having dinner with the Phelpses. Nowhere in *Adventures of Huckleberry Finn* is the sound of words in the mouth represented more vividly than here, and nowhere is the humor of character more delightfully realized. They are all expressing their amazement at the recent mixed-up and splendid "rescue" of Jim, believing that the slaves

rather than Tom and Huck had done it all. Old Mrs. Hotchkiss
leads off . . .

"Well, Sister Phelps, I've ransacked that-air cabin over an' I
b'lieve the nigger was crazy. I says so to Sister Damrell—didn't
I, Sister Damrell?—s'I, he's crazy, s'I—them's the very words I
said. You all hearn me: he's crazy, s'I; everything shows it, s'I.
Look at that-air grindstone, s'I; want to tell *me*'t any cretur 't's
in his right mind's agoin' to scrabble all them crazy things onto
a grindstone? s'I. . . . He's plumb crazy, s'I . . . —the nigger's
crazy—crazy's Nebokoodneezer, s'I."

"An' look at that-air ladder made out'n rags, Sister Hotchkiss," says old Mrs. Damrell; "what in the name o' goodness
could he ever want of—"

"The very words I was a'sayin' no longer ago th'n this minute
to Sister Utterback, 'n' she'll tell you so herself. Sh-she, look at
that-air rag ladder, sh-she; 'n' s'I, yes, *look* at it, s'I—what *could*
he a wanted of it? s'I. Sh-she, Sister Hotchkiss, sh-she—"

"But how in the nation'd they ever *git* that grindstone *in*
there, *any*-way? 'n' who dug that-air *hole?* 'n' who—"

"My very *words*, Brer Penrod! I was a-sayin'—pass that-air
sasser o' m'lasses, won't ye?—I was a sayin' to Sister Dunlap,
jist this minute, how *did* they git that grindstone in there, s'I.
Without *help,* mind you—'thout *help!* Thar's wher' 'tis. Don't
tell *me* s'I; there *wuz* help, s'I; 'n' ther' wuz a *plenty* help, too,
s'I; ther's ben a *dozen* a-helpin' that nigger, 'n' I lay I'd skin
every last nigger on this place, but *I'd* find out who done it, s'I;
'n' moreover, s'I—"

"A *dozen* says you!—*forty* couldn't 'a' done everything that's
been done. Look at them case-knife saws and things, how tedious they've been made; look at that bed-leg sawed off with
'm, a week's work for six men. . . ."

"You may *well* say it, Brer Hightower! It's jist as I was
a'sayin' to Brer Phelps, his own self. S'e, what do *you* think of
it, Sister Hotchkiss, s'e? think o' what, Brer Phelps, s'I? I lay it
never sawed *itself* off, s'I—somebody *sawed* it, s'I. . . . I says to
Sister Dunlap, s'I—"

"Why, dog my cats, they must 'a' ben a house-full o' niggers

in there every night for four weeks, to 'a' done all that work,
Sister Phelps. . . ."

Whereupon Aunt Sally Phelps, the hostess, tells Brother
Marples and the rest how mysteriously things disappeared
from the house, and how "low and behold you," the robbers
"actuly gets *away* with that nigger, safe and sound, and that
with sixteen men and twenty-two dogs right on their very
heels at that very time! I tell you, it just bangs anything I ever
heard of. Why, *sperits* couldn't a done better, and been no
smarter." The guests respond all at once:

> "Well, it does beat—"
> "Laws alive, I never—"
> "So help me, I wouldn't a be—"
> "*House*-thieves as well as—"
> "Goodnessgracioussakes, I'd a ben afeard to *live* in sich a—"

Aunt Sally interrupts her company to admit that she was "that
scared I dasn't hardly go to bed, or get up, or lay down, or *set*
down, Sister Ridgeway." She is even afraid the robbers might
steal some of her family, and thinks of her "two poor boys
asleep" upstairs—and it is at this point that she begins to suspect the truth, that Tom and Huck had done it all; and the
comedy ends (chap. 41).

Precisely what the comedy consists in is more difficult to
discover. In part it certainly arises from the talent possessed
by these farm folk of making much of relatively little, and from
their wildly mistaken notion that Jim and the Phelps slaves
rather than Huck and Tom imagined so quixotic and involved
an escape. It consists, that is, of naïve conclusions based on
wrong premises. Some small part of the fun is verbal—e.g.,
"crazy's Nebokoodneezer" or "how tedious they've ben made"
or "it just bangs anything I ever *heard* of." But chiefly it in-

heres in the infallible and poetic "sentencing," and the incremental repetitions within the sentencing.

We have seen that Mark Twain as writer favored tautology in certain instances, and here is a classic example of his ability to show how people repeat themselves, with gusto, and yet to keep the dialogue continually entertaining. Chief of the repeated elements in Aunt Sally's non-stop sentences is—fittingly enough for her flustered state—"and," a word that comes out " 'n' " in the printed imitation. The very breath of the dialogue leading up to Aunt Sally's conclusion, however, is "s'I," "sh-she," "says you" (once), and "s'e." The passage does not truly take hold of the reader until he tries it aloud, intermingling "s'I" and "s'e" and "sh-she" in a constant susurrus. This presumably is "the extremest form of the backwoods Southwestern dialect" mentioned among the other dialects at the beginning. While the reader is not likely to "sentence" the dialogue as Mark Twain did, the italics mark primary accents for him and he will miss much poetry and humor if he does not try.

The great and serious art of *Adventures of Huckleberry Finn* looks back to "A True Story," in which, perhaps for the first time in American literature, a Negro is presented as heroine, sympathetic, flawed, and credible, rather than as a comic character or a caricature, as in Cooper or William Gilmore Simms. Rachel anticipates Jim in half a dozen ways, notably in her love for her son Henry. All of a piece with this accomplishment is the author's ever so careful listening to and recording of "the best and reallest kind of black talk" [16] for pathetic and dramatic ends—a feat that looks forward to the revolutionary use of dialect and the "language of the street" in *Huckleberry Finn*. The art of this novel is also closely allied to "Old Times on the Mississippi" and *Life on the Mississippi*. Walter Blair in his *Mark Twain and Huck Finn* traces the connections closely, the "lifted" raftsmen chapter, the Grangerford-Shepherdson feud, precedents for Sherburn's defiance of the lynch mob, sources for the Royal Nonesuch, and much more, both from *Life on the Mississippi* and from Mark Twain's unconventional reading of history and biography and reminiscences.

Curiously, however, while Mark Twain thought well of *Life on the Mississippi,* having intended to make it "a standard work," he was never fully aware that *Huckleberry Finn* was his best full-length fiction. Or perhaps it is more accurate to say, he took a defensive attitude about "Huck, that abused child of mine who has had so much unfair mud slung at him." In March 1885 Mark Twain was offered membership in the Concord Free Trade Club at the very moment when the public library of Concord eliminated *Huckleberry Finn* from its shelves as "the veriest trash." [17] The heart of his response, to the Concord Free Trade Club, follows:

> . . . a committee of the public library of your town has condemned & excommunicated my last book, & doubled its sale. This generous action of theirs must necessarily benefit me in one or two additional ways. For instance, it will deter other libraries from buying the book; & you are doubtless aware that one book in a public library prevents the sale of a sure ten & a possible hundred of its mates. And secondly it will cause the purchasers of the book to read it, out of curiosity, instead of merely intending to do so after the usual way of the world & library committees; then they will discover, to my great advantage & their own indignant disappointment, that there is nothing objectionable in the book, after all.

He concludes his letter (which presumably he never sent) with an obeisance to the "moral icebergs" of the library committee. [18] Ten years after writing the Concord letter, he jotted down in a notebook a truly penetrating comment on the novel, calling it "a book of mine where a sound heart & a deformed conscience come into collision & conscience suffers defeat." [19]

What he had managed to make into an elaborate—and pro-found—joke in "The Facts Concerning the Recent Carnival of Crime in Connecticut" he now takes with utter seriousness. "Conscience" represents blind, Calvinistic, unfeeling acceptance of slavery; the sound heart has its own reasons and knows that *Homo sapiens* is of one blood.

Chapter 5

POLEMICAL PIECES

Numerous and varied, they flow from a "pen warmed up in hell." — "Gold-smith's Friend Abroad Again," the Chinese and the Irish in San Francisco. — "The Curious Republic of Gondour," a new Utopia. — The special delight of "Letter from the Recording Angel." — On Winston Churchill. — "A Salutation Speech from the Nineteenth Century to the Twentieth," and "To the Person Sitting in Darkness": cartoon-style attacks on imperialistic ventures.

Once when editor Joseph Goodman left the *Territorial Enterprise* in his charge for a whole week, Mark Twain developed an enduring admiration for journalists like Goodman capable of writing sound editorials day in and day out for years on end. In his record of this experience in *Roughing It,* he even totaled up their production, to show how far it exceeded in bulk the writings of Dickens or Thackery. Although he never wrote daily editorials, at the end of his life he might have looked back in wonder at the number of pieces he himself had written in the spirit of the social critic, satirist, reformer, judge, politi-

cal partisan, moralist, and Old Testament prophet. Many unpublished pieces of rhetorical or exhortatory thrust contained
in the Mark Twain Papers are becoming available in the new
editions of his work. But the hundreds of items already in
print, even as they give the lie to Van Wyck Brooks's contention that Mark Twain failed in his responsibilities as a satirist,
demonstrate that the humorist found the prophetic role conge-
nial from the first, and persisted in it to the last. The best of
the persuasive essays suggest as well that Mark Twain really
deserved the epithets he won as exhorter and rhetorician:
"Moralist of the Main," self-appointed missionary, "Ambas-
sador-at-large" of the United States of America, without salary. These same best essays won for Clemens "his claim to be
heard on any public matter" and even the "odd sort of pri-
macy" [1] as commentator-satirist-interpreter that Howells
claimed for him on his old friend's triumphal return from
Europe in the fall of 1900.

In general, writing designed primarily to praise, blame, persuade, or dissuade (despite Norman Mailer's recent books),
enjoys little prestige as literature in our time, perhaps because
so much of it is either venal or dull. Rhetoric (or persuasive
writing)—is it not flawed from the beginning by its purpose,
and does it not pass into oblivion when the issues it argues
are gone? Unquestionably the mass of rhetorical writing is
ephemeral, motivated as it is by political expediency or special
interest. Quite as unquestionably, Milton, Swift, Goldsmith,
Voltaire, Paine, Shelley, Melville, William Vaughn Moody,
Steinbeck, and Hemingway achieved memorable rhetoric out
of the same impulses and with the same craftsmanship that
governed their other writings. The body of memorably persuasive writing is comparatively small, and yet Milton's *Areo-
pagitica* and Swift's *A Modest Proposal* embody the special
quality that confers immortality on rhetorical literature: the
artful fusing of the momentary issue and the ancient racking

issues of liberty and license, have and have not, charity and justice.

The narrator, we know, warned readers of *Huckleberry Finn:*

> "Persons attempting to find a motive in this narrative will be prosecuted; persons attempting to find a moral in it will be banished; persons attempting to find a plot in it will be shot. By Order of the Author."

The warning, well taken for the novel, will serve as a reminder that he wrote rhetoric with a motive and a moral. Clemens as citizen used many rhetorical forms: speeches, private letters, letters to newspapers, interviews, sponsored pamphlets, magazine articles, direct lobbying in Washington, even a proposal for a hall of fame to remind Americans of the "civic significance" of Washington, Franklin, Jefferson, and Lincoln.[2] He tackled an astonishing variety of topics, problems, and people, among them the maltreatment of the Chinese in San Francisco; American "vandalism" in Europe; unlimited suffrage; woman's suffrage (Mark Twain finally favored it); the effects of chattel slavery on slave and master, and the rights of Negroes in post-Civil War America; the neglect of graveyards; the Hartford Gas Company; the Baltimore & Ohio Railroad; the Medicis and the Church in Italy; the Erie Ring; the "greed" of Jay Gould early and late, and the "California sudden-riches disease"; Tammany corruption; "insolence" among telegraph operators, railroad conductors, hotel clerks, cab drivers, and royalty; the "Sir Walter Scott disease" and feuding in the South; Bret Harte—"A liar, a thief, a swindler, a snob, a sot, a sponge, a coward, a Jeremy Diddler . . . ;"[3] the "superior character and accomplishments" of Anson G. Burlingame, W. D. Howells, Samuel E. Moffett, Ulysses S. Grant, Grover Cleveland, St. Joan of Arc, Captain Alfred Dreyfus, Henry H. Rogers, and others like them; the tragic effect of Wilbrandt's play, "The Master of Palmyra"; the "literary offenses" of J. F.

Cooper; religious quacks and pious undertakers; Cecil Rhodes and the policies of McKinley in the Philippines and Chamberlain in South Africa; the Great Powers in China during the Boxer Rebellion; party loyalty *vs.* mugwump independence; the character of American juries, and the insanity plea in murder trials; newspaper editors (a rich variety of praise and blame); lobbyists in Washington; flunkeyism before titles and wealth; the "abilities" of the Jews; the "disabilities" of the French; Theodore Roosevelt's "arrogance"; the "oppressive stupidity" of Czar Nicholas II; King Leopold of the Belgians' alleged atrocities in the Congo; Matthew Arnold's conception of "reverence"; cruelty to animals, including bullfighting; lynching in the United States; witch-hunting and mob violence everywhere; the "superiority" of the health food Plasmon; the debt of the race to inventors—except for James W. Paige; Heinrick Kellgren's "beneficial" osteopathic treatments; Mary Baker Eddy's "baleful" power; the doctrines of infant damnation and of papal infallibility; the "damned human race"; and the "moral cowardice" of one Samuel L. Clemens. Even though far from complete in this itemization, it *is* an amazing list. It is unquestionable that the monumental rage he let fly at his publishing partner and nephew, Charles L. Webster, was unjustified; and his affection for Henry H. Rogers was so strong that he could not and would not recognize his friend's piratical business practices. Unquestionably he picked trivial targets at times, such as the rude people who served the public. His early jape that the women of Virginia City might be raising money for a "Miscegenation Society somewhere in the East" [4] rather than for the U.S. Sanitary Commission reveals a provincial vulgarity from which he had to free himself, just as his hatred for the patrons of Italian Renaissance art blinded him almost totally to the glories of the art itself. Nonetheless, "that Christian devil" Mark Twain used all his literary cunning and a "pen warmed-up in hell" [5] against the shams and hypocrisies and cruelties of his day. "It is a matter not of argument, but of fact," as Archibald Henderson declared, "that he . . . made far more damaging admissions concerning America than any other nation"—which is the measure, I take it, of his true patriotism. And in Gamaliel Bradford's view, "He may have believed, in the abstract, that selfishness was the root of human action, but he scourged it in concrete cases with whips of scorpions." [6]

"Goldsmith's Friend Abroad Again" (1870–71) [7] articulates well the author's not wholly consistent views on race and civil rights, as well as a typical rhetorical stance of his mid-twenties. The convention he follows is Goldsmith's, in *A Citizen of the World*, adapted here to contemporary conditions in San Francisco. In a series of letters, Ah Song Hi, a very intelligent Chinese, tells a friend at home of his first experiences as a young cooly laborer. He learns quickly, the hard way, what an immense gap lies between the tenets of the Declaration of Independence and the actions of the San Francisco police. Even before taking ship, he must give two dollars of his total fortune of twelve to the American consul, and when he arrives he must pay ten dollars for a smallpox vaccination, despite the scars he bears of the disease. On his first walk through the city, young men (obviously Irish) set a vicious dog on him, the police standing by indifferently; and only the intervention of a stranger saves him. He is subsequently arrested, kicked, cuffed, and jailed for disturbing the peace, and left alone at last only when the police (who are also Irish) find that he has no money. He is thrown into a big general cell with men of various races and with two blowsy women separated behind a grating—all of them noisy and fighting drunk. The two women (also Irish), who have spent years in two-month sentences in the county jail, curse Ah Song Hi for a "bloody interlopin' loafer" taking the bread from "dacent people's mouths" and depressing workers' wages. A boy pimp is brought in, and a blackmailing photographer who sells phoney photographs of respectable young women's heads attached to the nude bodies of "another class of women." The pimp goes free. The blackmailer is fined a hundred dollars. The police bring in a man beaten so badly that toward daybreak he dies of his injuries.

This indignant excursion into San Francisco low-life in the police court reaches its climax when the court releases the Irishmen with minimum fines, metes out strict justice to the Frenchmen, Spaniards, and Italians, gives prompt punishment to Negroes, and administers severe, apparently unvarying, punishment to the Chinese. For Ah Song Hi, at least, the sentence is ten days in jail, because the stranger who had protested his harassment is bullied into silence by the arresting officers, and because, to his utter woe, Ah Song Hi learns that *"Chinamen ain't allowed to testify against white men!"* He remembers with much bitterness "that sentence [on freedom and equality] from the great and good American Declaration of Independence which we have copied in letters of gold in China and keep hung up over our family altars and in our temples." Ah Song Hi's reflection echoes Taji's observation twenty years earlier in Melville's *Mardi:* the inscription over the great temple of Vivenza, "All men are created free and equal" was followed, he had dryly noted, by the qualification (in very small letters), "Except the tribe of Hamo." [8]

"Goldsmith's Friend Abroad Again," chief among the author's several defenses of the civil rights of Chinese labor in California, is equally an attack on the brutality of the San Francisco police, with some admixture of the current and widespread anti-Irish feeling—though it will not do to call Mark Twain a detractor of any nation or race or creed, not even of the French. His letters to the illustrator of *Adventures of Huckleberry Finn* confirm what Huck's surname suggests, that he is Irish. [9] It is perhaps more to the point to recognize that his defense of the Chinese laborer is based on direct observation: "No experience," he opens the letter by saying, "is set down in the following letters which had to be invented." Thirty years later Mark Twain wrote that he was pro-China in the Boxer Rebellion—but by then he was for *all* persons sitting in non-Christian, "uncivilized" darkness—in the figure he, like Matthew, borrowed from Psalm 107.

A very different kind of rhetoric, beamed at a different body of readers, marks "The Curious Republic of Gondour," [10] Mark Twain's first venture into utopian literature. The audience for "Goldsmith's Friend Abroad Again" had been the readers of *Galaxy*, a New York magazine aspiring to rival the *Atlantic*, whereas "Gondour" appeared in the *Atlantic* itself. The first is a heated exposé intended to disgust its audience with the brutality of the police toward the Chinese; the second is a cool analysis of an imaginary country, the Republic of Gondour, where the franchise has been enlarged to give more power to the wealthy, educated, and talented. The author did not sign it: while he trusted the *Atlantic* readers' intelligence, he knew that his pseudonym would lead to an expectation of burlesque or humor. Here he was wholly serious.

Gondour *is* a curious republic, and much like the heaven that Mark Twain had envisioned for Captain Stormfield a few years earlier. Suffering from the misgovernment of officials elected under universal suffrage, Gondour resolved to preserve the constitutional right of every voter to a single vote—but then enlarged the suffrage so that "property, character, and intellect" could wield political influence and put forward the best candidates. A grammar-school education gave a citizen an extra vote; a high-school education gave him a total of four votes; a university education entitled him to nine. Similarly, property to the value of three thousand *sacos* meant one extra vote, and every fifty thousand *sacos* meant still another. The property votes were "mortal" and could be lost, whereas the learning votes were "immortal," and thus the citizens of Gondour soon came to strive for voting power—especially "immortal" votes—rather than money. A shoemaker's apprentice might rise to the heights of meriting twenty-two mortal votes and two immortal ones; but only the most illustrious astronomer of the state, possessing nine immortal votes, would be paid homage by fellow Gondourians by a doffing of hats to him. The Republic was governed by a ministry subject to the current administration, but the Grand Caliph was elected for a twenty-year term. Since the ministry and the parliament truly governed the land, and the Grand Caliph was subject to impeachment for misconduct, Gondour was well governed. The highest office of the land had twice been filled by women; and women had served ably in the cabinet.

The anonymous writer elicits much of this information from a friend in Gondour, and the utopian sketch ends upon the friend's explanation that the free schools and colleges are filled, since the education acquired by a child will make him powerful and honored. The friend speaks proudly of his country, and the narrator finds this pride annoying, for, as he concludes, one never hears that sort of music in *his* "dear native land."

Gondour is indeed curious. It is a country where "reverence" for wealth, but even more for accomplishment, has become customary; and yet only a decade later Mark Twain was to equate "reverence" with the worst sort of flunkeyism. His imagined Republic has achieved control over the scarcely mentioned *polloi*—half-literate emigrants from Europe, the Irish and the Jews in the cities, the Germans and Scandinavians in the West. Yet Mark Twain in other moods and at a later time was fiercely egalitarian. Samuel Clemens had almost no formal schooling, and yet he would award nine immortal votes to university graduates on the argument that "learning goes usually with uprightness, broad views, and humanity." In

Washoe he jested about women's suffrage. Here he envisages women as routinely filling the offices of the presidency and the cabinet. Every phase of political life in Gondour has of course a direct reference to contemporary politics in the United States, and distrust of a backwoods or an immigrant electorate was scarcely a new theme with him.

The pointed violence of Ah Song Hi's first experience in the "home of the free," as Mark Twain tells it, and his probing of the gilded age in "Gondour" deserved reprinting. For whatever reason, however, he never collected the two pieces; they were issued as a small book only nine years after his death. But the reason he suppressed the "Letter from the Recording Angel," which he had written in 1887, is clear.[11] An extravagantly funny attack on the character of his wife's uncle, Andrew Langdon, it may well have been written with no thought of publication but simply to relieve his feelings and to tease his wife. It is nonetheless a first-rate satirical characterization, in a genre Mark Twain favored all his life: one need mention only his attacks, more and less artful, upon Jay Gould, Andrew Carnegie, Charles Webster (his business manager), Bret Harte, Lillian Aldrich, Theodore Roosevelt, among dozens of others. (Of Mrs. Aldrich he wrote: "A strange and vanity-devoured, detestable woman! I do not believe I could ever learn to like her except on a raft at sea with no other provisions in sight." [12])

The genre of personal censure or detraction is rather special. It must steer the difficult course between the too easygoing, the too-forgiving, and "blasts of opinion which are so strongly worded as to repel instead of persuade." [13] But when it passes through this strait, it becomes, curiously enough, a pure delight. The author apparently reaches the state of Horace Bixby after cursing his cub's leather-headedness: "You could have drawn a seine through his system and not caught curses enough to disturb your mother with." [14] Certainly the reader, who knows nothing about this coal-dealer uncle of Livy Clemens, and could hardly care less, feels relieved of resentment and aggression on reading the angel's letter to him and enjoys remarkable peace of mind.

The recording angel, writing to Andrew Langdon, coal dealer of Buffalo, New York, opens his formal communication by observing that Langdon's recent benevolent act was more than extraordinary, it was unique in the entire course of Langdon's life to that moment. The "benevolent act" disclosed at the end of the letter is of course the snapper to the entire story. The first part of the record lists Langdon's recent Secret Supplications of the Heart—all of them having to do with crushing his rivals and achieving a sharp increase in hard-coal prices— along with the generally favorable reaction of heaven to them. The second part records Langdon's recent Public Prayers, and heavenly denials of nearly every one of them, since they conflict so sharply with the Secret Supplications. The recording angel then observes that over a forty-year period the subject has changed from Professing Christian to Professional Christian, from section A to section W of the Elect, and from 322 carats fine to 3 carats fine. "You seem," he concludes, "to have deteriorated." [15]

This disclosure of Langdon's lifelong hypocrisy leads up to the matter of charitable donations. Years ago, according to the record, he had sent two dollars (of his $100,000) to an impoverished cousin, a widow. When the widow's child had died, he had sent six dollars; and heaven was astonished and gratified. Sundays, the recording angel continues, "when your hand retires from the contribution plate, the glad shout is heard even to the ruddy walls of remote Sheol, 'Another nickel from Andrew!' " But "there was not a dry eye in the realms of bliss" when Andrew sent the widow a check for fifteen whole dollars—after adding up his recent $65,000 profit from his mines. Then the heavenly host decreed that Andrew—he is "affec-

tionately called Andrew here"—should be memorialized on a
page of his own in the Book called *Golden Deeds of Men,* since
the strain of his act exceeded that of ten thousand martyrs at
the fiery stake.[16] And all said,

> "What is the giving up of life, to a noble soul, or to ten thou-
> sand noble souls, compared with the giving up of fifteen dollars
> out of the greedy grip of the meanest white man that ever lived
> on the face of the earth?"

> And it was a true word. And Abraham, weeping, shook out
> the contents of his bosom and pasted the eloquent label there,
> "RESERVED"; and Peter, weeping, said, "He shall be received
> with a torchlight procession when he comes"; and then all
> heaven boomed, and was glad you were going there. And so
> was hell.

> [Signed]
> The Recording Angel
> [Seal]

> By command.[17]

When one remembers how few of the souls in Captain
Stormfield's heaven have ever *seen* Abraham and Peter, this
slangy hyperbole combined so judiciously with Biblical ca-
dences prepares the reader for the second snapper, "And so
was hell." The Reverend Mr. T. DeWitt Talmage, who expected to greet the heavenly patriarchs with tears and em-
braces, is thus a spiritual predecessor of Andrew Langdon.
More, one may suspect that Mark Twain's enthusiasm for the
songs and bawdry and anti-Presbyterian verse of Robert Burns
led him to "Holy Willie's Prayer," and that this fine dramatic
monologue suggested the hypocritical Public Prayers of Andrew Langdon. What presumably began in resentment, or
anger, then, in Mark Twain's mind, turned to pure, tranquil
art in "Letter from the Recording Angel." [18]

In the fall of 1900 Mark Twain initiated a crusade that would continue for six years against current imperialistic wars and tyrannies, and contributed several effective, enduring essays to it. As one looks back on the writing of these pieces, his crusade seems imbued with historical ironies. He wrote these essays while suffering intense personal grief and at the same time promoting his conviction that all men everywhere act only from selfish motives—that all men's acts are predetermined. He wrote them believing that he and fellow anti-imperialists like Howells and William James could alter public policy, but later he became convinced that their efforts had been almost wholly futile; and he did not live long enough to witness the overthrow of the Czar or the restoration of the Philippine Republic by the U.S. Government. But he was largely unconscious of any ironies in his acts at the time; or if he felt them he simply ignored them. In England, in a long letter written but never dispatched to Moberley Bell, editor of the London *Times*, he anticipates his later published protests against the role of the Great Powers in China. As he told an interviewer, "We have no more business in China than in any other country that is not ours." [19]

On home ground again, in New York City, Mark Twain received a warm and widespread welcome. Newspapers all over the country praised him for his long, finally successful struggle to free himself from bankruptcy and to pay every one of his creditors every cent he owed. His house on West Tenth Street in Greenwich Village swarmed with friends, reporters, and visitors—many of these last with axes to grind. Thus, in the winter of 1900–1901 Clemens was often in the public eye, and had a large audience every time he gave a lecture or an interview or published an article. He received strong private support for his political views from his wife, as also from Howells and the small but active anti-imperialist leagues. He had a distinguished forum in the *North American Review* and the Harper periodicals, and could count on newspapers to print his views, more often than not with editorial deprecation. Yet he realized perfectly well that he was taking a position that was highly unpopular and might seriously affect his living as a writer—and this when he had just freed himself from crushing debt. (As Edwin H. Cady has remarked, Howells at first-hand could warn him of the abuse *he* had suffered after asserting in a famous newspaper letter that the Haymarket (Chicago) anarchists, having in his belief been unfairly tried, deserved clemency.[20])

During that Fall, in lectures and interviews, Mark Twain expressed sympathy for the Boers in South Africa, asserted that he had favored the war to liberate Cuba from Spain but was now an anti-imperialist "opposed to having the eagle put its talons on any other land," and maintained that "the Boxer is a patriot . . . the only patriot China has, and I wish him success." [21] At a banquet in New York on December 13, he introduced Winston Spencer Churchill to a distinguished audience—as the young Englishman who had fought in South Africa, been captured by the Boers, secured release, and come to America to lecture. The introduction was filled with hands-across-the-sea sentiment and good humor, but it was also seasoned with pungent comment on the light-bringing nations and their *mission civilisatrice*. After establishing his good will and his qualifications to speak of an Anglo-American alliance, Mark Twain exclaimed with mounting irony:

> Behold America, the refuge of the oppressed from everywhere (who can pay $10 admission)—everyone except a Chinaman—standing up for human rights everywhere, even helping to make China let people in free when she wants to collect $50 from them. And how unselfishly England has wrought for the open door for all. And how piously America has wrought for that open door in all cases where it was not her own.
> How generous England and America have been in not com-

pelling China to pay exorbitantly for extinguished missionaries. They are willing to take produce for them—fire-crackers and such; while the Germans must have monuments and any other boodle that is lying around. They've made Christianity so expensive that China can't afford German missionaries any more.

The introduction concludes with a sting in its tail:

Yes, as a missionary I've sung my songs of praise; and yet I think that England sinned when she got herself into a war in South Africa which she could have avoided, just as we have sinned in getting into a similar war in the Philippines. Mr. Churchill by his father is an Englishman; by his mother he is an American; no doubt a blend that makes the perfect man. England and America: yes, we are kin. And now that we are also kin in sin, there is nothing more to be desired. The harmony is complete, the blend is perfect—like Mr. Churchill himself, whom I now have the honor to present to you.[22]

The religious diction, the rhetorical balance, the final epigram are carefully wrought, and hint strongly of what was to come.

The first fruit of "long talk and high" [23] with Howells concerning the Filipino, Boer, and Chinese troubles and of Mark Twain's increasing commitment to the "unpatriotic" anti-imperialist minority was his "A Salutation Speech from the Nineteenth Century to the Twentieth." This brief paragraph in the form of a toast was written for the Red Cross Society and was scheduled to be read aloud at watch-meetings throughout the country on New Year's Eve, along with "greetings" composed by other famous people. But Mark Twain was not sure of the company he was to appear in, and so wrote to the manager of the enterprise:

The list thus far issued by you contains only some vague generalities, and one definite name, mine—"Some kings and queens and Mark Twain." Now I am not enjoying this sparkling solitude and distinction, which has not been authorized by me, and which makes me feel like a circus-poster in a grave-yard or like any other advertisement improperly placed.

Since the Red Cross director could not publish the names as Mark Twain had requested, the "Greeting" was returned. It was then sent, with a copy of his note satirizing monarchs, to the New York *Herald,* which reproduced it in holograph and in print in the issue of 30 December 1900. Dated "New York, Dec. 31, 1900," the holograph reads:

> A Salutation-Speech from the 19th Century to the 20th, taken down in short-hand by Mark Twain: I bring you the stately ma-tron named Christendom, returning bedraggled, besmirched & dishonored from pirate-raids in Kiao-Chou, Manchuria, South Africa & the Philippines, with her soul full of meanness, her pocket full of boodle, & her mouth full of pious hypocrisies. Give her soap & a towel, but hide the looking-glass.[24]

Mark Twain had noted on the surviving manuscript in the Mark Twain Papers, "Original mailed Nov. 29." By "original" it seems likely that he meant the fair copy (presumably no longer existing) that he had sent to the Red Cross people, had had returned to him, and gave to the New York *Herald.* In the true original in the Mark Twain Papers, certain revisions are noteworthy. Mark Twain had altered "matron called Christendom" to "matron named Christendom." He had first written "soul full of meanness," then tried "treachery" for "mean-ness," and then returned to his first choice by writing "stet" under "meanness." At the bottom of his page he had jotted down the phrase, "her halo battered (awry)" but had finally decided not to use it. These revisions will serve as proof, once again, of his passionate interest in finding the right word or phrase, his fine sense of prose rhythm, and his skill in met-aphor—in this instance, personification.

The basic accent pattern is triadic: "Bedraggled / besmirched / dishonored" prepares for the Kiao-Chow, South Africa, Philippines sequence, and climaxes with the double-triad, "soul / meanness," "pocket / boodle," and "mouth / hypocrisies." Even the hortatory last sentence must be read as two triads, unobtrusive as their prose rhythm may be. Presumably the pictorial phrase "her halo battered (awry)" was discarded either because it would break up the tight epigrammatic structure of triplets if it were retained or because it was not strong enough to replace "soul" or "pocket" or "mouth."

The "Salutation-Speech" is structured also by the personification of the nineteenth and the twentieth centuries, figures who frame and present Christendom centrally as a "matron"—and here Mark Twain's gift for mixing formal and colloquial speech serves perfectly the satiric anticlimax he is building toward. Transparently masked as mere amanuensis, he reports overhearing a sardonic toast of the nineteenth century to the twentieth, which has betrayed its tradition of freedom. The first shock occurs when the "stately matron" returns as a kind of female pirate, disheveled, dirty, drunk, and by implication sexually promiscuous in the new imperialist wars. The irony and the matron's shame mount in the disclosure that her mean-spiritedness is matched only by her greed—the word "boodle" explodes in this context—and in her self-righteous attempts to justify her conduct. (Mark Twain was probably thinking of President McKinley's decision, after thought and prayer, to "Christianize" the Catholic Filipinos, as well as of certain Christian missionaries' demands for heavy reparations from the Chinese.) The flat injunction "Give her soap & a towel" reduces the "stately matron" to the level of a dirty girl, and the mock-pity of "but hide the looking-glass" covers the demand that the matron Christendom look at herself without further self-deception.

The "besmirched and dishonoured" matron figure points to Mark Twain's frequent and expert use of metaphor in his rhe-

torical writings. The opening scene in "Old Times on the Mississippi"—a "fresco" from the past, the author calls it—reveals
how naturally pictorial and even cinematic was his imagination. This ability to render the natural scene in writing and to
concretize abstractions went hand in hand, I feel certain, with
his close concern with illustrations—that prime feature of subscription books and subscription publishing. If Mark Twain
could make very little of the "old masters," he made much of
Audubon's great folio of American birds, of E. W. Kemble's
illustrations for *Huckleberry Finn,* and of Dan Beard's satirical
illustrations for *Connecticut Yankee.*[25] His taste for political car-
toons was equally strong, as witness his long friendship with
Thomas ("Nasty") Nast, like himself an enemy of the Erie
Ring and of Tammany Hall, and credited as much as any single factor with the downfall of Boss Tweed.[26]

Shortly after the "greeting" appeared, the New England
Anti-Imperialist League reprinted it on small cards and distributed them wholesale, but with an added couplet adapted
from Burns:

> Give her the glass; it may from error free her
> When she shall see herself as others see her.

The ironic final phrase, "Give her soap and a towel, but hide
the looking-glass" is converted into a direct appeal for the
Anti-Imperialist League, and thus the ironic frame is broken.
It seems unlikely that Clemens wrote the additional lines himself, though it is certain that he permitted them to be added to
his text.[27]

"A Salutation-Speech" is an almost perfect small piece of
rhetoric in that it is realized through the personification of
Christendom, that it is eloquent in its prose rhythms, shock-
ing by reason of its clashing ironies, humorous and collo-
quially strong in its final injunction. It is a small-scale in-

troduction to Mark Twain's strongest and most considered utterance on the subject of imperialistic war, "To the Person Sitting in Darkness." He finished this very substantial essay some time before 29 January 1901, the date of his remark to the Reverend Joseph Twichell, "I've written another article; you better hurry down and help Livy squelch it." [28] There is of course no trusting an ironist: according to his daughter Clara, he had "secured the approbation of both [her] mother and Mr. Howells, whose opinions alone could enable him to stand like the Statue of Liberty, unweakened by the waters of condemnation that washed up to his feet." [29] According to Dan Beard, he revealed that their fellow ironist Howells had advised him to publish the piece and then "go hang myself first." And when Clemens had asked why he should do that, Howells had replied, "To save the public the trouble" because they would surely hang him when the piece appeared in print.[30] This was the climate in which George Harvey's *North American Review* published the essay, and in which it reappeared as a pamphlet widely disseminated by the New York Anti-Imperialist League.[31]

Mark Twain's purpose in writing "To the Person Sitting in Darkness" was to censure as forcefully as possible the behavior of the American missionary William S. Ament after the Boxer Rebellion; that of the Czar and the Russians in China, of Kaiser Wilhelm, of Colonial Secretary Joseph Chamberlain in South Africa, and of President William McKinley in the Philippines. A portion of the article is devoted to a course of action proposed to still the alarm of "the person sitting in darkness," but the plan is wholly ironic, a "modest proposal," and is designed only to make clearer the moral and intellectual deficiencies of these men in power and of their administrations. The "person" is of course the Chinese, the Boer, the Afrikander, and the Filipino, to whom the imperialist nations are bringing the light of the Gospel or of civilization, and the ar-

ticle is addressed to the "person" ostensibly to reconcile him
to his present lot. The title (from Matthew 4:16, echoing Psalm
107:10) was chosen for its evangelistic connotations and its familiarity to the American reader.

The Reverend Mr. Ament of the American Board of Foreign
Missions comes under attack first. The article begins with a
New York *Sun* clipping of Christmas Eve, 1900, which quoted
the missionary extensively about a trip he had made to collect
indemnities for Boxer damages. The Chinese were usually
compelled to pay three hundred taels for each Chinese Christian killed, Ament observed; the Catholic missionaries demanded six hundred eighty severed heads; fines thirteen
times the amount of the indemnity were assessed by Ament
himself; and in Ament's words, the soft hand of the Americans was not so persuasive as the mailed fist of the Germans.
Mark Twain's comment was bitter:

> By happy luck, we get all these glad tidings on Christmas
> Eve—just in time to enable us to celebrate the day with proper
> gaiety and enthusiasm. Our spirits soar, and we find we can
> even make jokes: Taels I win, Heads you lose. (Pp. 162–63)

With this savage pun, Mark Twain began his ironic praise of
Ament, "the right man in the right place," who represents not
only the Christian virtues of grace, gentleness, loving-kind-
ness, and charity, but the "American spirit" as well, the ab-
origine American Pawnee spirit, which demands that the innocent suffer for the guilty. The missionary's magnanimity,
he goes on, deserves a monument, and the designs may be sent
to him, Mark Twain; they must include a representation of the
thirteen-fold indemnity, and must "exhibit 680 Heads, so dis-
posed as to give a pleasing and pretty effect; for the Catholics
have done nicely, and are entitled to notice in the monument"
(pp. 163–64). The final charge against Ament was calculated to
strike home. Squeezing blood money out of pauper peasants

to be *"used for the propagation of the Gospel,"* he noted, underlining Ament's words, does not flutter his serenity, "although the act and the words, taken together, concrete a blasphemy so hideous and so colossal that, without doubt, its mate is not findable in the history of this or of any other age" (p. 164).

The Reverend Mr. Ament's behavior and another newspaper clipping advocating the suppression of missionaries in the Orient because they act as "filibustering expeditions" for the Western Powers then introduce the general issue, which Mark Twain puts this way:

> *Shall we?* That is, shall we go on conferring our Civilization upon the peoples that sit in darkness, or shall we give those poor things a rest? Shall we bang right ahead in our old-time, loud, pious way, and commit the new century to the game; or shall we sober up and sit down and think it over first? Would it not be prudent to get our Civilization-tools together, and see how much stock is left on hand in the way of Glass Beads and Theology, and Maxim Guns and Hymn Books, and Trade-Gin and Torches of Progress and Enlightenment (patent adjustable ones, good to fire villages with, upon occasion), and balance the books, and arrive at the profit and loss, so that we may intelligently decide whether to continue the business or sell out the property and start a new Civilization Scheme on the proceeds? (Pp. 164–65)

In the past, he stated, the Blessings-of-Civilization Trust has paid extremely well, but Christendom has been playing the game so badly in recent years that the People who Sit in Darkness have become suspicious, and are beginning to examine those blessings; the business is being ruined by the ineptitude of Mr. McKinley, Mr. Chamberlain, the Kaiser, the Czar, and the French. They have, so the author alleged, been exporting Civilization *"with the outside cover left off"*: no longer does the customer believe he is buying Love, Justice, Liberty, Equality, Mercy, Education, Gentleness, Christianity, and so on. He then damned the governments of England, Germany, Russia, and the United States in turn, showing how each of them has ruined the business, has played the game badly.

England under Mr. Chamberlain, he continues, "manufactures a war out of materials so inadequate and so fanciful that they make the boxes grieve and the gallery laugh, and he tries hard to persuade himself that it isn't purely a private raid for cash." It is bad play, this "onslaught of an elephant upon a nest of field-mice," particularly so because England could stand three serious affronts from Russia, but not even a shadow of insolence from the Transvaal.

Similarly, the Kaiser got two hundred thousand dollars from China (Mark Twain noted), as well as twelve miles of territory worth twenty million dollars and a monument and a Christian church, all because two missionaries were killed in a Shantung riot. A missionary, like a doctor, or a sheriff, or an editor, Mark Twain assures his reader, is worth much, but he is not worth the earth. Here again the person sitting in darkness has not been deceived: he knows that the Chinese have been overcharged. The Kaiser thus played the game badly, because the Chinese revolt has been expensive to Germany.

Russia robs Japan of Port Arthur, hard-earned spoil swimming in Chinese blood, and seizes Manchuria, "raids its villages, and chokes its great river with the swollen corpses of countless massacred peasants," so Mark Twain asserted—with the Person noting every move that Russia makes, and perhaps saying to himself, "It is yet *another* Civilized Power, with its banner of the Prince of Peace in one hand and its loot-basket and its butcher-knife in the other" (pp. 166–69).

From this point on in the article, Mark Twain devoted his attention to America's war with Spain and the Philippines. With an effective contrast in mind, he first demonstrated how well McKinley, our "Master of the Game," played his cards in the Cuban campaign; playing the American game, he could not lose. The Master held the strength of seventy million sympathizers and the resources of the United States to back Cuba's struggle for freedom; "Nothing but Europe combined," he declared, "could call that hand and Europe cannot combine on anything." Moved by a high inspiration, the Master had even proclaimed forcible annexation to be "criminal aggression." The other half of the contrast follows: McKinley forgot what he had said of "criminal aggression" within a year, and began to play the Chamberlain game. The consequence is that those who sit in darkness are becoming convinced that just as there are two brands of civilization, one for home consumption and one for export, there must be two Americas, "one that sets the captive free, and one that takes a once-captive's new freedom away from him, and picks a quarrel with him with nothing to found it on; then kills him to get his land." This, he warns, is going to be bad for the Business (p. 170).

Having thus presented the problem, Clemens made his "modest proposal." It was simply, following Mr. Chamberlain and even going beyond him, to "present the whole of the facts, shirking none, then explain them according to Mr. Chamberlain's formula," which runs "twice 2 are 14, and 2 from 9 leaves 35." The "facts" follow in the form of an expertly summarized history of the Philippine war, written from the anti-imperialist point of view, of course. Mark Twain insisted upon the military and political capability of the Filipinos, their invaluable aid as allies, their patriotism and love of freedom, the deceitful course of action followed by the American command, the wholly inadequate pretext for fighting, and the unspeakable procedure of buying from Spain territory that she no longer owned.

The historical facts presented, Mark Twain was now ready to explain them to the "Person Sitting in Darkness" . . .

They look doubtful, but in reality they are not. There have been lies; yes, but they were told in a good cause. We have been treacherous; but that was only in order that real good might come out of apparent evil. True, we have crushed a deceived and confiding people; we have turned against the weak and the friendless who trusted us; we have stamped out a just and intelligent and well-ordered republic; we have stabbed an ally in the back and slapped the face of a guest; we have bought a Shadow from an enemy that hadn't it to sell; we have robbed a trusting friend of his land and his liberty; we have invited our clean young men to shoulder a discredited musket and do bandit's work under a flag which bandits have been accustomed to fear, not to follow; we have debauched America's honor and blackened her face before the world; but each detail was for the best. We know this. The Head of every State and Sovereignty in Christendom, and ninety per cent. of every legislative body in Christendom, including our Congress and our fifty State Legislatures, are members not only of the church, but also of the Blessings-of-Civilization Trust. This world-girdling accumulation of trained morals, high principles, and justice, cannot do an unright thing, an unfair thing, an ungenerous thing, an unclean thing. It knows what it is about. Give yourself no uneasiness; it is all right. (Pp. 174–75)

The diatribe ends with an appeal to two symbols: the American army uniform and the American flag. If the Business is to have a new start, Clemens insisted, a disguise instead of an honorable uniform must be worn by the soldiers in the Philippines. As for the flag, "We can have a special one—our States do it: we can have just our usual flag, with the white stripes painted black and the stars replaced by the skull and crossbones." The reassuring last word is, "By help of these suggested amendments, Progress and Civilization in that country can have a boom, and it will take in the Persons who are Sitting in Darkness, and we can resume Business at the old stand" (p. 176).

"To the Person Sitting in Darkness" was published at the

beginning of February, and almost immediately a storm of vituperation and a shower of praise descended on Mark Twain.
Much of the English and American press commented edi-
torially, with bitter denunciations or firm appreciation according to their convictions. Almost inevitably the tempest grew
worse when the article was distributed, in pamphlet form, by
the New York Anti-Imperialist League, the entire controversial
section on William Ament significantly omitted.[32] While the
storm was at its height Clemens had written to Andrew Carnegie:

> You seem to be in prosperity. Could you lend an admirer
> $1.50 to buy a hymn-book with? God will bless you. I feel it; I
> know it. . . . P.S.—Don't send the hymn-book; send the
> money; I want to make the selection myself.

And Carnegie had replied:

> Nothing less than a two-dollar & a half hymn-book *gilt* will
> do for you. Your place in the choir (celestial) demands that &
> you shall have it.
> There's a new Gospel of Saint Mark in the *North American*
> which I like better than anything I've read for many a day.
> I am willing to borrow a thousand dollars to distribute that
> sacred message in proper form, & if the author don't object may
> I send that sum, when I can raise it, to the Anti-Imperialist
> League, Boston, to which I am a contributor, the only mis-
> sionary work I am responsible for.
> Just tell me you are willing & many thousands of the holy
> little missals will go forth.[33]

The broad dissemination of the pamphlet reprint (which
Carnegie seems to have financed), and the number and nature
of reprintings and editorials in magazines and newspapers afford proof that the article stirred its audience deeply. This effect was owing in part to the writer's skill with irony, humor,
and invective. The article, moreover, follows a clear plan—that

of censuring the agents of imperialism—which reaches its climax with McKinley and the United States; and the terms in which the plan is unfolded derive largely from two related and sustained metaphors—conducting an unscrupulous business, and playing a "skin-game"—roulette or, more often, poker. Above all, Mark Twain conceived portions of the article in strong cartoon terms: e.g., a monument exhibiting six hundred eighty heads; the improper *packaging* of the Blessings of Civilization; the national deities represented by Washington (bearing the Sword of the Liberator), Lincoln (the slaves' broken chains), and McKinley (the chains repaired); and the skull and cross bones replacing the stars in the American flag. "To the Person Sitting in Darkness" is a remarkably coherent rhetorical work, free from digression, even in tone, and single in purpose.

Mark Twain wrote a good deal more about wars of conquest. "To My Missionary Critics" (April 1901) admitted the purity of intention of his critics but questioned their intelligence. "A Defense of General Funston" (May 1902) condemns the general for capturing Aguinaldo, the Filipino resistance leader, by what William James called "a bunco-steering trick." [34] "The Czar's Soliloquy" (May 1905) and "King Leopold's Soliloquy: A Defence of His Congo Rule" (1905) both contain telling passages, and the convention of self-revelation and consequent self-condemnation works well at times. In general, though, Mark Twain was too angry over both the Czar and the King, too much concerned to beat them both to "rags and pulp" to achieve complete success in satirizing and condemning them. More effective is the Christmas greeting in the style of Pudd'nhead Wilson, never published:

> It is my warm & world-embracing Christmas hope that all of us that deserve it may finally be gathered together in a heaven of rest & peace, & the others be permitted to retire to the clutches of Satan or the Emperor of Russia, according to preference—if they have a preference. [35]

Among the recently published pieces probably the most striking is "The Stupendous Procession," [36] written not long after the "Greeting" but before "To the Person Sitting in Darkness." It opens upon two female figures, "the twentieth century" appearing young, drunk, and disorderly, and again the majestic matron of Christendom, this time wearing a crown of thorns on which are impaled the bleeding heads of Boers, Boxers, and Filipinos. England, Spain, Russia, France, Germany, and America follow in order, appropriately accompanied; France, for example, is paired with the mutilated figure of Dreyfus, and America, with the Sultan of Sulu with his slaves and concubines. After a wild menagerie of American figures troop by, a pirate flag appears bearing the inscription, "All white men are born free and equal." The Statue of Liberty carries her torch extinguished and reversed; the American flag is furled and draped in crepe; and the shade of Lincoln "towering vast and dim" broods with pained aspect over the far-reaching pageant.

Chapter 6

THE PUDD'NHEAD
WILSON MAXIMS

Their wit, concentration, depth, and quotability. — On the professions, poli tics, nation and race, money, truth, lies, courage, cowardice, vanity, the art of literature, the mystery of humor.

Driven by his resolve to pay off all his creditors in full, Mark Twain wrote steadily throughout the 1890s and into the first years of the twentieth century, piling up unfinished manuscripts and publishing a procession of generally undistinguished books. *Tom Sawyer Abroad* (1894) and *The Tragedy of Pudd'nhead Wilson* (1894) are good and interesting compared to the pieties of *Personal Recollections of Joan of Arc* (1896) or the plot twistings of *The American Claimant* (1892) or the Sherlock Holmes burlesque of *A Double Barrelled Detective Story* (1902). *Following the Equator, A Journey Around the World* (1897) is a decidedly better book than all but a few critics have said in print, and the chapters devoted to India have never been surpassed. To my mind, however, the distinctive and distinguished pieces in the last decade of Mark Twain's writing life are a set of maxims, a reminiscence of people in Hannibal, and an unfinished tale concerning three boys and a mysterious stranger.

The Pudd'nhead Wilson maxims take their name from the detective character whose ironies pass over the heads of his fellow townsmen so that they consider him a kind of idiot—until his skill in fingerprinting reveals the true identity of Tom and Chambers, whose roles in life have been reversed by a slave mother, Roxy. These extracts from Pudd'nhead Wilson's Calendar, which figure as witty chapter openers in the melodramatic novel *The Tragedy of Pudd'nhead Wilson*, are purportedly the creation of David Wilson, attorney-at-law; and many of them bear some thematic relation to the chapter they introduce. Thus, the first maxim, on the effect of ridicule upon the ass, a choice spirit of almost perfect character, anticipates the townsmen's conclusion that Wilson is a "perfect jackass." But the relation of sayings to text in *Following the Equator* (with attribution to Pudd'nhead Wilson's New Calendar) is really no stronger than in the novel; so that in both books the maxims are independently memorable as assertions of Mark Twain, rather more than as utterances of the shadowy Pudd'nhead Wilson in the context of the story of Roxy and her "children."

There are about three hundred such sayings, published and unpublished,[1] and while they were written at nearly every stage of Mark Twain's career, most of them originated during the 1890s. His interest in apothegmatic statement developed early, linked as it was with his determination to achieve a pure, vigorous style and to find the right word. This interest seems a function as well of his appetite for clichés, inflated rhetoric, and etiquette books, which might be given a delightful or a cutting turn by a burlesque twist of some kind; and in this sense, the maxims relate closely to his earliest practice of turning upside down the melodramatic or didactic or sentimental formulae of his predecessors. Why he should have produced so many of the sayings in the 1890s is less clear. The definitions in Ambrose Bierce's *The Cynic's Word Book* (1906) or *The Devil's Dictionary* (1911) bear a slight resemblance to these sayings, but follow them at some years' distance, as do Howells's "reversible proverbs," or "old saws with new teeth" in a column of 1903.[2] Whatever the reason, the maxims possess the concentration of Stephen Crane's best "lines" and the memorability of poetry.

Such impression as readers have of the Pudd'nhead Wilson sayings is that they are witty and cynical, issuing as most of them do from the dark years of their author's bankruptcy and the onset of old age. A few of them deserve the label "cynical":

> It takes your enemy and your friend, working together, to hurt you to the heart; the one to slander you and the other to get the news to you.

> There is an old-time toast which is golden for its beauty. "When you ascend the hill of prosperity may you not meet a friend."[3]

But it is their range of subject and variation in tone that strikes the reader who attempts to see the maxims together as a distinct expression in the Mark Twain canon. The formal variety is quite as great as the variety of topics dealt with. Two of his most obvious devices for securing form are to hang the maxim on a calendar date, and to reverse a well-known proverb or quotation. Thus, of February:

> This is the blessedest of the months: there are two or three days less of sin in it, & toil, & sorrow, & weariness, & death, & expense.

—the reader being counted on to make the appropriate wry pause before "expense." *April 1* "is the day upon which we are reminded of what we are on the other three hundred and sixty-four," the crucial term omitted. And *Dec. 25* carries the calendar label: "Cheer up—it comes but once a year." This last stands on its head the familiar cliché about Christmas derived from Thomas Tusser's sixteenth-century poem, "The Farmer's Daily Diet": [4]

> At Christmas play and make good cheer,
> For Christmas comes but once a year.

Mark Twain took especial pleasure in giving "old saws new teeth." He claimed, for example, that, unlike the early bird, the man who got up at sunrise was bitten by a horse for his pains. Again, adapting the sentiment from *Proverbs* about the live dog and the dead lion, he counsels,

> CONSIDER well the proportions of things. It is better to be a young June-bug than an old bird of paradise. [5]

One of the funniest and most familiar of the maxims breaks down a rule of conduct: "WHEN angry, count four; when very angry, swear." In printed versions "ten" appeared once, and "one hundred" once; but evidently he found the new version better suited to swearers with short fuses. [6] Altering or adding merely a single word of a proverb or quotation produces a vivid result when Mark Twain chooses the word, as in this variation on a famous line from Robert Burns's "Man Was Made to Mourn": "God's inhumanity to man makes countless thousands mourn," or the sharp challenge of "Geological time is not money." Or Mark Twain will endorse a cliché with a straight face, thus:

> Even the clearest and most perfect circumstantial evidence is likely to be at fault, after all, and therefore ought to be received

with great caution. Take the case of any pencil, sharpened by
any woman: if you have witnesses, you will find she did it with
a knife; but if you take simply the aspect of the pencil, you will
say she did it with her teeth.

That the woman appears to have used a "pile-driver" was his
first idea—but he soon found a much subtler figure: that of her
working at the pencil like a beaver.[7] Flat denial carries conviction even in colloquialese:

> Truth is mighty and will prevail. There is nothing the matter
> with this, except that it ain't so.[8]

Metaphor was one of Mark Twain's strong "holds" as a
wrestler with language. He hangs a long maxim on a business
metaphor:

> Do not undervalue the headache. While it is at its sharpest it
> seems a bad investment; but when relief begins, the unexpired
> remainder is worth $4 a minute.

Or he creates metaphors with a simple, ironic comparison in
"He is as modest as a maxim," or "He is as self conceited as a
proverb"; or, in a sharp reversal of the anti-Semitic stereotype,
"As charitable as a Jew—." [9] But how profoundly he *could*
plunge appears in the rare, wholly serious metaphorical in-
sight in which he appears to look back to Melville and forward
to O'Neill: "Every one is a moon, and has a dark side which
he never shows to anybody." Later he delivers this variant:

> Men and women—even man and wife are foreigners. Each has
> reserves that the other cannot enter into, nor understand. These
> have the effect of frontiers.[10]

Euphemism served his purpose at least once: "He is useless
on top of the ground; he ought to be under it, inspiring the

cabbages." [11] The pause, leading to anticlimax, is rather more characteristic. For example, in 1866 he cautioned,

> Never refuse to do a kindness unless the act would work great injury to yourself, and never refuse to take a drink—under any circumstances.

With much the same levity he wrote in 1897, "Few of us can stand prosperity. Another man's, I mean," though we can "easily learn to endure adversity. Another man's, I mean." But in the "expansionist" years, he employed the rhetorical trick of deflation to profound ends, thus: "The universal brotherhood of man is our most precious possession, what there is of it." [12]

"Education consists mainly in what we have unlearned" takes the form of definition. "It takes me a long time to lose my temper, but once lost I could not find it with a dog" finds our author punning—in a biographical mood. The quip "It is easier for a cannibal to enter the Kingdom of Heaven through the eye of a rich man's needle than it is for any other foreigner to read the terrible German script" burlesques the Book of Proverbs, as other maxims burlesque *Hamlet*. [13] Mark Twain found the riddle and the questions of the Catechism especially useful as models. Thus he creates variations on a favorite idea of his later life:

> Who is richer than Croesus in his palace? The pauper in his grave.

> Who is luckiest of all the living? The dying.

> Why is it that we rejoice at a birth and grieve at a funeral? It is because we are not the person involved. [14]

And a second favorite late idea appears in the rhetorical question and answer: "What is the human being's other name? Slave." [15]

The range of subjects for Mark Twain's humor and of objects for his satire parallels the variety of form and technique in which the maxims are set forth, and is in fact wonderfully various. One finds a kind of epitome of the topics that concern him in his other writings. They are presented here with almost no regard for chronology, since most of them were written during the five-year period 1895–1900; yet by association they do roughly follow a sequence, and our task is to exhibit their sweep and scope and to uncover strains that qualify the *idée reçu* of Clemens's pessimism.

Naturally enough, heaven and biblical figures, God and the gods, predestination, the "damned human race" and death appear prominently in the Puddn'head Wilson maxims. "Adam and Eve," observes Mark Twain, displaying the dead-pan literal-mindedness of the Renaissance artist concerned whether to paint Adam and Eve with navels, "had many advantages, but the principal one was, that they escaped teething." Adam "was but human," he insists. "He did not want the apple for the apple's sake, he wanted it only because it was forbidden. The mistake was in not forbidding the serpent; then he would have eaten the serpent." Still, "Let us be grateful to Adam our benefactor. He cut us out of the 'blessing' of idleness and won for us the 'curse' of labor." [16] As for Eve's stolen fruit,

> The true Southern watermelon is a boon apart, and not to be mentioned with commoner things. It is chief of this world's luxuries, King by the grace of God over all the fruits of the earth. When one has tasted it, he knows what the angels eat. It was not a Southern watermelon that Eve took; we know it because she repented.[17]

Traditional views of heaven, especially the Biblical heaven and John Bunyan's heaven, were fascinating to Mark Twain, and hell only a little less so. But his concept of the Christian hereafter was scarcely traditional. "When I reflect upon the number of disagreeable people who I know have gone to a better world, I am moved to lead a different life," he exclaims, with massive irony directed at the "unco guid." The rather insipid injunction, "Let us swear while we may, for in heaven it will not be allowed," is transformed into the highly personal "If I cannot swear in heaven I shall not stay there." In a wholly different mood, one perhaps born of reading Shakespeare's *King Lear*, Mark Twain set down—though he never revised or published—this thought:

> An eternity of woe stands as a possibility before every child that is born into this life—a risk restricted to our race. Who, then, having the choice, would elect to be born a man if he could be born a bug, or a stone, or a weed? [18]

The God of this heaven is as paradoxical as the four-person'd deity of "The Chronicle of Young Satan." Intellectually, Clemens was capable of predicting that "Christianity will doubtless survive in the earth ten centuries hence—stuffed and in a museum" in a Godless universe; and yet emotionally he could not accept the atheist position. Relatively early, in 1877, "The old man (for whom we may read Samuel L. Clemens) said":

> When I think of the suffering which I see around me, and how it wrings my heart; and then remember what a drop in the ocean this is, compared with the measureless Atlantics of misery which God has to see every day, my resentment is roused against those thoughtless people who are so glib to glorify God, yet never have a word of pity for him. [19]

Basically, the same view minus the satiric edge, appears in the two maxims, "There has been only one Christian. They caught him and crucified Him early," and "If Christ were here now, there is one thing he would *not* be—a Christian." [20] Still, his animus is never far away, and indeed develops with his thought. "What God lacks is convictions," he writes in 1898, "stability of character. He ought to be a Presbyterian or a Catholic or *something*—not try to be everything." This is the God who "pours out love upon all with a lavish hand—but he reserves vengeance for his very own." On the other hand, "Man is saved one reproach—he didn't make himself," according to an unpublished maxim he labeled "usable," adding that "if a man had created man, he would have died of remorse." [21]

Given the God of vengeance whom he feared in his childhood and never forgot, belief in predestination and damnation would shade into determinism and pessimism in Mark Twain's maturity and old age. "Man is part angel, part rat; mainly rat" is a more vivid, colloquial condemnation than the magisterial assertion that "the human race consists of the damned and the ought-to-be-damned." [22] "The spirit of wrath," says that expert in wrathful expression "—not the words—is the sin; and the spirit of wrath is cursing. We begin to swear before we can talk." When Olivia Clemens once tried to shame her husband by repeating his curses *verbatim*, he told her gently that she had the words but not the tune. [23] Thus, the tune betrays the emotion, and even to *feel* wrath is sinful. More resignedly he counsels, "If you must, you'd better," and "It is easier to stay out than get out." He concludes that "circumstances make man, not man circumstances," condensing an earlier maxim:

> We are nothing but echoes. We have no thoughts of our own, no opinions of our own, we are but a compost heap made up of the decayed heredities, moral and physical. [24]

These sayings suggest a naturalistic variation of the doctrine of predestination. Perhaps the sharpest comment of all, on original sin, is the punning aphorism, "You can straighten a worm, but the crook is in him & only waiting." [25]

Maxims corroborating that man is "mainly rat" and is either damned or ought to be damned make up a rich vein in the lode of the maxims. Men, that is, are scoundrels or fools. So, "let us be thankful for the fools. But for them the rest of us could not succeed." Conversely, a long, unpublished maxim beginning with the Biblical equation of the adulterous wish with adultery, concludes by selection and compression—and perhaps an assist from Hamlet's "who should 'scape whipping"—with the polished saying, "If the desire to kill and the opportunity to kill came always together, who would escape hanging?" [26]

Ingratitude was another trait that drove Mark Twain to damn the human race. In one of the maxims he observes that

> Gratitude and treachery are merely the two extremities of the same procession. You have seen all of it that is worth staying for when the band and the gaudy officials have gone by. [27]

More subtly, perhaps more truly, Clemens laments that "There are people who can do all fine and heroic things but one: keep from telling their happinesses to the unhappy." [28] This is the "exquisite" Clemens in Howells's understanding of him. The sardonic Mark Twain can explain why men are what they are: "Man was made at the end of the week's work, when God was tired," and "Man alone is cruel wittingly" as compared with animals, who are unwittingly cruel. [29] "There has been a mistake," Mark Twain announces: "it is the beasts that should have been made in the image of God." His prime example:

> Of all God's creatures there is only one that cannot be made the slave of the lash. That one is the cat. If man could be crossed with the cat it would improve man, but it would deteriorate the cat. [30]

Severely limited freedom of choice and a moral sense that mostly leads men astray—these beliefs of Mark Twain's explain why his maxims praise death and are so many and sharp. The earlier "Pity is for the living, envy is for the dead" is elaborated into:

> Whoever has lived long enough to find out what life is, knows how deep a debt of gratitude we owe to Adam, the first great benefactor of our race. He brought death into the world.[31]

The sobriety of tone leads the reader to take seriously Mark Twain's belief that Adam brought peace (through death) along with "all that woe," as Milton had asserted in the opening lines of *Paradise Lost*. The remark "All say, 'How hard it is that we have to die'—a strange complaint to come from the mouths of people who have had to live" [32] is in fact more Hellenic than Miltonic or Christian in sentiment. The remedy for the living? "Of the demonstrably wise there are but two; those who commit suicide, and those who keep their reasoning faculties atrophied with drink"—a remarkable summary of the characters in Eugene O'Neill's late plays. The maxim "Don't part with your illusions; when they are gone you may still exist but you have ceased to live" might also come from the pen of O'Neill. By the age of forty-eight, however, Mark Twain had tempered this attitude:

> The man who is a pessimist before he is forty-eight knows too much; the man who is an optimist after he is forty-eight knows too little.[33]

The Pudd'nhead Wilson maxims dealt with so far tend to turn inward, into the human psyche, toward "the pain of living and the drug of dreams," as T. S. Eliot called it in "Animula." A second group of saws and sayings, quite as substantial and rather better known, deal humorously or satirically with society and people as social animals: with the professions, politics, with nation and race, money, truth and falsehood, courage and cowardice, vanity, the art of literature and the art of humor.

Himself a journalist, Mark Twain obviously relished this maxim based on an ancient pun:

> The old saw says, "Let a sleeping dog lie." Right. Still, when there is much at stake it is better to get a newspaper to do it.

One of his most famous aphorisms comes in three variants. "In the first place God made idiots. This was for practice. Then he made juries." Or school boards. Or proofreaders—depending on his *bête noir* of the moment.[34] Of lawyers the litigious Clemens observed, "To succeed in the other trades, capacity must be shown; in the law, concealment of it will do." Of doctors: *"Admonitions* harvested from the wisdom of the ages: Physician, heal thyself. Patient, heel thyself." Of hotelkeepers: "It is an art apart. Saint Francis of Assisi said—'All saints can do miracles, but few of them can keep hotel.' " Of plumbers: "In the island of Fiji they do not use turkeys, they use plumbers. It does not become you and me to sneer at Fiji." [35] And of inventors (with a hopeful glance at himself): "Neither a moneyed fool nor an inspired inventor is valuable by himself; but harnessed together they build civilizations." [36]

The political maxims are famous, the most widely known being the assertion that "It could probably be shown by facts and figures that there is no distinctly native American criminal class except Congress." With mock ferocity, he says of conservatives, "I have a rooted distaste for conservatives. I like them boiled, but otherwise I do not care for them." At the beginning of the Spanish-American War Clemens wrote in his notebook: "It is by the goodness of God that in our country we have those three unspeakably precious things: freedom of speech, freedom of conscience, and the prudence never to exercise either of them" [37]—surely a jape that strikes to the heart of the dilemma between democratic theory and practice in the late twentieth century as well as in the 1890s. The inflated rhetoric and the principles it embodies are punctured by the pause, the anticlimax, and the prudential inaction. It was also at the turn of the century, in the context of imperialistic warfare, that Clemens advised, "In statesmanship get the formalities right, never mind about the moralities." [38]

An especially memorable application of this principle appeared in *Following the Equator* of 1897, addressed to the British and their armies in South Africa, whom the Boer guerrilla soldiers were so often evading. "First catch your Boer, then kick him." [39] Mark Twain's sympathy for the revolting Boers and Boxers and Filipinos and Russian nihilists was of years standing. Not long after finishing *A Connecticut Yankee in King Arthur's Court* in 1889 he wrote:

> The first gospel of all monarchies should be Rebellion; the second should be Rebellion; and the third and all gospels and the only gospel in any monarchy should be Rebellion against Church and State. [40]

In the matter of nationality and race, Mark Twain takes the tone of the good Samaritan in a maxim of 1898:

> There is but one first thing to do when a man is wounded and suffering: *relieve* him. If we have a curiosity to know his nationality, that is a matter of no consequence, and can wait.

In the maxims the United States fares rather badly, as "the Impolite Nation," inventive and boastful and energetic like others, but in uncourteousness, incivility, impoliteness, "we stand alone—until hell shall be heard from." The French fare little better: "France has neither winter nor summer nor morals—apart from these drawbacks it is a fine country." The English get mixed comment. "The English are mentioned in the Bible: Blessed are the meek, for they shall inherit the earth" is ironic enough, but "I have traveled more than anyone else, and I have noticed that even the angels speak English with an accent" [41] is good-humored satire.

Mark Twain tended to sympathize with "the person sitting in darkness" (except for the Goshoot Indians) and with savages and black Americans, as his inventing of the word "snivelization" might suggest, or the aphorism, "The difference between savage & civilized man: one is painted, the other gilded." In 1884 Olivia Clemens made a maxim for her husband about Negroes, and he adopted and cherished it. Once when he lost his temper over a begging letter from a minister and controlled it immediately when he learned that the writer was a Negro, Livy advised him, "Consider everybody colored till he is proved white." In the *Notebook* for 1895 he argued that men and women were least equal and farthest apart in savagery—but that civilized men will not admit that "no civilization can be perfect until exact equality between man and woman is included." [42]

"The lack of money is the root of all evil" came from Mark Twain's heart, for he made a great deal of money from writing and lecturing, lost it all investing in a typesetting machine, paid off his debts fully, and re-emerged solvent but scarcely wiser. Similarly, "Prosperity is the best protector of principle." He learned, at considerable expense, that "there are two times in a man's life when he should not speculate: when he can't afford it, and when he can." [43] In the matter of saving money, he adapts one of Franklin's stories thus:

> To save half, when you are fired by an eager impulse to contribute to a charity, wait and count forty. To save three-quarters, count sixty. To save it all, count sixty-five. [44]

As for money in the moral realm, his most striking maxim was that "the holy passion of Friendship is of so sweet and steady and loyal and enduring a nature that it will last through a whole lifetime, if not asked to lend money." His tact and economy in maxim writing and his skill in using the pause before the "snapper" are all illustrated by this maxim on friendship and money. In the manuscript version, he originally had said, "through the frowns and smiles, the storms and sunshine, the joys and sorrows, and the manifold vicissitudes of fate and fortune of a whole lifetime"—a version pared down simply to "through a whole lifetime." [45] Many other maxims on money support the saw,

> Some men worship rank, some worship heroes, some worship power, some worship God, and over these ideals they dispute—but they all worship money. [46]

Moralist in disguise as he was, Mark Twain was fascinated by truthtellers and liars, as at least a dozen Pudd'nhead Wilson maxims show. Apparently he believed that the tendency to lie and to repeat lies was as basic as original sin in the human constitution. His remark that "One of the most striking differences between a cat and a lie is that a cat has only nine lives" presupposes such a tendency. Conversely, "It is often the case that the man who can't tell a lie thinks he is the best judge of one." Of the "869 different forms of lying," he asserts, "often, the surest way to convey misinformation is to tell the strict truth." [47] One of his cleverest bits of alliteration, one involving a metaphor from whist or bridge, resulted in the memorable maxim, "Tell the truth or trump—but get the trick." The wisdom or even the necessity of lying are hinted at in two even better-known maxims: "Truth is the most valuable thing we have. Let us economize it," and "When in doubt, tell the truth." [48]

Courage and cowardice found their way into the maxims. That men erect cowardice into principle is hinted at in the saying, "There are several good protections against temptations, but the surest is cowardice." In one frame of mind Mark Twain insists that strength and weakness are born in a man and therefore attributable to God; in another, that "Courage is resistance to fear, mastery of fear—not absence of fear," and cites the flea as "the bravest of all the creatures of God, if ignorance of fear were courage." [49]

Vanity struck Mark Twain as the most absolute and elemental motivating force in all human behavior, so that to expose it became a prime purpose in his maxim-making. "There are no grades of vanity," he felt sure, "there are only grades of ability in concealing it." As early as 1866 he mixed metaphors to wry effect in "A man never reaches that dizzy height of wisdom when he can no longer be led by the nose." In the following year he concluded that "Fame is a vapor; popularity an accident; the only earthly certainty is oblivion." Later, "Man will do many things to get himself loved," he observed; "he will do all things to get himself envied." Yet, ironically, "The lust of admiration in us proves our kinship with the Gods. It is the divine spark." [50] For illustrations of the force of vanity, Mark Twain drew on Alfred Russel Wallace, Satan, and the Russian Emperor:

Mr. Wallace has proved that the universe was made for this world, & that this world was made for man. There being twenty-two billion microbes in each man & feeding upon him, we now perceive who the whole outfit was made for.

SATAN (impatiently) to NEW-COMER. The trouble with you Chicago people is, that you think you are the best people down here; whereas you are merely the most numerous.

The Autocrat of Russia possesses more power than any other man in the earth; but he cannot stop a sneeze. [51]

"Pull down thy vanity, I say, pull down" is in short a firmly held sentiment of Samuel L. Clemens, as well as a striking injunction from Ezra Pound's *Cantos*.

On the themes of literature and of humor, however, Mark Twain worked out his most intense sayings, devoting to them the energy of a true literary craftsman. "It is more trouble to make a maxim than it is to do right," he claims with comic understatement. For him a good part of that trouble lay in finding the exact word or expression. So, he finds, "the difference between the *almost* right word and the *right* word is really a large matter—'tis the difference between the lightning-bug and the lightning." In consequence, "I have found that one can do without principles but not without the Standard Dic[tionary]." Classic pre-Hemingway advice by now appears in his dictum, "As to the Adjective: when in doubt, strike it out." [52] He was equally sensitive to sentimentality, inflated rhetoric, and clichés, as this maxim shows:

> Some of our commonest expressions are of a very high antiquity. When the parents of mankind came upon the corpse of their son Abel & perceived how torn & bruised it was, Adam said, "What do you think of this?" and Eve replied, "It beggars description." Adam rejoined, with a sigh, "It will cast a gloom over the whole community." And it did.

This preoccupation with language extended beyond traditional English. "There is no such thing as 'the Queen's English,' " he declared. "The property has gone into the hands of a joint stock company and we own the bulk of the shares!" As for the German language, it afforded him unfailing entertainment. "Some of the German words are so long that they have a perspective. When one casts his glance along down one of these it gradually tapers to a point, like the receding lines of a railway track." [53]

The aphorisms on literature cover still other topics. Thus,

on probability: "Truth is stranger than fiction, but it is because Fiction is obliged to stick to possibilities; Truth isn't."
On originality: "In literature imitations do not imitate."
Among his definitions: " 'Classic.' A book which people praise
and don't read." On characterization:

> Surely the test of a novel's characters is that you feel a strong in-
> terest in them and their affairs—the good to be successful, the
> bad to suffer failure. Well, in John Ward you feel *no* divided in-
> terest, no discriminating interest—you want them all to land in
> hell together, and right away.

And on revision: "The time to begin writing an article is when
you have finished it to your satisfaction." [54]
    Humor was of course the Mark Twain trademark, and dur-
ing his lifetime he was considered by nearly everyone merely
a humorist. He himself thought of humor otherwise, as the
maxims he wrote about it plainly show. In 1885, for example,
he made these notes:

> Wit and Humor—if any difference it is in duration—lightning
> and electric light. Same material, apparently; but one is vivid,
> brief, and can do damage—the other fools along and enjoys
> elaboration.

In his mind wit apparently is closely related to satire and can
do damage and hurt. The observation "Irreverence is the
champion of liberty and its only sure defense," which dates
from 1888, is clearly connected with the satire of *A Connecticut
Yankee* and with Matthew Arnold's writings on reverence. So
is the aphorism, "No god and no religion can survive ridicule.
No church, no nobility, no royalty or other fraud, can face ridicule in a fair field and live." [55]
    Wit, irreverence, ridicule, satire—all are variant terms for
the character Philip Traum's "humor" in his assertion (in "The

Chronicle of Young Satan") that humor is one of mankind's few weapons against humbug and fraud. It is even, Mark Twain claimed more than once, a uniquely human power. The metaphor of *seeing* clearly and steadily appears in the maxim, "The function of humor is that of the screw in the opera glass—it adjusts one's focus." More than a uniquely human capability, humor has to be socially exercised. As he once wrote,

> Funniness has no place in an interview, because it takes two to produce mental effervescences in this world—in oratory, poetry, humor & the other airy & fleeting products of the mind: the spark stays in the flint till the steel strikes it out.

In this social sense, humor is like joy: "Grief can take care of itself; but to get the full value of a joy you must have somebody to divide it with." [56] This leads us to his profoundest meditation on the subject: "Everything human is pathetic. The secret source of Humor itself is not joy but sorrow. There is no humor in heaven." [57]

What does this mean? Are human beings, whom he elsewhere exposes as vain or cruel or ignorant, pathetic in that they live so short a time? We know that, for example, the humor of Charlie Chaplin (who rarely smiled) trembled on the edge of tears in the midst of his audience's laughter. Does Mark Twain foretoken something of Chaplin's special genius in holding that humor stems from sorrow, from a Virgilian sense of the "tears of things"? Why is there no humor in heaven? Is it that the blessed have no need to laugh and that God therefore has no "sense of humor"? However one observes it, it is the power in Mark Twain that led Howells to class his friend with Cervantes.

Chapter 7

◆·◆

DREAMS AND
THE INNER LIFE

The early skit, "Facts Concerning the Recent Carnival of Crime in Connecticut," a Freudian drama of conscience and superego before Freud. — The late vision, "The Chronicle of Young Satan," the mysterious stranger. — Its dark motifs, satire, melancholy—tempered by the creative forces, music and laughter.

Any number of the humorous or witty or sardonic elements in the Pudd'nhead Wilson maxims reappear in developed form in "The Chronicle of Young Satan," the first of three pieces by Mark Twain about a mysterious angelic stranger visiting the earth. The moral superiority of the animals to humans is one such element. Another appears in the Mark Twain maxim, "When we remember that we are all mad, the mysteries disappear and life stands explained," [1] which anticipates the fate of Father Peter, the benevolent priest who goes mad at the moment of his acquittal in the trial for theft. Still another strain is the concept of man's moral sense, or conscience, which appeared early in 1876 in a remarkable story with the almost opaque title, "The Facts Concerning the Recent Carnival of Crime in Connecticut." [2] Perhaps the role of "the moral sense" in "The Chronicle of Young Satan" may best be seen in the lurid light of "Mark Twain's" murdering conscience in the "Carnival of Crime." This is a fanciful narrative, and so intensely dramatic that it might be adapted to the stage without difficulty. It is also an allegory of the human psyche— foreshadowing Freud and depth psychology, and an astonishing bit of Clemens's autobiography spoken through the mask of Mark Twain.

The "Carnival of Crime" is told, first-person colloquial, in Mark Twain's best confidential—even confessional—manner. It gives every appearance of being no more than a "humorous story" floating along in a leisurely way, open to elaboration. It involves in fact a tightly wrought confrontation between the storyteller and his conscience, full of growing anguish and suspense, in which the narrator's loved and honored Aunt Mary plays a vital (if small) role. The story opens with Mark Twain feeling "blithe, almost jocund" as he lights his cigar and learns with great satisfaction from the morning mail that his Aunt Mary is to visit him and will in fact be arriving soon. She could still stir his "torpid conscience" in the matter of his "pernicious habit" of smoking—but only faintly. So strong is his euphoria that he feels he might now make peace with his "most pitiless enemy."

At this very moment the door opens, admitting a two-foot-tall dwarf who bears a caricature resemblance to the narrator and is covered with a "fuzzy greenish mould." The manikin insolently demands a match, lights one of Mark Twain's pipes, and in a mocking drawl remarks that it's "devilish odd weather." The pigmy with the weasel eyes ignores his host's resentment and opens attack upon him, with increasingly

alarming inside knowledge of misdeeds which "Mark Twain"
has been ashamed of. That very morning he had turned a
hungry tramp from the door with a lie, and the other day he
had refused to read a young woman's manuscript and made
her weep—so the "small fiend" reminds him. He had pun-
ished his children unjustly, and had "disloyally allowed old
friends to be traduced" in his hearing—so the dwarf persists,
taking obvious pleasure in the narrator's increasing remorse.
Worse still, Mark Twain is reminded of his tricking his
younger brother into an ice-filled brook when they were boys
together; and worst of all, there was that "peculiarly mean
and pitiful act . . . toward a poor ignorant Indian . . . in the
winter of eighteen hundred and—," a memory so painful that
he cannot permit the dwarf to go on with his recital. The ac-
cusations grow stronger and move back in time into the narrator's youth and childhood. Challenged as Satan—the Devil
himself—the dwarf reveals to Mark Twain that he is his *Conscience*.

In a murderous rage the narrator fires the poker, books, ink-
stands, and chunks of coal at his tormentor, but Conscience,
"light as a feather," darts to the top of a high bookcase and
laughs at his "slave." Locking the door and declaring a truce
for the moment, he begins to catechize Conscience, rather in
the spirit of Dr. Faustus querying Mephistopheles, and learns
that Conscience is usually invisible and insubstantial, but still
quite mortal. More, Conscience, that "ashcat," is neither his
friend nor his equal: he is enemy and master—and takes the
profoundest satisfaction in punishing his slave, pegging at
him night and day, year in and year out, never letting his subject off for any offense. While the effect may be to improve a
man, the intent of Conscience is to punish. He and other Consciences take special pleasure, for example, in hazing people of
a "peculiarly sensitive nature," and it is his *business* to make

the author suffer, whether he feeds a tramp and encourages vagrancy or refuses food to the tramp and feels mean, to repent of *everything* he does.

The debate turns to the size of consciences, and Conscience reveals that he was seven feet tall and "pretty as a picture" when Mark Twain was a boy, but had since shriveled and grown mouldy and lethargic. Mark Twain wants to know about his neighbor Thompson's conscience. Once eleven feet tall and of faultless figure (Conscience replies), he is now rusty and dull—and "sleeps in a cigar box." Robinson's? Robinson's conscience is four and one-half feet tall, shapely and comely still. Tom Smith's? When Smith was two years old, his conscience was thirteen inches tall and sluggish—like others in babyhood; now, however, he is thirty-seven feet tall and still growing, and never sleeps. Smith is president of the New England Conscience Club and is always heartbroken "because he cannot be good!" His Aunt Mary's? Her conscience lives out-of-doors entirely, for no door is big enough to admit her. And what of the publisher who once stole some Mark Twain sketches for a "series," and made him pay the law expenses to "choke him off"? At a recent exhibit of consciences (Conscience replies) the publisher's conscience was to have been the main feature—but no one could see it, since the management's microscope magnified only to thirty thousand diameters.

When Aunt Mary arrives, and in her mild, good-hearted way is soon reproaching her nephew for neglecting a poor family in the neighborhood, Conscience droops heavily on his bookcase perch. She reminds him how he has neglected her protégée at the almshouse—and Conscience falls to the floor, squirming feebly. Only when Aunt Mary supplicates her nephew to give up "this hateful slavery of tobacco" does Conscience reel drowsily and fall fast asleep. With an exultant shout, Mark Twain seizes Conscience by the throat, tears him to bloody fragments, and burns the fragments in the fire. Conscience is dead, and he is a free man.

In a change like that of Dr. Jekyll into Mr. Hyde—except for the narrator's comic exaggeration and the sympathy the reader still must feel for him—"Mark Twain," a "man WITHOUT A CONSCIENCE," rejects his Aunt Mary's paupers and reform and pestilential morals, and ejects her from the house.[3] His life since that day is unalloyed bliss, he tells us. He kills thirty-eight people whom he has old grudges against; burns down a building that spoils his view; swindles a widow and orphans of their last cow, and enters on a carnival of crime. The anti-climatic order of these crimes prevents the reader from taking "Mark Twain" the narrator of this story as a Raskolnikof, and the business jargon and flat prose of the last paragraph set firmly the key of burlesque:

> In conclusion I wish to state, by way of advertisement, that medical colleges desiring assorted tramps for scientific purposes, either by the gross, by cord measurement, or per ton, will do well to examine the lot in my cellar before purchasing elsewhere, as these were all selected and prepared by myself, and can be had at a low rate, because I wish to clear out my stock and get ready for the spring trade.

The tone is burlesque, but the author still manages his point: his *persona*, free of conscience, has murdered those who annoy him, and will murder more who do so in the future.

The autobiographical element in the "Carnival of Crime" is fairly strong. Although Aunt Mary is fictional and typical, like Aunt Polly in *Tom Sawyer* (which was scheduled for publication a few months later), the portrait owes several traits to Olivia Clemens, especially her early aversion to her husband's smoking. The allusion to the larcenous publisher would be clear enough to Mark Twain's friends, for W. F. Gill had included "An Encounter with an Interviewer" in the first volume of *The Treasure Trove Series,* and used the Mark Twain *nom de plume* without permission.[4] Gill's conscience, one notes, is so small as to be all but invisible. The "budding authoress" certainly seems real. She may be composite. But the contemptuous and mocking reference by Conscience to "your o-w-n s-n-i-v-e-l-l-i-n-g d-r-a-w-l—baby!" ıs a direct and personal reference to Clemens's "drawling infirmity of speech." Howells queried the phrase; his friend asked whether it seemed too personal; the speech remained unaltered.[5]

One wonders, too, whether the unidentified trick played on an Indian—perhaps a Goshoot, of a tribe he detested—was based on a deed he had perpetrated or was a creation of Mark Twain's imagination. Similarly, while young Sam Clemens may not have pushed a trusting younger brother blindfolded into an icy brook, the episode figures in "No. 44, The Mysterious Stranger" and in "Villagers of 1840–3", and Clemens *did* play practical jokes on his younger brother Henry.[6] Above all, self-blame and Conscience's "hazing" of a man of "peculiarly sensitive nature," and the rebellion against a rarely-still conscience are recognizable facts of the history of Clemens's inner life. The "Carnival of Crime" makes unusually frank—and effective—use of the author's own experience.

The Freudian dimension of the tale might be defined fully by a practicing Freudian critic, which I am not. Nonetheless, anyone with an elementary awareness of psychoanalytical concepts can see that Mark Twain anticipated Freud (who, we know, read the humorist with pleasure) in several striking ways, particularly in his chapter "The Anatomy of the Mental Personality" in *New Introductory Lectures on Psycho-Analysis.*[7] In his description of "the anatomy of the mental personality," for example, Freud occasionally uses effective metaphors, such as a cracked crystal for the complex relations of Germans, Magyars, and Slovaks, and the sustained metaphors of geography, exploration, and the "anatomy" of the psyche. Most vividly, he personifies superego, id, and external world as "harsh masters," and creates a genuine drama in which the ego, crying "Life is not easy," must make a go of life by reconciling the divergent and even incompatible demands of its three masters.[8]

Freud begins with the astonishing fact that the ego can take itself as an object of study or observation, criticize itself, and "do Heaven knows what besides with itself." It can even, in the case of Mark Twain, write a profound and very funny "metaphysical" narrative arising from the power of conscience, the conscious portion of the superego, to observe, criticize, and sustain ideals.[9] Thus, in the "Carnival of Crime," the narrator plays the role of the tormented ego, his Aunt Mary represents parents and other authority figures as a "vehicle of tradition" in training the superego, the mouldy dwarf is the narrator's conscience or conscious part of the superego, and the id approximately remains invisible in the unconscious, but quite evident in the compulsively demonic behavior of the narrator-ego at the end of the "Carnival." Freud observes that the superego abuses and humiliates the ego and threatens it with severest punishment, just as (conscious) Conscience torments Mark Twain's narrator, especially for "long-forgotten actions" [10] such as his ill-treatment of his brother or the bad turn done to the Indian in the Rocky Mountain West. Freud theorizes that conscience works intermittently, and may be heavy or light in different people: "A great many men have only a limited share of it or scarcely enough to be worth mentioning." [11]

Mark Twain prefigures the proposition in the change of his conscience from seven feet tall and attractive to dwarfish and disgusting; and in the varying sizes and weights of those of Thompson, Robinson, Smith, Aunt Mary, and the publisher. Even the remark that "small children are notoriously amoral" is prefigured in the statement that Robinson's conscience, now thirty-seven feet tall, had been thirteen inches tall "and rather sluggish, when he was two years old—as nearly all of us are, at that age," [12] and shares Freud's view that the superego is acquired, not innately present, like sexuality.

And so the drama is played out: Mark Twain as ego destroys his master or lord,[13] Conscience, terrifies and banishes his Aunt Mary, and enters upon a joyful "carnival of crime." Freud concluded his essay with the famous dictum, "Where id was, there shall ego be." Mark Twain dramatizes the reverse idea, "Where superego was, there shall id be." Bernard Shaw attributed to Mark Twain a piece of wisdom to the effect that "telling the truth's the funniest joke in the world." [14] This is the distinction of "Carnival of Crime," and the product of Mark Twain's high art and thorough craftsmanship. As he wrote Howells, he spent two days producing seventy manu-script pages of the story (or about 4,000 words each day), but then spent three more days "trimming, altering & working at it," and intended to put in one more day polishing it before reading it aloud to the Monday Evening Club of Hartford. Howells clearly thought well of it, for he gave it first place in the June *Atlantic*.[15]

"The Facts Concerning the Recent Carnival of Crime in Con-necticut" initiates a body of late writing that is concerned largely with the anatomy and physiology of the mental person-ality. In a long Notebook entry of January 1897 Clemens re-viewed his effort to solve the "haunting mystery" of the human psyche. In "Carnival of Crime" he had dealt with "duality" and the master conscience in the form of a malignant dwarf. Robert Louis Stevenson took another step with duality in "Dr. Jekyll and Mr. Hyde" (1886), though he was wrong in suggesting that the dual persons could communicate with each other. The French experimenting with hypnosis provided Clemens with the germ of a new theory, of the waking self and the dream self, this latter possessing extraordinary powers and

free from aging and mortality.[16] Mark Twain's Notebook obser-
vations in turn led to speculation in "No. 44, The Mysterious
Stranger" about waking self, dream self, and immortal soul—
phenomena he used in this rambling, unfinished story at least
as much for farce as for pathos or other serious ends.[17]

Of the three late tales of an unfallen, incarnated angel who
as hero and *raisonneur* visits the planet earth, the one we could
not do without is "The Chronicle of Young Satan." Even
though never finished—"Schoolhouse Hill" and "No. 44, The
Mysterious Stranger" were not completed, either—it is a major
piece in the canon because it embodies a transcendent Satanic
figure befriending and judging and fraternizing with a group
of memorable characters; and the story, which is long enough
to be finishable, has weight and breadth.

The task of interpreting this fragment is of rather recent ori-
gin, since the text as actually written was published only in
1969, in *The Mysterious Stranger Manuscripts.* In 1916, six years
after Mark Twain's death, A. B. Paine, his official biographer
and first literary executor, and F. A. Duneka, an editor at
Harper & Brothers, published a heavily cut and bowdlerized
version of the manuscript, which they made complete in appearance by appending a chapter written as the conclusion for
"No. 44," and entitled the "composite" *The Mysterious
Stranger, A Romance.* They changed the worst features of a bad
priest into an astrologer lifted from "No. 44," they concealed
their omissions with their own bridgework, and they altered
the names 44 and August to Satan and Theodor in the chapter
silently borrowed from "No. 44." It says something about
Paine and Duneka's taste and their determination to keep
Mark Twain before the reading public that they had N. C.
Wyeth, a talented painter, illustrate the book and paint the
nonexistent astrologer for the front cover, and issued it as a
children's Christmas gift book. The two "editors" must have
felt that they were enhancing Mark Twain's reputation; but

they must have known, too, that the real Samuel L. Clemens would have been enraged at their presumption and their editorial fraud.

"The Chronicle of Young Satan" (Bernard DeVoto referred to it as "Eseldorf") is Mark Twain's own title for a story of some four hundred twenty-five manuscript pages which breaks off in mid-chapter in the court of an Indian rajah, where Satan is competing with the court magician. The main setting is Eseldorf, an Austrian village, in 1702; the action begins in May. The chief characters are the narrator Theodor Fischer, who in maturity looks back on his youthful adventures; his boyhood companions Seppi Wohlmeyer and Nikolaus Baumann; the good and evil priests of the village, Father Peter and Father Adolf; Marget, the niece of Father Peter, and Ursula, their servant; Wilhelm Meidling, Marget's suitor, and Joseph Fuchs, who is courting Theodor's sister, Lilly Fischer; Lisa Brandt and her mother; and finally the stranger, known to the villagers as Philip Traum, although at home in Himmelreich he is called Satan, after his uncle.

The composition of "The Chronicle of Young Satan," its sources, and its place in the author's development are admirably set forth by John S. Tuckey in his monograph *Mark Twain and Little Satan*.[18] He examined thoroughly the three manuscripts in the light of the whole body of holographs in the Mark Twain Papers from 1897 through 1908, comparing papers, inks, and handwriting for dating clues, and making skilled use of internal evidence as well. Other evidence cited in *The Mysterious Stranger Manuscripts* supports Tuckey's dating at every point.[19] My dating of the "Chronicle" follows closely Tuckey's conclusions. Apparently, then, the "Chronicle" was composed in three periods between November 1897 and September 1900, not long before the author returned from Europe, free from his "long nightmare" of debt. During the first period, from November 1897 through January 1898 in

Vienna, he reworked the "St. Petersburg Fragment"—a false start, so to speak, reviving Tom Sawyer and Huck Finn and based in Hannibal of the 1840s—into a plot sequence recounting the boys' first encounter with Satan, Father Peter's trial on the charge of stealing Father Adolf's gold, and Father Peter's vindication. In *The Mysterious Stranger Manuscripts,* this sequence occupies Chapters 1 and 2, the opening of Chapter 3, and part of Chapter 10.

During the following months, however, Mark Twain apparently decided that he had resolved the conflict between the priests too rapidly, and that for Satan to drive Father Peter into a state of "happy insanity" at the very moment when the old man was proved innocent might provide the true ending he was seeking. Accordingly, when he returned to his manuscript between May and October 1899, he put aside the trial scene and developed the intervening episodes, splicing them with Socratic dialogues on the workings of the "Moral Sense." (These episodes, written in London and in Sanna, Sweden, constitute Chapters 3, 4, and 5 of the "Chronicle."), Theodor recalls the story of the girls burned as witches because of flea-bite "signs" and tells how Gottfried Narr's grandmother had suffered the same fate in their village. The village is forced to choose between charging Father Adolf with witchcraft and receiving an Interdict (ecclesiastical proscription of public ceremonies). Fuchs and Meidling suffer pangs of jealousy when Lilly Fischer and Marget become infatuated with Satan's angelic charm and skills.

This spurt of sustained composition ended approximately with the summary passage early in Chapter 6:

> What a lot of dismal haps had befallen the village, and certainly Satan seemed to be the father of the whole of them: Father Peter in prison . . . Marget's household shunned . . . Father Adolf acquiring a frightful and odious reputation . . . my parents worried . . . Joseph crushed . . . Wilhelm's heart broken . . .

Marget gone silly, and our Lilly following after; the whole village prodded and pestered into a pathetic delirium about nonexistent witches . . . the whole wide wreck and desolation . . .
the work of Satan's enthusiastic diligence and morbid passion
for business.[20]

The remaining half of the "Chronicle" was composed between
June and the end of August of 1900, in London and at nearby
Dollis Hill. The author's hatred of cruelty (which would lead
him to begin a book about lynchings in the United States [21])
continued to manifest itself in passages on the burning of Frau
Brandt at the stake for blasphemy, the punishment of the
gamekeepers, the pressing to death of a gentlewoman in Scot-
land, and the Eseldorf mob's stoning and hanging of a "born
lady."

Satan's freedom in time and space and his godlike powers
also make possible two new strands of action: he changes the
lives of Nick and Lisa to bring on their drowning, and he
refers to future—that is, contemporaneous—events. During
the spring and summer of 1900 Mark Twain was increasingly
angered by the role of the European powers in the Boxer Rebellion in China; and, despite his admiration for the British
and their institutions, he became increasingly committed to
the cause of the Boer Republics in South Africa. In Chapters 6
and 8 Satan refers sardonically to both wars.

Nearly all the episodes thus far lead to the deferred episode
wherein Father Peter is exonerated in the civil court—and
goes mad, the conclusion toward which Mark Twain had presumably been working. But the pressure of world events and
his sense that this story would probably not be published in
his lifetime carried him on. Thus, when King Humbert "the
Good" of Italy, assassinated by an anarchist at Monza on 29
July 1900, died excommunicated, and Pope Leo XIII subsequently forbade priests throughout the country to recite a
"tender prayer" composed by Queen Margherita and already

widely repeated in Italy and the Catholic world, Mark Twain must almost at once have seized upon this as "proof" of the doctrine of papal infallibility,[22] which he related thematically to the Interdict. His version of the event seems to have inspired the memorable generalization on the power of laughter, along with the comment on the failure of the race to make use of its one really effective weapon. Then he added a parable on the price the British might have to pay for their tenure in India; and the Indian setting led him to begin another repetitious "adventure" of Satan and Theodor in the court of a rajah. At this point the narrative ends.

Initially Mark Twain had located his fable of man's meanness and misery in "St. Petersburg" and during his boyhood years, but found it necessary to move it to Austria and a remoter era. Though he tended to regard time and place as unimportant and easily changeable, this effort to revive the "Matter of Hannibal" [23] suggests that he may have been drawing characters from memory. The likelihood grows as one reads "Villagers of 1840–3," a fragment of late 1897 written shortly before Mark Twain began the first sequence of the "Chronicle." An impressive set of thumbnail biographies of people in Hannibal, "Villagers" suggests total recall modified by black humor, as if Hannibal were Spoon River.

Most of the names, as Dixon Wecter and Walter Blair have shown, were of real persons, though a few, including certain Clemenses, were disguised.[24] In the "St. Petersburg Fragment," for example, "Mr. Black" (Father Peter in the "Chronicle") was inspired by Orion Clemens, the good-hearted and dreamy older brother who vacillated for a lifetime in his religions, jobs, and moods, and had no trace of unkindness in him. Contemporaneous events in Vienna as well as in family and Hannibal history provided further ideas for characters. Deputies Wohlmeyer and Fuchs of the Austrian parliament of 1897 furnished only names, but Father Adolf—originally Fa-

ther Lueger in the manuscript—derived his unpleasant traits
from the writer's impressions of Dr. Karl Lueger, Burgomeister
of Vienna and leader of the anti-Semitic Christian Socialists.
The priest's bull voice and gross physique come to mind in
descriptions of Deputy Schönerer: "vast and muscular, and
endowed with the most powerful voice in the Reichsrath." [25]

Satan is the primary character in the "Chronicle," as he is in
the other two manuscripts, and the most complex in his acts,
his satirical bent, the "fatal music of his voice," his Socratic
way of speaking, and his origins. To adapt Whitman's figure,
he forms one side of a Square Deific.[26] In the Mark Twain
theology he is the truth-speaker come down from heaven, the
preacher Koheleth, the new Prometheus. He thus usurps certain functions of Christ the Consoler who, says the head clerk
in "Captain Stormfield's Visit to Heaven," has saved as many
worlds as there are gates into heaven—"none can count
them." The Father of Old Testament and Missouri Presby-
terianism forms the second side of the square—severe, jealous,
and vengeful. He is distinct from but sometimes shades into
the eternal Creator, the third side, whom Mark Twain thought
of in astronomical terms—as a supernal Power not so much indifferent to men as wholly unaware of them. Satan personifies
this last, greatest deity when he informs Theodor that "man is
to [him]as the red spider is to the elephant." [27]

Of the Quadernity, it is nonetheless Satan the rebel, the
fourth and finishing face of the deity, who figures most often
and exhibits the richest development in Mark Twain's writings.[28]

Young Clemens's first imaginings of the devil, recorded
sixty years later, were so strong, he says, that he tried at age
seven to write Satan's biography, only to be frustrated by the
paucity of facts and his Sunday-school teacher's shocked resistance.[29] If this remembrance strikes the reader as something
less than petrified fact, one should take more seriously Mark

Twain's claim that he had read the entire Bible by the time he entered his teens, and his remembered fear, during a thunderstorm, that the devil was coming to claim the soul of the original Injun Joe. Even more significant is his recollection of the way he and other boys conspired to abuse the character of Satan in his mother's presence, to see how she would react. As they had expected, Jane Clemens was "beguiled into saying a soft word for the devil himself": she could not remain silent or passive when "hurt or shame [was] inflicted upon some defenceless person or creature"—not even the arch-sinner.[30] Years later, when as a cub pilot on the Mississippi he was reading Shakespeare and Milton, he observed in a letter to Orion, "What is the grandest thing in 'Paradise Lost'—the Arch-Fiend's terrible energy!" [31]

Then in 1867, shortly before he sailed for the Holy Land, the journalist encountered in a New York library another memorable prototype in the Apocryphal Books of the New Testament. For his *Alta California* readers he quoted:

> Jesus and other boys play together and make clay figures of animals. Jesus causes them to walk; also clay birds which he causes to fly, and eat and drink. The children's parents are alarmed and take Jesus for a sorcerer. . . .

The resemblance of the boy Jesus to Philip Traum in the first scenes is unmistakable.[32]

Satan in the Bible and *Paradise Lost* and the youthful Jesus of the Apocrypha are thus essential components of the matrix in which the "Mysterious Stranger" was shaped. Three decades later the character began to take form. The process began, it appears, with Clemens's bankruptcy, the death of his daughter Susy, and his daughter Jean's first epileptic seizures, and it continued during Olivia's decline into invalidism. In 1895 he recorded a dominant mood and a ruling idea in this Notebook entry:

> It is the strangest thing, that the world is not full of books that
> scoff at the pitiful world, and the useless universe and the vile
> and contemptible human race—books that laugh at the whole
> paltry scheme and deride it. . . . Why don't *I* write such a
> book? Because I have a family. There is no other reason.[33]

That this question relates to the "Chronicle" as well as to Mark
Twain's "gospel," *What Is Man?*, which he would begin in
1898, is hinted at in a cryptic entry of one month later, "What
uncle Satan said." [34] By the summer of 1897 Mark Twain was
writing "Letters to Satan," inviting His Grace to "make a pleasure tour through the world," assuring Him, "You have many
friends in the world; more than you think"—specifically Cecil
Rhodes and the "European Concert." [35] Then comes the nota-
tion late in June, "Satan's boyhood—going around with other
boys and surpising them with devilish miracles"; and in these
words "The Chronicle of Young Satan" was born.[36]

Mark Twain's opening allegation in "Concerning the Jews"
(September 1899), is that he has no prejudices of race, color,
caste, or creed—not even a prejudice against Satan, "on account of his not having a fair show." A crucial passage follows
in which he defends Captain Dreyfus, announces that he will
undertake Satan's rehabilitation himself, and concludes that
"A person who has for untold centuries maintained the im-
posing position of spiritual head of four-fifths of the human
race, and political head of the whole of it, must be granted the
possession of executive abilities of the loftiest order." [37] This
elegantly ironic passage (which may refer to the "Chronicle"
as his means of rehabilitating Satan in effect) ends his periph-
eral attempts to delineate Satan and to use him for immediate
argumentative ends. From the autumn of 1899 on, his attention was concentrated on full-length portraits of Philip Traum
(Satan), and of No. 44, in the "Mysterious Stranger" stories.
During the last decade of his writing life he began many other
fables and fictions and managed to complete a few. But the Sa-

tanic stranger who visits the earth and pities and judges and
scorns men dominated his imagination and guided his pen as
did no other figure in those years, trailing dozens of lesser
characters in his demonic wake.

Just as one may glimpse in Clemens's own experience the
origins of certain characters in the "Chronicle," so one also
finds in the events of his life adumbrations of themes in the
unfinished tale. These may be termed, by a kind of shorthand,
death-by-water, mob cowardice and cruelty, the Creation derided, quarrels and warfare, and the Moral Sense. Developing
such motifs with varying degrees of success, Mark Twain was
arguing that ultimately men and women have no need of any
hell "except the one we live in from the cradle to the grave," [38]
and for the reason that the race was irrevocably damned, either by an indifferent-unconscious God or by its own defec-
tive nature—he could never decide which. Three other themes
he identifies as the powers of laughter, music, and thought.
They qualify, though they cannot finally counterbalance, the
negative acts and concepts.

Under the heading of death-by-water belongs Theodor Fischer's futile attempt to save Lisa Brandt and Nikolaus Baumann from drowning, a fictional event that stems from a memory of the writer's boyhood recalled in 1906. Sam Clemens and
Tom Nash had been skating on the Mississippi one frigid
winter night when the ice broke up under them; he reached
the shore safely, but the perspiring Nash boy had fallen into
the icy water near shore, and in consequence contracted scarlet
fever, which left him stone-deaf and with speech impaired.[39]
As for Theodor, even if he had managed to save his friends, he
would have been left paralyzed for forty-six years as the result
of a bout of scarlet fever. The examples in the other stories of
good persons who suffer blasted lives are also intended to
arouse pity and indignation, though the writer's countermood
of bitter resignation is never far away. As the older Theodor

Fischer muses after telling of the death of his friends, "Many a time, since then, I have heard people pray to God to spare the life of sick persons, but I have never done it."

Mob cowardice and mob cruelty, often abetted by the orthodox, figure again and again in the "Chronicle." Eleven girls of Eseldorf had been burned together as witches because of "witch signs" or fleabites on their bodies. The grandmother of Gottfried Narr is burned as a witch because she relieves pain by massage. Lisa Brandt's mother burns at the stake for blasphemy after her daughter drowns and the blacksmith holds her daughter's body in ransom for a debt. And while an Eseldorf mob stones and hangs a "born lady" suspected of collusion with the devil, Satan tells Theodor how in the future a Scottish mob will stone and crush to death a gentlewoman because they suspect her of Catholic sympathies.

Sources for some of these episodes may be found in W. E. H. Lecky's *A History of England in the Eighteenth Century*, Cotton Mather's *The Wonders of the Invisible World*, and Sir Walter Scott's *Letters on Demonology and Witchcraft*—but no reader of "Goldsmith's Friend Abroad Again," or *The Prince and the Pauper*, or *Huckleberry Finn* or *A Connecticut Yankee* or "The United States of Lyncherdom" would be surprised to find such scenes in the "Chronicle." The reader may also be reminded of traumas Clemens suffered when he was young. As a boy he once gave matches to a drunken tramp in the Hannibal jail so that he might smoke; during the night, before the jailer could be found to unlock the door, he had to watch the man at the barred door burning to death. As a young man he also sat helplessly by while his beloved younger brother, Henry, suffered and died of burns from a steamboat explosion.

One of the most memorable acts in all three tales is Philip Traum's creation and then destruction of a race of Lilliputian men and women, apparently for the sole purpose of amusing

the three boys of the "Chronicle": "Oh, it is no matter," he
said, "we can make more." Mark Twain thus derides or mini-
mizes the creation of man. If memory and imagination are the
great gifts in a writer, as John Hay once wrote him,[40] they are
evinced in this demonstration by Satan. Here, in 1897, Mark
Twain developed a dramatic idea that he had noted only
briefly thirty years earlier, from the Apocrypha, the youthful
Saviour of those books often crippling or killing those who opposed his will.[41] From the apocryphal anecdote and his memory of *Gulliver's Travels*, the artist Mark Twain developed his
own version of the Creation, the Fall, and the Day of Doom, in
which the unfallen angel and nephew of Satan acts the part of
God. The Fall, in the Mark Twain "Bible," is due to a quarrel
between two workmen, who grapple like Cain and Abel in "a
life and death struggle" until Satan crushes them with his
fingers. As for the Judgment Day, it comes about by whim.
Annoyed by the lamentation of the "fingerling" mourners
around the two bodies, Satan mashes them into the ground
with the seat from the boys' swing, then wipes out the whole
race by fire and earthquake. Mark Twain may well have had in
mind Gloucester's speech in *King Lear:* "As flies to wanton
boys, are we to the gods / They kill us for their sport." Less effective are Satan's satirical reference to God's concern for the
fall of a sparrow, and the parodies of the miracle of the loaves
and fishes, of Christ's changing water into wine at the mar-
riage feast at Cana, and of Lot's wife being turned to a pillar of
salt.

A succession of personal quarrels and their enlargement into
national wars in the "Chronicle" tend to substantiate Mark
Twain's contention that if the human race is not already
damned, it ought to be. As he said in 1899, he had proposed
to the Emperor Franz Joseph "a plan to exterminate the human
race by withdrawing the oxygen from the air for a period of
two minutes." [42] Behind this savage mockery of mankind

lurks an old animus reawakened by turn-of-the-century warfare: revulsion against Christian nations warring anew against
other Christian nations, and overwhelming pagan countries
by conquest.

To illustrate, in the "Chronicle," Theodor promises to tell,
by and by, why Satan "chose China for this excursion." In
1897 Mark Twain was defending the Emperor of China, and in
1899 he clearly sided with the "cautious Chinaman" against
the "Western missionary." [43] By 1900 he was writing his
friend the Reverend Joseph H. Twichell, "It is all China, now,
and my sympathies are with the Chinese. They have," he
said, "been villainously dealt with by the sceptred thieves of
Europe, and I hope they will drive all the foreigners out and
keep them out for good." [44] Presumably he meant to make
some exemplary use of the Chinese Boxers' struggle against
the Powers, East and West. Satan develops the war motif to
the full by showing the boys a theatrical or visionary "history
of the progress of the human race" from Cain and Abel down
through the sixty wars fought during the reign of Queen Vic-
toria. And Mark Twain's last cartoon or cinema frames depict
England as fighting what he called elsewhere a "sordid &
criminal war" against the Transvaal Republic and the Orange
Free State in South Africa, and Europe as "swallowing
China"—proof, he commented, that "all the competent killers
are Christian." [45] Even Satan and Theodor's adventure with
the "foreigner in white linen and sun-helmet," who canes the
native juggler, thereby destroying the many-fruited tree and
bringing a fearful penalty upon himself, is a parable of British
imperialism in India and even a prediction of its end. Compare the tree-growing juggler in Ceylon with Dan Beard's
drawing of "The White Man's World," which shows the white
man in the sun-helmet and illustrates the Mark Twain assertion in the text: "The world was made for man—the white
man." [46]

The author's frame of mind, so often reflected in these war scenes and "stupendous processions," may be summed up in a statement from the summer of 1900:

> The time is grave. The future is blacker than has been any future which any person now living has tried to peer into.[47]

Small wonder, then, that Philip Traum should recount an up-to-date history of private and public murder in the "Chronicle." But the very heart of the matter, for Mark Twain, lay in man's foolish pride in his conscience, or the Moral Sense, its built-in unreliability as a moral guide, and its power to place him not only a little lower than the angels but decidedly lower than the animals. Philip Traum introduces the term "Moral Sense" to the boys, explaining that the difference between men and angels is almost incalculable—like the difference between Homer and a wood louse—and that men alone possess a Moral Sense that sets them off from angels and animals alike.[48] In Mark Twain's theology the Moral Sense parallels the original sin of Calvinism; but to Father Peter, who takes the traditional Christian view, it is "the one thing that lifts man above the beasts that perish and makes him heir to immortality" (p. 60).

The motif persists throughout the narrative. Satan, it follows, does not know right from wrong and lies harmlessly to Ursula. The episode of Hans Oppert's drunken clubbing of his dog develops the distinction: the act was not brutal, it was not inhuman, Satan tells the boys; it was "quite distinctly human" (p. 75). Perhaps, thinks Theodor, God would accept the dog's forgiveness of his master in place of the priest's. In other words, none of the higher animals is tainted with the disease called the Moral Sense. In the same way, after Theodor recalls to Satan the burning of the eleven schoolgirls as witches, Satan talks to a bullock from the fields, and represents the bullock as

stating that it would never "drive children mad with hunger
and fright and loneliness and then burn them for confessing to
things . . . which had never happened" (p. 80).

Then, when Theodor tries to reform Satan's "random-ness,"
the angel explains that the villagers have no sense, no intellect,
"Only the Moral Sense." Man, in short, is to Satan "as the red
spider" not so big as a pinhead "is to the elephant"; so that in
"power, intellect and dignity" the distance between them is
"simply astronomical" (pp. 113–14). Mark Twain may have
drawn his metaphor from the Jonathan Edwards sermon, "Sin-
ners in the Hands of an Angry God." Although Satan, with
perverse inconsistency, calls the villagers sheep for stoning,
out of fear, a lady who nursed the sick unconventionally, and
considers mankind mutton for following minority leadership
into war, he is vividly pictured in one scene as a kind of St.
Francis of Assisi among the animals, fascinating and fascinated, because he and they are kin in their freedom from the
Moral Sense.

The indictment of men as suffering, mortal, cowardly, cruel,
and foolish—and therefore inferior to angels and animals
alike—would seem to be fairly comprehensive. But Mark
Twain never quite gave up on men and women, just as he
never quite ceased writing about them. In the "Chronicle" the
power of the Immortal Mind to create is an angelic power, not
a human power—but the paradox is resolved in Clemens's creation of Satan, who calmly asserts:

> Man's mind clumsily and tediously and laboriously patches lit-
> tle trivialities together, and gets a result—such as it is. My mind
> *creates!* . . . Creates anything it desires—and in a moment.
> Creates without materials; creates fluids, solids, colors—
> anything, everything—out of the airy nothing which is called
> Thought. . . . I *think* a poem—music—the record of a game of
> chess—anything—and it is there. This is the immortal mind—
> nothing is beyond its reach. (P. 114)

The power of music had been demonstrated, rather in the style of Tom Sawyer, when Philip Traum had set Meidling's narrative poem to music, *extempore*. But for Samuel L. Clemens the power was real, whether it came from the Negro spirituals he sang with such fervor and artistry or from the music he liked so much from his *Orchestrelle,* a kind of proto-phonograph he had brought back from Switzerland. Ultimately it was, as Theodor claims, the ability to laugh, however poorly developed, that distinguished the race; and Satan, in his sharp fashion, admits it:

> Will a day come when the race will detect the funniness of these juvenilities and laugh at them—and by laughing destroy them? For your race, in its poverty, has unquestionably one really effective weapon—laughter. Power, Money, Persuasion, Supplication, Persecution—these can lift at a colossal humbug,—push it a little—crowd it a little—weaken it a little, century by century: but only Laughter can blow it to rags and atoms at a blast. Against the assault of Laughter nothing can stand. (Pp. 165–66).

So, thematically, the "Chronicle" is built on alternatives of these negative and positive strains. Perhaps it was this contrast that wrung from Livy Clemens, when her husband read her the opening chapters, the tribute, "It is perfectly horrible—and perfectly beautiful." [49] Humor and music as catharsis, and satire as corrective and perspective, are omnipresent in Mark Twain's theory and writings. The citizens of Hadleyburg, we recall, restore their town's reputation for honesty by laughing down their "incorruptible" leading citizens, whom another "mysterious stranger" had beguiled and exposed. But in these stories and other late writings, the author could never quite decide whether laughter was divine or only human. Of all the paradoxes in the "Chronicle" none is more paradoxical, or more sanative, than the humorist's demonstrations of the power of laughter—could it be *merely* human?—in the empty spaces of the universe.

The art of the "Chronicle," my argument concludes, is in kind if not in magnitude the art of Michelangelo's figures in the partly finished, roughly finished, unfinished stone. The kinesthetic thrust of the emerging figures, the pattern of actions and thoughts, are sufficiently there, though the witness cannot predict what the artist might finally have achieved. One clear element in Mark Twain's art is the invention of the adult narrator (in this case Theodor Fischer) looking back on his youthful encounter with an angel, for Theodor resists Satan's arguments sometimes in unconscious superstition, sometimes persuasively, sometimes rebelliously—but nearly always with a boyish love of Satan's power and knowledge. Theodor is Faust in his boyhood. A second element creating imaginative force in the "Chronicle" is the alternation of terror and pathos. The pattern is set in Philip Traum's first deed—that of creating and then destroying a small community. Like a red thread, it follows through the burning at the stake of the schoolgirls, old Mrs. Narr warming her hands at the fire and choosing to burn rather than to starve, Theodor and Seppi's kindness to their doomed friend Nikolaus, and Theodor's stoning the dying lady—like nearly all the other villagers, out of fear. It culminates in Satan's bloody pageant of men at war and his ridicule of the shamed trio of boys—then gently drinking a health with them in wine that he brings down from heaven.

There are, apparently, fissures in the character of Philip Traum/Satan. But while he is indifferent to men and contemptuous of them, he is friendly to the boys and more than willing to "show off" in front of Lilly Fischer and Marget. In one of his avatars he behaves like Tom Sawyer granted magical powers, and in another he is a god, omnipresent and immortal. Yet finally the "Chronicle" revolves around this flawed figure, and Mark Twain succeeds with the protean characterization very much as he did, though more consistently, with Huckleberry Finn.

Satan is in fact a Prospero figure, endowed with the poet's wit and charm and vitality. For the boys' pleasure he produces fire and ice with his breath, and vanishes into thin air like a soap bubble, "a strange and beautiful thing to see." He makes the boys glad before he reappears, and affects Ursula and the thin kitten like a "fresh breeze." When he appears at Marget's party, the atmosphere becomes "cool and fresh" though the sun was strong outside. At Marget's house, later, he "brought that winy atmosphere of his" with him. At the Fischers' he came in "cheerful as a bird, and his coming was like the sea-breeze invading a sick-room." Philip Traum's influence is a dramatizing of Pudd'nhead Wilson's aphorism, "It is your human environment that makes climate."

The last secret of Satan's force as a character, however, lies in "the fatal music of his voice," which is to say, the vitality of his author's rhetoric, whether he is describing the fate of characters whose life course he has altered at the boys' pleading, or predicting dreadful wars in the future, or confounding a murderous gamekeeper with secret knowledge of his past, or rewarding Father Peter with happy insanity. In sum, the hands are the hands of Philip Traum, creating the Lilliputian villagers or juggling a hundred balls in the skin of Father Adolf—but the voice is the voice of Samuel Clemens–Mark Twain, the artist, that "veteran trader in shadows."

Appendix

———◆·◆———

Twice in his lifetime Mark Twain had to defend his "abused child," *Huckleberry Finn*. In the summer of 1902 the Denver Public Library eliminated *Huckleberry Finn* from its shelves, along with Kate Chopin's *The Awakening*. The Denver *Post* wired Mark Twain for a comment. Apparently the novel was replaced on the library shelves "as soon as the appropriation" permitted its purchase. The *Post* printed his reply in full, on page 1 of the issue of 18 August 1902—thus:

Your telegram reached me (per post) from "York Village" (which is a short brickbat throw from my house) yesterday afternoon when it was thirty hours old. And yet, in my experience, that was not only abnormally quick work for a telegraph company to do, but abnormally intelligent work for that kind of mummy to be whirling off out of its alleged mind.

Twenty-four hours earlier the Country club had noticed me that a stranger in Portsmouth (a half-hour from here) wished me to come to the club at 7:30 p.m. and call him up and talk upon a matter of business. I said: "Let him take the trolley and come over, if his business is worth the time and the fare to him." It was doubtless yourself—and not in Portsmouth, but in Denver. I was not thinking much about business at the time, for the reason that a consultation of physicians was appointed for that hour (7:30) at my house to consider if means might be devised to save my wife's life. At the present writing—Thursday afternoon—it is believed that she will recover.

When the watch was relieved an hour ago and I left the sick chamber to take my respite I began to frame answers to your dispatch, but it was only to entertain myself, for I am aware that I am not privileged to speak freely in this matter, funny as the occasion is and dearly as I should like to laugh at it; and when I can't speak freely I don't speak at all.

You see, there are two or three pointers:

First—Huck Finn was turned out of a New England library seventeen years ago—ostensibly on account of his morals; really to curry favor with a personage. There has been no other instance until now.

Second—A few months ago I published an article which threw mud at that pinchbeck hero, Funston, and his extraordinary morals.

Third—Huck's morals have stood the strain in Denver and in every English, German and French-speaking community in the world—save one—for seventeen years until now.

Fourth—The strain breaks the connection now.

Fifth—In Denver alone.

Sixth—Funston commands there.

Seventh—And has dependents and influence.

When one puts these things together the cat that is in the meal is disclosed—and quite unmistakably.

Said cat consists of a few persons who wish to curry favor with Funston, and whom God has not dealt kindly with in the matter of wisdom.

Everybody in Denver knows this, even the dead people in the cemeteries. It may be that Funston has wit enough to know that these good idiots are adding another howling absurdity to his funny history; it may be that God has charitably spared him that degree of penetration, slight as it is; in any case he is—as usual—a proper object of compassion, and the bowels of my sympathy are moved toward him.

There's nobody for me to attack in this matter even with soft and gentle ridicule—and I shouldn't ever think of using a grown-up weapon in this kind of nursery. Above all, I couldn't venture to attack the clergymen whom you mention for I have their habits and live in the same glass house which they are occupying. I am always reading immoral books on the sly and then selfishly trying to prevent other people from having the same wicked good time.

No, if Satan's morals and Funston's are preferable to Huck's, let Huck's take a back seat; they can stand any ordinary competition, but not a combination like that. And I'm not going to defend them anyway.

York Harbor, Aug. 14, 1902. Sincerely yours, S. L. CLEMENS.

The tone of the reply is to be understood only as one realizes that it was originally a private letter to a "Denver friend." In an interview with a reporter on the New York *World* some two weeks later, Clemens remarked: "Now, that was a very funny thing about that letter getting into print. You see I sent it to my man marked 'Private,' and that was a sure sign that it was going to be published." [1] The reference to Livy's serious illness, the admitted reluctance to respond at all to so foolish an action, and the rambling nature of the letter all indicate that it was intended as a private communication, though the allusions to General Funston echo the polemics of his "Defence of General Funston," published in the *North American Review* in May, just three months earlier. But the letter is more a fact in Mark Twain's biography than it is a commentary on *Adventures of Huckleberry Finn*.

1. New York *World*, 7 September 1902, as cited in Charles Neider, *Mark Twain Life As I Find It* (Garden City, N.Y.: Hanover House, 1961), p. 362.

Abbreviations

Some of the references to published works in the footnotes are double. The first reference is to an early form of Mark Twain's printed text, usually the first edition, and *the quotation is taken from this text.* The second reference, within parentheses, is for the convenience of the reader and is to a more generally available text, such as "Nat Ed," the Author's National Edition published by Harper & Brothers and reprinted from the same plates by P. F. Collier & Son.

MS   Manuscript
MT   Mark Twain
MTP   The Mark Twain Papers, University of California, Berkeley
Nat Ed   Author's National Edition, *The Writings of Mark Twain,* 24 vols.
SLC   Samuel Langhorne Clemens
TS   Typescript
WDH   W. D. Howells

AHF   *Adventures of Huckleberry Finn.* New York: Webster, 1885. AHF Nat Ed.

ATS   *The Adventures of Tom Sawyer.* Hartford: American Publishing Co., 1876. ATS Nat Ed.

CSS   *Complete Short Stories of Mark Twain,* ed. Charles Neider. Garden City, N.Y.: Doubleday, 1957.

CY   *A Connecticut Yankee in King Arthur's Court.* New York: Webster, 1889. CY Nat Ed.

EE   *Europe and Elsewhere,* ed. A. B. Paine. New York: Harper, 1923.

FE　*Following the Equator, A Journey Around the World.* Hartford: American Publishing Co., 1897.

IL　In holograph of Isabel Lyon.

LoM　*Life on the Mississippi.* Boston: Osgood, 1883. LoM Nat Ed, 2 vols.

MSM ChYS　"The Chronicle of Young Satan," *The Mysterious Stranger Manuscripts,* ed. William M. Gibson. Berkeley: University of California Press, 1969.

MSM No. 44　"No. 44, The Mysterious Stranger," *The Mysterious Stranger Manuscripts.* Berkeley: University of California Press, 1969.

MTB　Albert Bigelow Paine, *Mark Twain, a Biography.* New York: Harper, 1912.

MTHL　*Mark Twain-Howells Letters,* ed. Henry Nash Smith and William M. Gibson. 2 vols. Cambridge: Harvard University Press, 1960.

MTJB　Howard G. Baetzhold, *Mark Twain and John Bull.* Bloomington: Indiana University Press, 1970.

MTL　*Mark Twain's Letters,* ed. A. B. Paine. 2 vols. New York: Harper, 1917.

MTLS　John S. Tuckey, *Mark Twain and Little Satan, the Writing of The Mysterious Stranger.* West Lafayette, Ind.: Purdue University Press, 1963.

MTN　*Mark Twain's Notebook,* ed. A. B. Paine. New York: Harper, 1935.

NYPL　New York Public Library.

PortMT　*The Portable Mark Twain,* ed. Bernard DeVoto. New York: Viking Press, 1946.

TPW　*The Tragedy of Pudd'nhead Wilson . . .* Hartford: American Publishing Co., 1894. TPW Nat Ed.

RI　*Roughing It.* Hartford: American Publishing Co., 1872. RI Nat Ed, 2 vols.

SNO　*Sketches New and Old.* Hartford: American Publishing Co., 1875. SNO Nat Ed.

SWE　*The Stolen White Elephant Etc.* Boston: Osgood, 1882.

TA　*A Tramp Abroad.* Hartford: American Publishing Co., 1880. TA Nat Ed.

NOTES

CHAPTER 1

1. William M. Gibson, ed., in *Howells and James; A Double Billing* (New York: New York Public Library, 1958); *My Mark Twain* (New York: Harper, 1910), p. 101.
2. T. S. Eliot, introd., AHF (New York: Chanticleer Press, 1950), p. vii.
3. Quoted in George Bainton, ed., *The Art of Authorship* (New York: Appleton, 1890), pp. 87–88.
4. In LoM, p. 389; Nat Ed, pp. 306–7.
5. MSM ChYS, p. 50. This music is a prime source of Philip Traum's power over the boys of the tale.
6. In *The Curious Republic of Gondour and Other Whimsical Sketches* (New York: Boni and Liveright, 1919), pp. 36–41.
7. See *Satires and Burlesques* (Berkeley: University of California Press, 1967).
8. See MTHL, p. 370 n1.
9. From Alma B. Martin, *A Vocabulary Study of "The Gilded Age"* (Webster Groves, Mo.: Mark Twain Society, 1930), p. 3, as quoted in MTHL, p. 321. RI, p. 124; Nat Ed, 1:107.
10. Robert L. Ramsay and Frances G. Emberson, *A Mark Twain Lexicon* (1938; reprint ed., New York: Russell & Russell, 1963), p. xiii.
11. PortMT, pp. 773–75.
12. MSM No. 44, pp. 221–405.
13. MTHL, pp. 652, 653 n2.

14. Supplement, 1938, to the *Oxford English Dictionary; Webster's Third New International Dictionary*, 1966.
15. RI, p. 200 (Nat Ed, 1:191).
16. RI, pp. 228–29 (Nat Ed, 1:221).
17. SWE, pp. 286–87.
18. SNO, pp. 148, 145 (Nat Ed, pp. 167, 164).
19. SNO, pp. 23, 22 (Nat Ed, pp. 9, 7).
20. TPW, pp. 408–9 (Nat Ed, pp. 278–79).
21. See MTJB, p. 36.
22. *A Horse's Tale* (New York: Harper, 1907), pp. 57–58; CSS, p. 537.
23. In MTHL, p. 765.
24. *The Gilded Age* (1873), pp. 246–47 (Nat Ed, 1:267–70).
25. MTHL, p. 235.
26. MTL, 1:183.
27. Franklin Rogers, ed. *Satires and Burlesques*, p. 165. See also William M. Gibson, a note on "snivelization," forthcoming in *American Speech.*
28. RI, pp. 335–36 (Nat Ed, 2:50).
29. Quoted in MTHL, pp. 160–61.
30. See Henry Seidel Canby, *Turn West, Turn East, Mark Twain and Henry James* (Boston: Houghton Mifflin, 1951), p. 180.
31. In Howells, *A Fearful Responsibility* (Boston: Osgood, 1881), p. 109; William Safire, *The New Language of Politics* (New York: Macmillan, Collier Books, 1972), pp. 416–18.
32. Gerard Manley Hopkins, "Pied Beauty," *Poems of Gerard Manley Hopkins* (London: Oxford, 1931), 2d edition, p. 30.
33. Ford quoted in Bernard DeVoto, *Mark Twain's America* (Boston: Little, Brown, 1932), pp. 265, 317.
34. "The Turning Point of My Life," *What Is Man? and Other Essays* (New York: Harper, 1917), p. 136.
35. *The Spirit of American Literature* (Garden City: Doubleday, Page, 1913) as quoted in Gladys Carmen Bellamy, *Mark Twain as a Literary Artist* (Norman: University of Oklahoma Press, 1950), p. 22.
36. A. B. Paine, ed., *Mark Twain's Speeches* (New York: Harper, 1923), pp. 2–4, "On Speech-Making Reform."
37. MTHL, p. 46.
38. MTHL, p. 26.
39. Respectively, TA, p. 37 (Nat Ed, 1:17); MTHL, p. 761; AHF, p. 60 (Nat Ed, p. 49); *Eve's Diary* (New York: Harper, 1906), p. 59; *A Horse's Tale* (New York: Harper, 1907), p. 6; CSS, p. 524; AHF, p. 93 (Nat Ed, p. 88).

40. LoM, p. 574 (Nat Ed, p. 478); PortMT, p. 774; CY, p. 292 (Nat Ed, p. 215).
41. SWE, p. 118.
42. "To the Person Sitting in Darkness," EE, p. 255.
43. See "William Dean Howells," *What Is Man? and Other Essays* (New York: Harper, 1917), pp. 228–39.
44. MTB, p. 1073; Hamlin Hill, *Mark Twain: God's Fool* (New York: Harper & Row, 1973), p. 12.
45. In MTHL, p. 112.
46. From "The Contributors' Club," *Atlantic,* 45 (June 1880): 851, as quoted in MTHL, p. 321.
47. SNO, p. 24; CSS, p.62.
48. RI, p. 383 (Nat Ed, 2:98).
49. RI, p. 441 (Nat Ed, 2:161).
50. "Fenimore Cooper's Literary Offences," *How to Tell a Story and Other Essays* (New York: Harper, 1897), p. 96; *Literary Essays,* Nat Ed, p. 62.
51. AHF, p. 108 (Nat Ed, p. 105); ATS, pp. 21, 31, 31 (Nat Ed, pp. 6,17,18). "New Century Greeting Which Mark Twain Recalled," New York *Herald* (30 December 1900), p. 7 (EE, p. xxxiv.)
52. TA, p. 37 (Nat Ed, 1:17).
53. TPW, p. 130 (Nat Ed, p. 83).
54. LoM, pp. 63–64 (Nat Ed, pp. 32–33).
55. From "The McWilliamses and the Burglar Alarm," *The Mysterious Stranger and Other Stories* (New York: Harper, 1922), pp. 316–17.
56. Eliot in the figure of the "dark brown god" in *Four Quartets;* Trilling in introd. to AHF (New York: Holt, Rinehart & Winston, 1948); and Smith in "Mark Twain as an Interpreter of the Far West: The Structure of *Roughing It,*" in *The Frontier in Perspective* (Madison: University of Wisconsin Press, 1957), pp. 205–28.
57. In "Mark Twain's Use of the Comic Pose," *PMLA,* 77 (June 1962):297.
58. See *My Mark Twain* (New York: Harper, 1910), p. 5.
59. Bernard DeVoto, ed., *Mark Twain in Eruption* (New York: Harper, 1940), pp. 110–11.
60. MSM No. 44, pp. 354–56.
61. This letter from Carson City, appearing in the *Territorial Enterprise* of 3 February 1863, is the first piece by Clemens known to be signed "Mark Twain." See Henry Nash Smith, *Mark Twain of the Enterprise . . . 1862–1864* (Berkeley: University of California Press, 1957), p. 50.

CHAPTER 2

1. Henry James to Henry Adams, 21 March 1914, in Leon Edel, ed., *The Selected Letters of Henry James* (New York: Farrar, Straus & Cudahy, 1955), p. 174.

2. MTB, pp. 433–39; Henry Nash Smith, "Mark Twain as Interpreter of the Far West: The Structure of *Roughing It*," in *The Frontier in Perspective* (Madison: University of Wisconsin Press, 1957), pp. 206–28.

3. RI, p. 19 (Nat Ed, 1:1–2). Hereafter cited in the text by page number or chapter number.

4. MTB, p. 440.

5. RI, chaps. 31–33 (Nat Ed, 1, ibid.).

6. MTB, pp. 438–40.

7. MTB, p. 273.

8. *My Mark Twain* (New York: Harper, 1910), p.29.

9. RI, chaps. 22–29 (Nat Ed, 1, ibid.).

10. MTB, pp. 201–2.

11. RI, chaps. 58–60, 78 (Nat Ed, 2:17–19, 37). Mark Twain probably exaggerates his poverty. Failing to read the note and missing the steamer at the dock sound suspiciously like the denouement of the Wide West Mine story. The "luxurious vagrancy" in the Sandwich Islands was filled with writing, and concluded with a journalistic scoop—the stories of the survivors of the clipper ship *Hornet*. "The Celebrated Jumping Frog" had made Mark Twain widely known in the United States even earlier. He mentions neither of these coups. Nor does he ever hint that he had addressed audiences before with distinct success.

12. Louis J. Budd, *Mark Twain: Social Philosopher* (Bloomington: Indiana University Press, 1962), p. 46.

13. Smith, "Mark Twain as Interpreter of the Far West . . . ," pp. 210–12; Gerber, "Mark Twain's Use of the Comic Pose," *PMLA*, 77 (June 1962):301–2.

14. Johnson Jones Hooper, *Some Adventures of Captain Simon Suggs* (Philadelphia: H. C. Baird, 1850), p. 12.

15. RI, pp. 23, 295 (Nat Ed, 1:5, 2:4).

16. Other anecdotes serve the same thematic end: Jack's preferring Ben Halliday to Moses as a guide in the desert; Jim Townsend's tunnel or trestle-work; the adventure of Colonel Jim and Colonel Jack, nabobs, in New York City; the miners who "fetched out" an

emigrant's sick wife and presented to her husband a hatful of gold, just for the glimpse of a woman; the splendid Blucher, who when he was hungry and had only a dime fed an even hungrier man a six-dollar dinner on his credit. Conversely, Mark Twain might better have eliminated or used in some other work his coat-eating camel, or the simpletons who fall spectacularly from Mont Blanc, or the four-times-repeated "joke" of Hank Monk and Horace Greeley.

17. RI, chaps. 7, 15, 24, 34, 47, 50, 53, 61, 62, 70, 77 (correspondingly, Nat Ed, 1:7, 15, 24, 34, and 2:6, 9, 12, 20, 21, 29, 36).

18. From the 1879 text as quoted in Constance Rourke, *American Humor: A Study of the National Character* (New York: Harcourt Brace, 1931), p. 247.

19. Dixon Wecter, ed., *The Love Letters of Mark Twain* (New York: Harper, 1949), p. 166; MTHL, pp. 34–35.

20. MTHL, p. 49. Mark Twain's awareness of his audience of readers as well as listeners and his capacity to profit from intelligent criticism are scarcely recognized as yet and therefore not understood. He kept a clipping file and read attentively newspaper criticism of his lectures.

21. MTHL, p. 46.

22. At the height of his success as pilot of the *City of Memphis*, Clemens admitted to his brother Orion that certain young rivals had believed he would never learn the river. But Clemens learned the river quickly, in eighteen months rather than the usual two and one-half years; he had a fine memory for its changing complexities; he became an excellent pilot and had only one minor accident in four years at the wheel, surely a superior record. Horace Bixby told Paine many years later that "Sam was a fine pilot" (MTB, p. 146).

23. LoM, chap. 5. Hereafter referred to in the text by chapter or page number.

24. Odell Shepard, ed., *The Heart of Thoreau's Journals* (Boston: Houghton Mifflin, 1927), p. 11.

25. As Emerson writes in "The Poet": "We are not pans and barrows, nor even porters of the fire and torch-bearers, but children of the fire." Stephen E. Whicher, ed., *Selections from Ralph Waldo Emerson* (Boston: Houghton Mifflin, 1957), p. 223.

26. Bernard DeVoto, *Mark Twain's America* (Boston: Little, Brown, 1932), p. 59.

27. TA, pp. 156–59 (Nat Ed, 1:136–39). Mark Twain had produced his own version of "The Raging Canal" earlier in RI (chap. 51), under the title "The Aged Pilot Man."
28. See James, "The New Novel," *Notes on Novelists* (London: Dent, 1914), pp. 273–79.
29. *The Mysterious Stranger and Other Stories* (New York: Harper, 1922), p. 284. "A Fable" was first published in 1909.

CHAPTER 3

1. "Jim Blaine and His Grandfather's Ram," part of chap. 53 of *Roughing It;* "A Medieval Romance," Buffalo *Express,* 1 January 1870, and CSS, pp. 50–56.
2. "The Notorious Jumping Frog of Calaveras County," in *The Celebrated Jumping Frog of Calaveras County, and Other Sketches* (New York: C. H. Webb, 1867), pp. 7–19. Hereafter by page number. Originally "The Notorious Jumping Frog of Calaveras County," *Saturday Press,* 18 November and 16 December, 1865; see also CSS, pp. 1–6.
3. SLC to Jane Clemens, 20 January 1866; MTL, p. 101.
4. See Bernard DeVoto, *Mark Twain's America* (Boston: Little, Brown, 1932), p. 174 and Appendix B.
5. 28 January 1866, as reprinted in *The Washoe Giant in San Francisco,* ed. Franklin Walker (San Francisco: George Fields, 1938), pp. 104–5.
6. Letter 16 April 1867 to the *Alta California.* In *Mark Twain's Travels with Mr. Brown,* eds. Franklin Walker and G. Ezra Dane (New York: Knopf, 1940), p. 144.
7. Ibid., pp. 188–89, Letter of 18 May 1867.
8. "A True Story," *Atlantic,* 34 (November 1874): 591–94. See MTB, p. 509.
9. MTHL, pp. 22–23.
10. Jer. 31:15. See *Moby-Dick* (New York: Norton, 1967), chap. 128, "The Pequod Meets the Rachel."
11. "A True Story," p. 594. Hereafter cited in text by page number.
12. Mary Lawton, *A Lifetime with Mark Twain* (New York: Harcourt Brace, 1925), p. 213.
13. MTHL, p. 25.
14. Ibid., pp. 25–26.
15. Reproduced respectively in SNO, pp. 85–92, SWE, pp. 206–16, and *Harper's Christmas,* pp. 28–29.

16. *The Mysterious Stranger and Other Stories* (New York: Harper, 1922), p. 315. Hereafter cited in text by page.

17. "Some Rambling Notes of an Idle Excursion, The Invalid's Story," SWE, p. 102; CSS, p. 191.

18. MTHL, pp. 701–2.

19. The text quoted and discussed here is from this edition from the manuscripts, by Dixon Wecter (New York: Harper, 1952).

20. *Report from Paradise*, Introduction, p. xi. Hereafter *Report*.

21. Ibid.

22. Bernard DeVoto, ed., *Mark Twain in Eruption* (New York: Harper, 1940), p. 247. Dictation of 29 August 1906.

23. Elizabeth Stuart Phelps Ward, *The Gates Ajar* (Boston: Fields, Osgood, 1868). The relevant passages are on pp. 10, 77–78, 81, 88, 115, 120, 125, 142–44, 154, 163, 188, 224, and 238.

24. *The Curious Republic of Gondour . . .* , pp. 25–29.

25. *Gates Ajar*, p. 78.

26. *Report*, pp. 60–61. Hereafter cited in text by page number.

27. *Report*, pp. 33–34. Stormfield remembers being at the Pi-Ute's funeral. He had been cremated, and the other Indians had gaumed their faces with his ashes and howled like wildcats. Compare the comment by Elizabeth Phelps's *raisonneur*: "Picture the touching scene, when that devoted husband, King Mausolas, whose widow had him burned and ate the ashes, should feel moved to institute a search for his body!" *Gates Ajar*, p. 115.

28. "Novel-Reading and Novel-Writing," in *Howells and James: A Double Billing*, p. 23. *The Man That Corrupted Hadleyburg and Other Stories and Essays* (New York: Harper, 1900), pp. 1–83. Hereafter cited in text by page number.

29. In *The $30,000 Bequest and Other Stories* (New York: Harper, 1906), pp. 160–65 (Nat Ed, pp. 218–23).

30. A. E. Housman trans., in Mark Van Doren, ed., *An Anthology of World Poetry* (New York: Albert and Charles Boni, 1929), pp. 276–77.

31. FE, 19:184 (Nat Ed, 1:167). MTHL, p. 854.

CHAPTER 4

1. Walter Blair, *Mark Twain and Huck Finn* (Berkeley: University of California Press, 1960), pp. 66–67.

2. ATS, pp. 189–90 (Nat Ed, p. 198).

3. ATS, p. 160 (Nat Ed, pp. 168–69).
4. J. D. Salinger, *Catcher in the Rye* (Boston: Little, Brown, 1951), p. 182.
5. ATS, p. 96 (Nat Ed, pp. 91–92). The convention bears some resemblance to Clemens's writing a 400-page manuscript on the rascality, as he saw it, of Isabel Lyon, his former secretary, in the form of a letter to WDH. See MTHL, pp. 844–45, and Hamlin Hill, *Mark Twain: God's Fool* (New York: Harper & Row, 1973), pp. 228–32.
6. In *Howells and James : A Double Billing*, pp. 22–23.
7. In his introd. to AHF, p. viii.
8. ATS, chaps. 18, 19.
9. In Lowell's *Poetical Works* (Boston: Houghton Mifflin, 1890), 1:180, 181.
10. Cable collected his articles and addresses on the rights of Negroes in *The Silent South* (1885) and *The Negro Question* (1890).
11. John 13:34. "A new commandment I give unto you, that ye love one another; as I have loved you, that ye also love one another."
12. Auction Catalogue, Anderson Galleries, February 7 and 8, 1911, item 373, p. 56. MS in MTP.
13. See Philip S. Foner, *Mark Twain Social Critic* (New York: International Press, 1958), pp. 220–21. EE, pp. 239–49.
14. Notebook 35 (1902), TS in MTP; as quoted in *The Mysterious Stranger Manuscripts*, p. 26.
15. In *The Liberal Imagination* (New York: Viking, 1950), p. 222.
16. MTHL, p. 24.
17. Arthur L. Vogelback, "The Publication and Reception of *Huckleberry Finn* in America," *American Literature*, 11 (November 1939): 260–72, esp. p. 270.
18. MTHL, pp. 877–78.
19. Notebook No. 28a TS, p. 35(1895), MTP, as quoted in Henry Nash Smith, AHF (Boston: Houghton Mifflin, 1958), p. xvi, n11.

CHAPTER 5

1. William M. Gibson, "Mark Twain and Howells, Anti-Imperialists," *New England Quarterly*, 20 (December 1947):455, quoting "Mark Twain: An Inquiry," *North American Review*, 172 (February 1901): 321; *My Mark Twain*, p. 185.

2. "Mark Twain and Howells, Anti-Imperialists," p. 468.
3. MTHL, p. 235.
4. Henry Nash Smith, ed., *Mark Twain of the Enterprise* (Berkeley: University of California Press, 1957), p. 200.
5. MTHL, p. 613.
6. Quoted in Arthur L. Scott, ed., *Mark Twain: Selected Criticism* (Dallas: Southern Methodist University Press, 1955), pp. 103, 171.
7. *Galaxy*, 10 and 11 (October, November 1870, January 1871): 569–71, 727–31, 156–58; *The Curious Republic of Gondour and Other Whimsical Sketches*, pp. 75–109.
8. See Herman Melville, *Mardi and A Voyage Thither* (Evanston and Chicago: Northwestern-Newberry, 1970), pp. 512–13.
9. In Samuel C. Webster, *Mark Twain, Business Man* (Boston: Little, Brown, 1946), pp. 253, 255–56.
10. *Atlantic*, 36 (October 1875):461–63; *The Curious Republic of Gondour . . .* , pp. 1–11.
11. Included in Dixon Wecter, ed., *Report*, pp. 87–94.
12. Quoted in Bernard DeVoto, ed., *Mark Twain in Eruption*, p. 293.
13. MTHL, p. 609.
14. LoM, p. 87 (Nat Ed, p. 50).
15. *Report*, p. 90.
16. Ibid., p. 93.
17. Ibid., pp. 93–94.
18. The difference in mood is clear in Mark Twain's explanation to Howells:

> I wish I *could* give those sharp satires on European life which you mention, but of course a man can't write successful satire except he be in a calm judicial good-humor—whereas I *hate* travel, & I *hate* hotels, & I *hate* the opera, & I *hate* the Old Masters—in truth I don't ever seem to be in a good enough humor with ANYthing to *satirize* it; no, I want to stand up before it & *curse* it, & foam at the mouth,—or take a club & pound it to rags & pulp. (MTHL, pp. 248–49)

19. MTB, p. 1097; New York *World* (14 October 1900), p. 3; quoted in "Mark Twain and Howells, Anti-Imperialists," p. 444.
20. Edwin H. Cady, *The Realist at War . . .* (Syracuse: Syracuse University Press, 1958), pp. 67–80, 147–48.
21. As reported in New York *Herald* (16 October 1900), p. 4; New York *Times Saturday Review of Books and Art* (24 November 1900), p. 9.

22. As quoted in Boston *Evening Transcript* (14 December 1900), p. 9.
23. *Life in Letters of William Dean Howells* (Garden City: Doubleday, Doran, 1928), 2:141.
24. New York *Herald* (30 December 1900), p. 7.
25. Respectively, MTHL, pp. 318–19; MTB, p. 772; MTHL, pp. 611–12, 624.
26. See Arthur L. Vogelback, "Mark Twain and the Tammany Ring," *PMLA*, 77 (March 1955): 69–77.
27. At the top of the card appears the line, "Copies supplied by Albert S. Parsons, Lexington, Mass."; William Augustus Croffut Papers, Library of Congress.
28. MTL, 2:706.
29. *My Father Mark Twain* (New York: Harper, 1931), p. 220.
30. Merle Johnson, *Mark Twain Bibliography* (New York: Harper, 1935), p. 73.
31. *North American Review*, 172 (February 1901):161–76; *To the Person Sitting in Darkness. . . . Reprinted by Permission from the North American Review, February, 1901* (New York, 1901). Published between February 1901 and 8 May 1901, the accession date of the Library of Congress copy. Hereafter cited in text by page number.
32. MTB, p. 1129; *Mark Twain Bibliography*, p. 73.
33. MTB, pp. 1132–33.
34. Elizabeth G. Evans, "William James and His Wife," *Atlantic*, 144 (September 1929):378.
35. Mark Twain Papers, DV 128 (7).
36. In John S. Tuckey, ed., *Mark Twain's Fables of Man* (Berkeley: University of California Press, 1972), pp. 405–19.

CHAPTER 6

1. The chief sources for these maxims, apart from *The Tragedy of Pudd'nhead Wilson* and *Following the Equator* are A. B. Paine, ed., *Mark Twain's Notebook* (New York: Harper, 1935), pp. 327–28, 343–47, 379–82, and 385 (some 75 maxims), and the Mark Twain Papers (a large group published and unpublished).
2. "Diversions of the Higher Journalist, Reversible Proverbs," *Harper's Weekly*, 47 (12 September 1903):1472.
3. FE, chaps. 45, 41; MS of both in MTP.
4. MTP; TPW, chap. 21, MS in MTP; MTP. Previously unpublished material.

5. MTN, p. 12 (1866); TPW, chap. 8.
6. TPW, chap. 10; variant versions in MTP.
7. MTN, p. 344, 1898; MTP, TS and MS in I. L.; TPW, chap. 20, and MS in MTP. Previously unpublished material.
8. MTN, p. 345.
9. FE, chap. 54, MS in MTP; MS in MTP from IL; MS in MTP in Olivia Clemens's handwriting; MTP. Previously unpublished material.
10. FE, chap. 66, MTN, p. 327 (1897), and MS in MTP; variant in MS notebook prior to June 1904, quoted by Hamlin Hill in *Mark Twain, God's Fool* (New York: Harper & Row, 1973), p. 61.
11. TPW, chap. 21.
12. MTN, p. 12; FE, chaps. 40, 39, MSS in MTP; FE, chap. 27, MTN, p. 347 (1898).
13. MTN, p. 346 (1898); MTN, p. 240 (late 1894); MTN, p. 346.
14. MS in NYPL, copy in MTP; MS in NYPL, copy in MTP; MS in MTP, TPW, chap. 9. Previously unpublished material.
15. MS in NYPL, copy in MTP. Previously unpublished material.
16. TPW, chap. 4; TPW, chap. 2, long MS variant in MTP and MTN, p. 275 (post January 1896); MS in MTP, revised in FE, chap. 33.
17. MS in MTP, cut and revised in TPW, chap. 14.
18. TPW, chap. 13, MS in MTP; MTN, pp. 344, 345; MS in MTP.
19. MTN, p. 346 (1898); MTN, p. 128, variant version, p. 182 (1885).
20. MTN, p. 344; MTN, p. 328.
21. MTN, p. 344; MTN, p. 237 (1894); MS in IL, copy in MTP; MS in IL, copy in MTP. Previously unpublished material.
22. Quoted in Anderson Galleries Catalogue (1911), p. 56, MS in MTP; MTN, p. 346 (1898).
23. FE, chap. 39, MS in MTP; MTB, p. 559.
24. TS in MTP; MTN, p. 347 (1898), and FE, chap. 18; MS in IL, copy in MTP, MTN, p. 379 (December 1902), and MTN, p. 312 (December 1896). Previously unpublished material.
25. MS in IL, TS in MTP. Previously unpublished material.
26. MS in MTP, FE, chap. 28; MS in MTP, revised in FE, chap. 46.
27. MS in MTP, cut and revised in TPW, chap. 18.
28. FE, chap. 26; MTN, p. 235 (1894).
29. MTN, p. 381 (May 1903); MS in MTP, quoted only in part. Previously unpublished material.
30. MS in MTP, quoted only in part; MTN, pp. 236–37 (1894). Previously unpublished material.

31. FE, chap. 19; TPW, chap. 3.
32. TPW, chap. 10.
33. MTN, p. 344 (1898); MS in MTP, FE, chap. 59; MTB, p. 706, revised, MTN, p. 380 (December 1902); and MS in IL, copy in MTP. Previously unpublished material.
34. FE, chap. 44, MS in MTP; MS in MTP; FE, chap. 61; MTN, p. 235 (1893). Previously unpublished material.
35. FE, chap. 37; TS of Aphorisms, vol. 20, p. 3 in MTP; MTN, p. 346 (1898); MS in MTP. Previously unpublished material.
36. MS in MTP. Previously unpublished material.
37. FE, chap 8, longer MS version in MTP; TS in MTP; MTN, p. 347 (summer 1898). Previously unpublished material.
38. FE, chap. 65, MS in MTP.
39. FE, chap. 67.
40. MTN, p. 217 (1891).
41. MTN, p. 344; MTN, p. 298 (1896 more fully); MTN, p. 153, 1879; FE, chap. 17; FE, "Conclusion."
42. MS in IL, copy in MTP; MTN, p. 170 (1884), and MTHL, pp. 509–10; MTN, p. 256. Previously unpublished material.
43. MS in IL, TS under vol. 2 in MTP; FE, chap. 38, MS in MTP; FE, chap. 56, MS in MTP. Previously unpublished material.
44. FE, chap. 47, MS in MTP.
45. TPW, chap. 8, fuller MS version in MTP.
46. MTN, p. 343 (1898).
47. TPW, chap. 7 and two MS variant versions in MTP; TPW "Conclusion", MS in MTP, and MTN, p. 261, Dec. 1895; FE, chap. 55, and FE, chap. 59, MSS in MTP.
48. TPW, chap. 1, MS in MTP; FE, chap. 7, MTN, p. 237 (1894); FE, chap. 2, MTN, p. 237 (1894).
49. FE, chap. 36, MTN, p. 347, variant MS in IL, TS in MTP; MS in MTP; TPW, chap. 12. Previously unpublished material.
50. MTN, p. 345 (1898); MTN, p. 30 (1866); MTN, p. 114 (1867); FE, chap. 21; and MS in IL, TS in MTP. Previously unpublished material.
51. MS in NYPL, TS in MTP; FE, chap. 60; FE, chap. 35. Previously unpublished material.
52. FE, chap. 3; G. Bainton, ed., The Art of Authorship (London, 1890), pp. 87–88; TS in MTP; TPW, chap. 11. Previously unpublished material.
53. MS in MTP; FE, chap. 24, MTN, p. 327 (1897); MTN, p. 137 (1878). Previously unpublished material.

54. FE, chap. 15, MTN, p. 347; TS in MTP; FE, chap. 25; MTN, p. 206 (1889, in reference to Margaret Deland's *John Ward Preacher*, Boston: Houghton Mifflin, 1889); MS in IL, TS in MTP, MTN, p. 380 (December 1902). Previously unpublished material.
55. MTN, p. 187 (1885); MTN, p. 195 (after March 1888); MTN, pp. 195, 198 (after March 1888).
56. MS in IL, TS in MTP; MS in MTP; FE, chap. 48, MTN, p. 309 (1896). Previously unpublished material.
57. FE, chap. 10.

CHAPTER 7

1. MTN, p. 345.
2. SWE, pp. 106–30; first published in the *Atlantic*, 37 (June 1876):641–50.
3. SWE, pp. 129–30. Baetzhold advances the Jekyll-Hyde comparison in MTJB, p. 205. Mark Twain is just possibly making a passing jape at E. E. Hale's popular story "The Man Without a Country" (1863), whose hero lived a long life of sentimental remorse.
4. MTHL, p. 93.
5. MTHL, p. 129.
6. MSM No. 44, pp. 321–23; Walter Blair, ed., *Hannibal, Huck and Tom* (Berkeley: University of California Press, 1969), p. 31; MTB, pp. 52–53.
7. *New Introductory Lectures in Psycho-Analysis,* trans. W. J. H. Spratt (New York: Norton, 1933), pp. 82–112. Hereafter "Anatomy."
8. "Anatomy," p. 109.
9. Ibid., p. 84.
10. Ibid., p. 109.
11. Ibid., p. 88.
12. SWE, p. 125.
13. "Lord" is Freud's own word in translation.
14. MTB, p. 1398; quoted in MTJB, p. 251.
15. MTHL, pp. 119, 131.
16. MTN, pp. 348–51.
17. MSM No. 44, pp. 369–70.
18. MTLS, chaps. 1–4, 7.
19. See, e.g., MSM, Explanatory Notes, p. 470.
20. MSM ChrYS, p. 111.

21. See "The United States of Lyncherdom," EE, pp. 239–49.
22. MTLS, pp. 49–50.
23. "Mark Twain's Images of Hannibal: From St. Petersburg to Eseldorf," *Texas Studies in English*, 37 (1958):3–23.
24. "Villagers of 1840–3," *Mark Twain's Hannibal, Huck and Tom* (Berkeley: University of California Press, 1969), pp. 23–40; Dixon Wecter, *Sam Clemens of Hannibal* (Boston: Houghton Mifflin, 1952), *passim;* Appendix A, "A Biographical Directory," in *Hannibal, Huck and Tom*, especially pp. 348–49 on the Carpenter (*alias* Clemens) family.
25. "Stirring Times in Austria," *The Man That Corrupted Hadleyburg* . . . (New York: Harper, 1900), p. 323.
26. I am expanding the trinity defined by Coleman O. Parsons in his "The Devil and Samuel Clemens," *Virginia Quarterly Review*, 23 (Autumn 1947):595–600.
27. MSM ChrYS, p. 113.
28. Satan's genealogy in Mark Twain's thought has been impressively outlined by Parsons, in "The Background of *The Mysterious Stranger*," *American Literature*, 32 (March 1960), 55–74. I expand the outline somewhat in MSM ChrYS, pp. 14–19.
29. "Is Shakespeare Dead?" *What Is Man? and Other Essays* (New York: Harper, 1917), pp. 307–10.
30. *Hannibal, Huck and Tom*, pp. 44–45.
31. MTB, p. 146; "The Devil and Samuel Clemens," p. 593.
32. Franklin Walker and G. Ezra Dane, eds., *Mark Twain's Travels with Mr. Brown* (New York: Knopf, 1940), pp. 252–53. This key source was first noted by Gladys Bellamy in *Mark Twain as a Literary Artist*, pp. 352–53. See *The Apocryphal New Testament*, 2d ed. (London: William Hone, 1820), I. *Infancy*, 15:1–7 and 19:3; and II. *Infancy*, 1.
33. Notebook 28, TS pp. 34–35 (10 November 1895), in MTP.
34. Ibid., TS p. 51 (8 December 1895), in MTP.
35. EE, pp. 212, 219–20.
36. Notebook 32a, TS p. 37, in MTP; MTLS, p. 31.
37. *Literary Essays* (New York: Harper, 1918), pp. 264–65 (Nat Ed, pp. 264–65).
38. Notebook 30, TS p. 53 (post 19 June 1896), in MTP.
39. *Mark Twain's Autobiography* (New York: Harper, 1924), 2:97–98.
40. MTHL, p. 55.
41. See Bellamy, *Mark Twain as a Literary Artist*, pp. 252–53.

42. MTB, pp. 1079, 1235.
43. MTL, p. 683.
44. Ibid., p. 699.
45. MTHL, p. 715; MSM ChrYS, pp. 136, 137.
46. MSM ChrYS, p. 169; FE, pp. 399, 186–87.
47. "The Missionary in World-Politics," with letter to C. Moberly Bell, ed., (London) *Times*; unpublished MSS in MTP.
48. MSM ChrYS, chap. 2. Hereafter cited in text by page number.
49. MTHL, p. 699.

Index